PROLOGUE TO LEWIS AND CLARK

THE AMERICAN EXPLORATION AND TRAVEL SERIES

Prologue to Lewis and Clark
THE MACKAY AND EVANS EXPEDITION

W. RAYMOND WOOD

FOREWORD BY JAMES P. RONDA

UNIVERSITY OF OKLAHOMA PRESS : NORMAN

ALSO BY W. RAYMOND WOOD

(with Thomas D. Thiessen) *Early Fur Trade on the Northern Plains: Canadian Traders among the Mandan and Hidatsa Indians, 1738–1818* (Norman, 1985)
Or Go Down in Flame: The Death of a Navigator over Schweinfurt (New York, 1993; London, 1993)
(ed.) *Archaeology on the Great Plains* (Lawrence, 1998)
(with Michael J. O'Brien) *The Prehistory of Missouri* (Columbia, 1998)

Publication of this book is made possible through the generosity of Edith Kinney Gaylord.

Library of Congress Cataloging-in-Publication Data

Wood, W. Raymond.
    Prologue to Lewis and Clark: the Mackay and Evans expedition / W. Raymond Wood; foreword by James P. Ronda.
        p.   cm.— (The American exploration and travel series; v. 79)
    Includes bibliographical references (p.) and index.
    ISBN 0-8061-3491-7 (alk. paper)
        1. Missouri River Valley—Discovery and exploration. 2. Missouri River Valley—Discovery and exploration—Spanish. 3. Missouri River Valley—Description and travel. 4. Great Plains—Discovery and exploration. 5. Mackay, James, 1759–1822. 6. Evans, John, 1770–1799. 7. Explorers—Missouri River Valley—Biography. 8. Indian traders— Missouri River Valley—Biography. 9. Mandan Indians—History—18th Century. 10. Hidatsa Indians—History—18th century. I. Title. II. Series.

F598 .W66 2003
978'.01—dc21

2002075431

Prologue to Lewis and Clark: The Mackay and Evans Expedition is Volume 79 in The American Exploration and Travel Series.

The paper in this book meets the guidelines for permanence and durability of the Committee on Production Guidelines for Book Longevity of the Council on Library Resources, Inc.∞

To
Aubrey Diller, Abraham P. Nasatir,
and John L. Champe,
who pointed the way

CONTENTS

ILLUSTRATIONS

FOREWORD

Tuesday, January 10, 1803, was not William Clark's best day at Camp Dubois outside St. Louis. The day before he had fallen through the ice while attempting to cross a nearby pond. Now he admitted in his journal, "I am verry unwell today, owing I believe to the Ducking and excessive Cold which I underwent yesterday." But sometime that Tuesday Clark entertained a noteworthy guest. This was no ordinary visitor at the Corps of Discovery's camp, but James Mackay, surely one of the most widely traveled fur-trade explorers of the age. Just a few days before, important exploration journals and maps from Mackay had come into Meriwether Lewis's hands. Those materials would give the American explorers an unparalleled view of the Missouri River up to the Mandan villages. Now it was Clark's turn to hear firsthand about the recently acquired West up the river and out across the Great Plains. Despite the momentary miseries of the day, Clark's career was on the rise; Mackay's great days as a western explorer were over, and he was about to slip into undeserved obscurity. But it had not always been so. In the decade before the Lewis and Clark expedition, Mackay and his able lieutenant John Thomas Evans were—so one Spanish official put it—"the two most famous travelers of the northern countries of this continent." To follow the journeys made by Mackay and Evans up the Missouri and across the plains in 1795–97 is to begin to appreciate the kind of world Lewis and Clark found when they voyaged up the river in 1804. Thomas Jefferson's Corps of Discovery followed in the wake of James Mackay and John Evans.

W. Raymond Wood's *Prologue to Lewis and Clark: The Mackay and Evans Expedition* is really two books in one. It is the remarkable story of James Mackay—Scotsman turned Spanish citizen, fur trader, explorer, entrepreneur, and agent of empire. And it is also the intriguing tale of John Thomas Evans, Welsh nationalist, visionary, traveler, and star-crossed adventurer. This improbable pair—the tough-minded trader and the dreamer—were bound together by a common enterprise in an expedition up the Missouri and into the country of the Mandan and Hidatsa people. That story alone, and its connections to the Lewis and Clark journey, is worth the telling. But this is also a book that illuminates some of the central themes in the history of the American West. One theme is the story of western rivers. Of all those waterways, none has captured the American imagination more than the Missouri. "Across the wide Missouri" is not only a song lyric; it represents both a highway into the West and a boundary in western migrations. The Missouri runs like a thread through this book. It is a river of promise, of dreams, and of dreams denied. Like Bernard DeVoto, Wood knows that to write about the Missouri is to explore the larger West.

Another theme that runs through the book is the clash of empires. Beginning in the sixteenth century, the political and cultural future of North America was shaped by imperial rivalries. In those struggles the West was both battleground and prize. England, France, Spain, Russia, and ultimately the United States all sought imperial sway in the West. And in those contests for power and place, explorers were the advance guard of empire. At the end of the eighteenth century, Spanish officials believed they had much to fear for their North American empire. Everywhere they looked there were rivals busy encroaching upon the Spanish domain. From its base at New Archangel (modern Sitka), the Russian-America Company was on the move along the northwest coast. British maritime fur traders, hard on the heels of voyages by Capt. James Cook and Capt. George Vancouver, were intent on capturing the rich trade in sea otter pelts. And there were growing fears about the expansionist energies of the new American Republic. In 1792 the French trader and explorer Jacques D'Eglise reached the Mandan villages and brought news to St. Louis confirming what Spanish officers feared—that British traders from Canada had engrossed the fur business at the northern reaches of Spanish Louisiana. This was not just an economic threat; it was a direct challenge to Spain's sovereignty in the West. That news and the desire to expel British traders set in motion the Mackay and Evans expedition.

Like the river itself, what threads its way through the lives and travels of Mackay and Evans were compelling illusions about continental geography and the native peoples of the West. The quest for a passage from the Atlantic to the Pacific had fascinated explorers and imperial planners since the time of Columbus. Lewis and Clark were part of that quest, so were Mackay and Evans. In the years after Fr. Jacques Marquette and Louis Jolliet first identified the mouth of the Missouri and then speculated on its course, cartographers and imperial planners pondered the possibility that the river might stretch to the Pacific. By the end of the eighteenth century, many geographers believed that the Missouri was the key river in the passage through the West. Following the Missouri might lead travelers to the eastern edge of the Rockies. Once over what was envisioned as a narrow ridge of mountains, travelers were sure to find rivers flowing directly into the Pacific. Here was the elusive Northwest Passage, and Spanish officials such as Governor General baron de Carondelet were determined that Spain should control this plain path to the Pacific. Prompted by Carondelet and a substantial financial reward, Mackay hoped Evans could make the transcontinental passage. What Mackay prepared for Evans were exploration instructions similar in Enlightenment spirit to those drafted for Lewis and Clark and the Russian explorer Nikolai Rezanov. But the dream of the Northwest Passage was not the only illusion to dance in Evans's mind. Welsh nationalism burned with renewed fire, a cultural aspect of which was the search for ancient roots, a search that involved the mythic journey of Prince Madoc to America. Now, so the legend went, there were Welsh Indians with blue eyes and pale hair living along the upper Missouri. These lost Welsh needed to be found and brought into the ethnic fold. Perhaps more important for Welsh cultural nationalism, Wales could now claim to be the real home of the European discoverers of America. John Evans went up the Missouri to find Madoc's descendents and claim Wales's place in the history of exploration.

Prologue to Lewis and Clark is one of those remarkable books that draw on many disciplines to tell an important story. Ray Wood has had a distinguished career as one of the foremost northern plains archaeologists. His work on Mandan and Hidatsa sites is a monument to painstaking fieldwork and meticulous research. Wood has also been a pioneer in the use of historical evidence to expand and explain the archaeological record. His discussion of the origin and various versions of the landmark Antoine Soulard map as well as his masterful analysis of the map of the Missouri held by Yale's Beinecke Library and the other cartographic sources associated with the Mackay and Evans expedition suggest how much can be learned by knowing both the ground and the written record. *Prologue* is informed by this kind of superb, interdisciplinary scholarship. And no reader should miss Wood's remarkable tour de force near the end of the book—a remarkable recreation of Mackay's journey into northeastern Nebraska in company with Omaha buffalo hunters during the fall of 1796. James Mackay and John Evans will never enjoy the public recognition accorded to Lewis and Clark, but thanks to Ray Wood they now have a secure place in the larger history of the exploration of the West.

                                                      James P. Ronda

Tulsa, Oklahoma

PREFACE

The first systematic exploration, mapping, and description of the Missouri River was carried out nearly a decade before the epic exploration of that river by Lewis and Clark. This landmark investigation, nearly forgotten today, was carried out by an improbable pair of men: a Scotsman and a Welshman employed by merchants and speculators of Spanish St. Louis. The history of the Mackay and Evans expedition, 1795–97—truly the prologue to Lewis and Clark—brings together research that has occupied me from the beginning of my professional career, indeed, even as an undergraduate student. This endpoint probably was predictable, for the principal arena of their expedition took place in my native state of Nebraska; in Missouri, where I have taught for nearly forty years; and in two other states that I have adopted as a research area, North and South Dakota, in which I have traveled, studied, and spent more time than I can recall. Much of my career (and many of my publications) unconsciously has been spent in preparation for this particular end. Rather than a set of collected essays, however, this book has taken an alternative form best described as an integrated, highly elaborated, augmented set of extracts from a number of my studies and fleshed out with information from many other kinds of sources, both published and from personal observation.

My infatuation with the Mackay and Evans expedition dates back to undergraduate research that I conducted on Ná ⁿza, the Ponca Fort, the only known Ponca Indian earth-lodge village, at the mouth of Ponca Creek in northeastern Nebraska and on the villages of the even earlier Redbird-phase peoples in the same locality. These were my first two independent archaeological and ethnohistorical studies, both of them leading, directly and indirectly, to a study of

Mackay and Evans under the tutelage of my major professor at the University of Nebraska, John L. Champe. I am even guilty of naming in my master's thesis two putative Ponca pottery types after that improbable duo.

It is above all necessary to acknowledge the great debt that all historians of the early Missouri River owe to Abraham P. Nasatir. Before he published his preliminary studies in 1929 and 1930 and the appearance in 1952 of his classic two-volume study, *Before Lewis and Clark,* our knowledge of the early history of the Missouri River was rudimentary at best despite the pioneering studies of Louis Houck and other early historians. Nasatir deserves further and heartfelt commendation: not only did he publish well and exhaustively, but he also was generous with his knowledge in informal settings and belonged among those rare individuals for whom the accolade "a gentleman and a scholar" fits like a glove. He was as kind and helpful to esteemed colleagues as he was to me at the time of our first contact, a rank, unwashed initiate.

I have leaned on and cited here a variety of my own publications, appropriately acknowledged in the text, but in some cases there has been more substantive self-plagiarism. I thank the *Great Plains Quarterly* for acquiescing to my use of text from "The John Evans 1796–1797 Map of the Missouri River" (vol. 1, winter 1981) and "The Missouri River Basin on the 1795 Soulard Map: A Cartographic Landmark" (vol. 16, summer 1996); *Nebraska History* for "Fort Charles or 'Mr. Mackey's Trading House'" (vol. 76, spring 1995); J&L Reprint Company for excerpts from *Ná ⁿza, the Ponca Fort,* 2d edition (1993); and the *Missouri Historical Review* for "Nicolas de Finiels: Mapping the Mississippi and Missouri Rivers, 1797–1798" (vol. 81, July 1987). Permission to use excerpts from the Brandon House journals was kindly granted by Judith Hudson Beattie, keeper, Hudson's Bay Company Archives, Provincial Archives of Manitoba, Winnipeg. Daniel S. Glover, computer-graphic artist for the American Archaeology Division, University of Missouri–Columbia, prepared the several new maps that appear here and otherwise provided essential help in computer graphics.

If there is one article concerning the early Missouri River that I would like to have authored, it is the classic essay by Aubrey Diller that appeared in 1946, "Maps of the Missouri River before Lewis and Clark." In a very real way, this article set the cartographic stage for not only Nasatir's book but also a substantial part of my own research in the historical cartography of the Missouri River valley, which has used that essay as a benchmark and point of departure. If *Prologue to Lewis and Clark* has a genealogy, it may be traced to the inspiration that Diller and Nasatir provided—and to the training in

historical method by John L. Champe, who directed my anthropology training during the early to middle 1950s.

The primary documents by James Mackay, John Evans, and related figures
are appended since they are first-person accounts of the expedition. Also
included are hard-to-obtain published documents written by or based on the
writings of John Evans relating to his quest for the legendary Welsh Indians
and a newspaper obituary of the expedition leader, James Mackay.

I am deeply indebted to Thomas C. Danisi for his generosity in sharing
with me his very extensive research concerning the life and activities of John
Mackay, especially his insights into Mackay's cartographic competence and
previously underappreciated role in creating charts of the upper Missouri
River that were so informative to Lewis and Clark.

I am grateful to Peter Walker of the Historical Resources Branch, Manitoba
Culture Heritage and Tourism Department, for the artist's reconstruction of
Brandon House (figure 19) and to James Denny of the Missouri Department
of Natural Resources for the photograph of Boone's Lick, formerly known as
Mackay's Saline (figure 28). Peter Leach, a descendant of James Mackay, provided useful biographical information, and Dr. Geraint Evans, University of
Wales at Aberystwyth, provided me a hard-to-obtain Welsh-to-English translation (of the first paragraph of Document 10). Walter A. Schroeder generously helped with Missouri place names. Paul R. Picha and Susan Dingle gra-
ciously checked the manuscript's content for accuracy. John Ludwickson
offered valuable advice and corrections on matters relating to the Omaha
Indians and the expedition itself. Dale R. Russell generously shared his
knowledge of the northern fur trade with me when I was struggling with
Mackay's Canadian itinerary. Norman Brown, Missouri Department of Natural Resources, Rolla, corrected my misconceptions concerning early means
for determining latitude and longitude. Finally, Alan R. Woolworth provided
photocopies of documents relevant to the British presence on the Missouri
River, not to mention his always sound advice in ethnohistorical matters.

Thank you one and all for your generous scholarly help and for your
healthy skepticism. I hope the result pleases each of you.

Prologue to Lewis and Clark

CHAPTER ONE

Before Mackay and Evans

"La Rivière Pekittanoui"

By September 1806, Meriwether Lewis and William Clark had returned triumphantly and been greeted with much celebration after their three-year, eight-thousand-mile roundtrip trek across the North American continent. At that time one would assume that the knowledge accumulated by their Corps of Discovery constituted the most concentrated information then available on western North America. Who could possibly know as much about the West as Lewis and Clark and their men?

Several men, in fact, did hold such knowledge, but the Corps of Discovery had a very close competitor in a single man: James Mackay. This Scotsman had traveled the width of Canada to the very foothills of the Rocky Mountains; had entered the present United States from Canada on a visit to the Mandan Indians along the Missouri River; had gone up the Red River of the North probably to its source near Lake Traverse (between present-day Minnesota and South Dakota); had ascended the Missouri River from St. Louis to a point halfway to the Mandan villages; and had explored much of what is now northeastern Nebraska—accomplishing all of this in the two decades before the return of Lewis and Clark to St. Louis. Other competitors for overall knowledge of the continent included Alexander Mackenzie, who had traversed much of Canada and discovered that the river bearing his name today entered the Arctic Ocean rather than the Pacific. He later descended the Fraser River (which he believed to be the "River of the West," or the Columbia) to become the first man to cross North America from coast to coast. David Thompson and other explorers of the northern wilderness also had covered thousands of miles of what is today Canada, although—except for Mackenzie's travels—these discoveries were largely unknown outside the fur-trading community in that region.[1]

Mackenzie's published account spurred action in the still-new United States. Perhaps no one read the book more intently than that nation's recently elected president, Thomas Jefferson, for the volume contained nothing less than a blueprint for the British acquisition of western North America and its commerce, a coup that would deny its riches to the ever expanding Republic. Jefferson would have been understandably nervous when he put the book down, for he too believed that the river Mackenzie had descended to the Pacific was in reality the Columbia and not the Fraser, which enters the Pacific much farther north in present-day southern British Columbia. Jefferson may have taken Mackenzie's feat as a personal challenge; in any event it undoubtedly was the major stimulus for the president to mount his own expedition to stem the international rivalry for the Pacific Northwest and place the United States on a continental stage.[2]

Lewis and Clark's explorations thereby jelled in the mind of Thomas Jefferson through his long planned dream, now realized, for American expansion. But there had been several geographical probes and explorations, some of them aborted, up the Missouri River long before the Corps of Discovery left St. Louis. Jefferson was involved in one way or another in each expedition that had not originated in Spanish St. Louis, for he had advocated western exploration from the time he entered politics. While he was a member of the Continental Congress in 1783, he wrote to Gen. George Rogers Clark (William Clark's older brother) to see if he would lead a mission into the trans-Mississippi West. Jefferson had become aware of a plan by Britain to dispatch an expedition from the Mississippi to California to promote their geographical knowledge. The British plan never materialized, however, and General Clark declined Jefferson's offer because he had exhausted his personal finances in winning from Britain the Old Northwest for the colonies.

A second proposed western exploration was more chimerical. While Jefferson was in Paris as the United States' minister plenipotentiary to the Court of France, he met John Ledyard, a dreamer of wholly impractical schemes. Ledyard had hatched a plan to cross North America on foot beginning from the northwestern coast, an area that was familiar to him as a former crewmember of Capt. James Cook's third voyage. Unable to find backers for his scheme in the United States, he sought support overseas, and in 1785 he met Jefferson in Paris. The American proposed an alternative scheme: that Ledyard cross Siberia to its east coast and obtain passage to the northwest coast on a

Russian fur-trader's boat. Ledyard acted on this advice and, leaving London, actually managed to reach Okhotsk in eastern Siberia in 1787. There, Russian officials became suspicious of his interest in their western American fur trade, and he was arrested and expelled from Russia through Poland. Despite this setback he persisted, and at the time of his death in 1789, he was concocting a scheme to explore North America in the opposite direction from Kentucky.

In 1793, while Jefferson was serving as secretary of state under Pres. George Washington, he was also a distinguished member of the American Philosophical Society in Philadelphia. That year he proposed that the society send André Michaux, a prominent French botanist, on a scientific tour across the Mississippi River to the Pacific. Jefferson himself wrote the instructions for Michaux—instructions that were closely mirrored in those he later provided for Lewis and Clark. Michaux's tour, however, never materialized, nor did another proposed expedition to penetrate to the Pacific by way of the Missouri River. In December 1789 the War Department came up with another idea and assigned Lt. John Armstrong to undertake the task. Because the area was under Spanish control, Secretary of War Henry Knox urged secrecy in the matter. Lieutenant Armstrong arrived in Cahokia, Illinois, and crossed the Mississippi into St. Louis in 1790, but he quickly learned the difficulties of taking a small party into the wilderness, and the venture was abandoned.[3]

Were these American efforts to reach the west coast known to the Spanish officials in St. Louis? If they were known, did this knowledge help spur the Spaniards' own explorations of the Missouri River during the waning years of their rule? We probably shall never know, though it is possible that if they had intelligence of American ambitions, it may have been among the elements that influenced the formation of the Missouri Company in St. Louis in 1794, a move designed to solidify Spain's control of Upper Louisiana. Jefferson himself did not approach the Spanish about exploring the West until he became president in 1801. Toward the end of 1802, he met in Washington with Don Carlos Martinez, Marqués de Casa Yrujo, the Spanish ambassador to the United States. Martinez rebuffed Jefferson's proposal to explore the West for geographical knowledge, being justifiably suspicious of American intentions in the area. The matter was dropped.

By the beginning of his administration, however, much of the available geographical knowledge concerning the western part of what was to become the United States had become known to Jefferson. Now in the position to sponsor his own exploration of the West, the president proceeded to form the Lewis and Clark expedition, and he forwarded to those leaders all of the information that he could obtain relevant to their travels. Indeed, the explorers carried with them a small library in geography and natural history, including a copy of Mackenzie's *Voyages from Montreal*.[4] But the Corps of Discovery also carried with it a variety of manuscript maps and narratives that had been created by James Mackay and his deputy, John Thomas Evans, during their explorations far up the Missouri River in 1795–97, nine years before Lewis and Clark left St. Louis. The Mackay and Evans expedition had penetrated far above the mouth of the Platte River, and they had built Fort Charles nearly 800 miles above the mouth of the Missouri. Evans then proceeded to ascend the river for another 750 miles to visit the Mandan Indians.

What were the documents left by Mackay and Evans and how did they come into Lewis and Clark's hands? Mackay had visited Camp Dubois, their base camp near the mouth of the Missouri River, on January 10, 1804, only a few months before the expedition's departure. On that day Clark mentions that "Cap. Mackey" visited them, having just returned to his home near St. Charles after surveying some property he held up the Missouri River. There is no record of their conversation, but Mackay's extensive travels in Canada, his visit to the Mandans nearly twenty years earlier, and the details he could provide about the Missouri River and the tribes that lived along its banks surely were primary topics of mutual interest. A few days earlier Lewis had written President Jefferson that he had obtained, apparently also from Mackay, the journals of both Mackay and Evans that covered parts of their 1795–97 expedition. The documents, in French, were being translated by John Hay of Cahokia. The journals included two fragments of Mackay's account of his ascent of the Missouri and the construction of Fort Charles in what is now northeastern Nebraska; his "Table of Distances," a roster of natural features from St. Charles to the White River; fragments of John Evans's journal of his trip from Fort Charles to the Mandans; and Mackay's postexpeditionary "Notes on Indian Tribes" of the Missouri River area.[5]

These narratives were augmented by two maps that Lewis and Clark also carried with them on their expedition. One of them, known as the "Indian Office map," depicts in detail the Missouri River from St. Charles to the Mandans, and the other chart illustrates Evans's trip from Fort Charles to the Mandan villages. William Clark obtained both of these maps from William Henry Harrison, the governor of Indiana Territory.[6] One of the curious turns of Great Plains history is that the first accurate eyewitness map of the Missouri River in what is now northern Nebraska and North and South Dakota— the historic home of the Mandan, Hidatsa, and Arikara Indians and of their nomadic neighbors—was produced by Evans, a Welshman who had come to the United States to seek evidence for something that never existed: the mythological "Welsh Indians." Bernard DeVoto did not exaggerate when he said that "In the United States [that tale] became our most elaborate historical myth and exercised a direct influence on our history."[7] The inquisitive explorer John Evans did not find what he came to discover, but he produced what was to be one of the most important maps available to Lewis and Clark in planning and executing their expedition up the Missouri River.

These maps and journals were vitally important to the Corps of Discovery. Although the general contours of the Missouri River were well known before Lewis and Clark, maps depicting it often were wildly in error. Without modern knowledge of geography, an observer today could make little sense of some northerly parts of most contemporary maps. Consequently, the eyewitness maps made by Mackay and Evans provided the Corps of Discovery with extraordinarily precise "road maps" of the geography that they would cover for the first full year of their expedition, for these charts accurately showed the course of the Missouri and every significant tributary of the river as far as the Mandan villages.[8] Only a few of the less important streams remained for Lewis and Clark to name. (It is interesting to note that most of the streams named on Mackay's and Evans's maps still bear the same designations today, albeit sometimes in translation. Some of these names had been given by French voyageurs more than a century earlier. See the appendix.) The journal narratives by Mackay and Evans provided supplementary data for Lewis and Clark, not the least of which were details on some of the Indian tribes they would meet en route.

A list of adjectives that would accurately portray geographer, scientist, and then-president Thomas Jefferson would have embarrassed him and, at the same time, been inadequate to express the full range of his intellect. But Jefferson's instructions to Lewis and Clark for the conduct of their mission did not spring from his mind alone but "embrace years of study and wonder, the collected wisdom of his government colleagues and his Philadelphia friends." It is sometimes, and falsely, claimed that Jefferson's directions were modeled in part on those written by James Mackay to John Evans for his transcontinental journey.[9] The Spanish had directed Mackay to send a party across North America and reach the western coast of the continent. This group was to open to Spanish traders the Missouri valley and the Northwest Passage to the Orient, a goal that had plagued and eluded explorers for three centuries. Both the Spanish and the American expeditions, however, were to fail in this endeavor because of one factor over which they had no control: the goal was impossible since the passage did not exist. Nevertheless, Lewis and Clark, unlike their predecessors, succeeded by reaching the Pacific coast and returning.

But during the closing decade of the eighteenth century, Spanish officials in St. Louis were alarmed by British traders from the upper Mississippi River and from Canada penetrating Spanish territory and trading with the Indians on the northern plains. British traders from the Mississippi River (that is, from Prairie du Chien), the Minnesota River, and from posts along the Assiniboine River in Canada (including Fort Montagne à la Bosse) were indeed busily trading with Indians as far south as the Omahas and Poncas and as far north as the Mandans. These incursions incensed the Spanish, even though their own St. Louis traders were doing little to satisfy that market. When, however, Spanish officials learned that British traders had actually built a "fort"— now usually called Jusseaume's Post—among the Mandans, some fifteen hundred river miles up the Missouri from its mouth, they were moved to send three expeditions to combat and expel them. These excursions were sponsored by the Company of Explorers of the Upper Missouri, known also by many similar names but commonly known simply as the Missouri Company. It all began, of course, with the discovery of the Missouri River.

DISCOVERY AND EARLY EXPLORATION
OF THE MISSOURI RIVER

Missouri. It was the name of a tribe of Indians later all but annihilated by smallpox and intertribal warfare; it was to become the name of a U.S. territory and then a state; but first and foremost, it was the latest of a series of names for the river that drains the great interior grasslands of North America. Today it is credited with a length of only 2,723 miles from its source to its junction with the Mississippi. But if we accept the idea that the Mississippi River above its confluence with the Missouri is but a tributary (after all, less than half of the Mississippi's length is above that junction), then the Missouri is the longest river on earth, coursing from the Rocky Mountains to the Gulf of Mexico. If it is not the longest such river, certainly it is "the largest tributary stream in the world."[10]

Powerful human dramas have been played out along the banks of the Missouri River, and it is safe to say that few streams in American history have evoked such notoriety and passion as "the Wide Missouri." Composing any

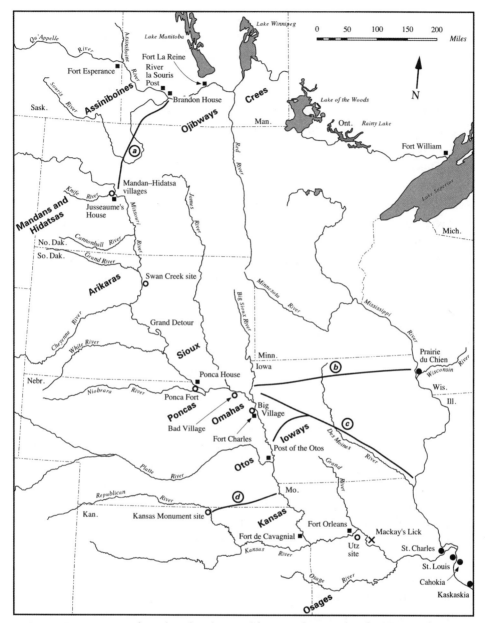

Fig. 1. Location map for cultural and natural features discussed in the Missouri basin. (W. R. Wood, ©2001)

characterization of the river is a challenge, for it is impossible to compete with descriptions of it by Jesuit Father DeSmet, interpretations by historians Hiram M. Chittenden and Donald Jackson, the epics of John G. Neihardt, and a host of other distinguished writers. There are many neglected aspects of this natural marvel, a river longer than the United States is wide and whose water, as a wag once said, was "all right to drink if you have some other water to wash it down with."[11] Then too some have said you can eat it with a fork (which is perhaps even more true today than it was in the past).

This roiling, muddy stream first became known to Europeans by the discoveries of Fr. Jacques Marquette and Louis Jolliet, although it is possible if not probable that far-ranging French traders had known of, or perhaps even traveled on, the Missouri prior to that "discovery." Marquette and Jolliet—in addition to the souls that Marquette planned to save—hoped to find a way to the South Sea, that is, the Pacific Ocean, and to the riches of what is today known as the American Southwest. They arrived along the banks of the Mississippi on June 17, 1673, and proceeded downstream.

The two men passed the confluence of the Missouri with the Mississippi in late June 1673 and were the first to place that turbulent river on maps. They called it "la rivière Pekittanouï," a name that later had a number of other, but still recognizable, variant spellings.[12] Others called it, for a time, the "River of the Osages" after the powerful tribe that controlled much of the Ozark Highland and its environs to the south and west of the Missouri's mouth. The actual maps and journals of Marquette and Jolliet's exploration were tragically lost on their return to Montreal, but both men produced maps from memory that reconstructed the major outlines of their journey. The "autograph map" that Father Marquette produced in this fashion provides us with our first glimpse of the locations of the tribes of the lower Missouri.[13] It shows a mere stub of the Missouri River, but the placement of tribal names along that section and upriver from it accurately reflects what we know of tribal locations along the river in early historic times. Moving upstream from its mouth, he records the 8chage (Osage), 8Emess8rit (Missouri), Kansa (Kansas), Paniassa (Pawnee), and farther on the Otontanta (Oto), Pana (Ponca), Maha (Omaha), and the Pah8tet (Ioway).

Marquette believed that ascending the Pekittanouï would be the route to the Vermillion or California Sea—the Pacific Ocean. His dream of making that voyage would be terminated by his early death, and Marquette's vision was not to be accomplished until Lewis and Clark did so 132 years later.

It is impossible to say who the first Frenchmen were to penetrate the lower Missouri valley, for we know of their early activities on the river only by hearsay. These early *coureurs du bois*—literally, "wood runners"—were independent, unlicensed traders who operated far from the frontier on small inventories. In 1680 or 1681 René Robert Cavalier de La Salle wrote of two French *coureurs du bois* who had been captured by the Missouri Indians and taken to their village, the earliest recorded white men to have been on the Missouri. In 1683 La Salle mentioned two Frenchmen and some Kaskaskia Indians who had been living among the Missouri and Osage tribes. At that time the Missouris were living along the river in the heart of the present-day state of Missouri. Since about the time of Columbus, they had been living in the general vicinity of the juncture of the Grand River and the Missouri, where their archaeological remains are embedded in numerous prehistoric and early historic village sites. (The most conspicuous of these is the Utz site, a prominent part of today's Van Meter State Park.)[14]

In the spring of 1693, some Kaskaskia Indians (residents along the Mississippi River below what was to become St. Louis) either accompanied or guided two French traders to the Missouri tribe, with whom the French hoped to establish a general peace and a trade relationship. A priest, Father St. Cosme, also traveled upriver in 1698 and reported that many Indians lived on the river.[15]

On February 9, 1792, Medad Mitchell, then in Philadelphia, wrote U.S. Secretary of the Treasury Alexander Hamilton a short but informative letter in which he summarized the commerce of the Illinois region. "Having been Employed in the Illinois Country last Autumn, beg leave to lay before You some information which I acquired relative to the commerce of that Country. The Missouri is navigated near 1200 Miles among various Tribes of Savages—it employs annually from 50 to 100 boats. The whole of the Mississippi from the Natches to its source is supply'd by Canadaian Merchts."[16] Mitchell's brief employment on the Mississippi had been sufficient to see the threat to American commerce by British traders entering the upper Mississippi valley from Canada. His letter to Hamilton contained suggestions for combating this by arming vessels to deny the British the use of the Illinois and Wisconsin Rivers.

Clearly, by the last decade of the seventeenth century, dozens of French had gone or were annually going up the Missouri River. How far they went is a matter for speculation, and, while the twelve hundred miles that Mitchell mentions may be an exaggeration, there is no doubt they went far beyond the Kansa Indian lands near present-day Kansas City, had traded with the Pawnees in central Nebraska, and had gone overland across the plains to the Southwest in an effort to reach Spanish Taos or Santa Fe.

The Mission of the Holy Family of the Tamoroa was established in March 1699 on the future site of Cahokia, Illinois. In the fall of the following year, the Kaskaskias left their ancestral homes along the Illinois River and settled at or near the mouth of the stream later called Des Peres, which flows into the Mississippi in modern south St. Louis. This budding settlement was soon augmented by a number of Frenchmen from east of the Mississippi, thus becoming the first village founded on the west bank of that river in what is now Missouri.

As early as March 1702, seventeen Frenchmen from Tamoroa planned to build a fort on the Missouri River between the Pawnees and the Ioways. The fort, according to the pastor at Tamoroa, Fr. Marc Bergier, was to be about two hundred leagues upriver. This would have placed the establishment somewhere near the mouth of the Platte River. The Frenchmen undertaking this venture, however, were attacked en route to their destination, and whereas the results of this encounter remain cloudy, probably one can safely assume that the fort was never built. These results notwithstanding, this expedition appears to have been the first such organized venture by Europeans on the Missouri River.[17]

Baron Marc de Villiers du Terrage makes allusions to French penetration of the Missouri River before 1700 and cites documents in French archives referring to others in the first fifteen years of the eighteenth century. Since traders had discovered that the source of the Missouri was to the north or northwest, in the direction of Canada, the French did not attempt to travel above the Platte River. Rather, they ascended it to the Osage or Kansas Rivers, hoping thereby to reach the mines of Spanish New Mexico by going overland. On June 20, 1710, Nicolas de La Salle wrote to Paris providing the name of the first French officer ordered to navigate the Missouri: La Sieur Darac, a Canadian. J. B. Lemoyne, Sieur de Bienville, governor of Louisiana territory, ordered Darac and two soldiers to go eight hundred or nine hundred leagues upstream to give presents to Indians who were friendly to the French. The success of his mission is not reported in the document, but it is clear the men went no such distance, for eight hundred leagues would have placed them somewhere in eastern Montana. Four years later Le Maire announced that the Missouri had been ascended some five hundred leagues.[18] Taken literally, this would have meant the French had reached the Mandans in the vicinity of modern Bismarck, North Dakota—an improbable eight hundred miles above the Platte, which surely represented the maximum known exploration at the time.

There is a somewhat later account of an ascent of the Missouri by Derbanne (later the commandant at Natchitoches); his mission was to record details for upstream navigation by the French. On June 12, 1724, he wrote: "I should gladly speak to you of the Missouri which I entered nearly 18 years ago [1706]. We ascended nearly 400 leagues from its mouth. These are the first of the French to have been so far into the interior." If Derbanne's ascent of four hundred leagues is correct, he would have reached a point well to the north of the White River in present-day South Dakota.[19]

More than a half-century before the founding of St. Louis, then, French traders were entering the basin of the Missouri valley and in all probability transporting a small flood of furs downstream. But the first European to explore, chart, and describe the Missouri above the villages of the Missouri Indians was Etienne Véniard de Bourgmont. This young Frenchman began his ascent on March 29, 1714, and made his way to the Missouris then living somewhere in the vicinity of the Utz site, their old village on the bluffs overlooking the Missouri nearly opposite the mouth of the Grand River. That village had been abandoned about 1712, and, although they remained in the neighborhood for a time—and certainly did so during Bourgmont's time—the Missouris had left their old territory sometime before 1794.[20]

For the next five years, Bourgmont made his home among the Missouris and Osages, and like so many Frenchmen before and after him, he found that adjusting to life among the Indians came readily. Taking a native wife, he even sired a son among the Missouris. But by 1719 he was back in France, where the following year he was commissioned Commandant de la Rivière du Missouri. He was told to establish contact with the Kansa and Padouca (that is, Apache) Indians, as well as with any other potentially hostile tribes to their south and west, and to enter into peace treaties with them. This he was to do from a fort he was to establish on the Missouri River within two years' time. It was 1723, however, before Bourgmont was able to reenter the Missouri and reestablish contact with his old native friends. On November 9, 1723, he and his party of some forty men began building Fort Orleans. Although a grand plan of the establishment exists, probably little of it was actually constructed.[21] Later maps show that it was erected on the northern bank of the Missouri River a short distance upstream from the mouth of the Grand River, not far from the Missouri Indian village.

The following year Bourgmont was able to obtain the men and supplies necessary to explore farther up the Missouri River. In June he set out, reaching the vicinity of present-day Atchison, Kansas, where he struck southwest across the plains. Meeting the Apaches somewhere in north-central Kansas, he concluded a peace treaty with them, one of the missions his royal charter had demanded.[22] On his return to Fort Orleans, Bourgmont prepared to return to France to visit King Louis XV. He successfully persuaded a delegation of chiefs of the Missouri, Osage, Oto, and Illinois peoples to accompany him, including the mother of his son, the daughter of a head chief of the Missouris. Despite the success of his visit to His Catholic Majesty, however, Fort Orleans was abandoned sometime around 1728. Its general location remained known as late as Lewis and Clark's journey, but the exact site is now lost, though still being sought. More than likely, having been built by the water's edge, it is now in the channel of the ever-shifting Missouri River.[23]

But although official exploration ended, French *coureurs du bois* continued to move west to exploit the furs they were obtaining along the lower Missouri and its tributaries. It is clear that they had been trapping the area for decades, for by 1718 enough information had accumulated that Guillaume Delisle produced in Paris one of the landmark maps of the Missouri valley: his "Carte de la Lousiane" provides good information on the Missouri from its mouth to the Omaha and Ioway Indians, who were then living along what appears to be the lower reaches of the Big Sioux River near modern Sioux City, Iowa.[24]

One of the earliest settlements in the Mississippi valley was the little town of Kaskaskia on the east bank of the river some seventy miles below the mouth of the Missouri. The wealth of deeds, depositions, wills, marriage contracts, and inventories produced there between 1714 and 1816 allow us a glimpse of the fur trade during that period by Frenchmen who made their living by "going up the Missouri." These documents record the names of no less than thirty engagés who plied their trade—at least at times—on the Missouri. *Engagés* were the common laborers of the fur trade, drawing the least pay and performing manual labor of every sort, from dragging boats upriver to chopping firewood. Four *engagés* are specified as having been involved in trade at the "Post of the Missouris" between 1743 and 1747. Inasmuch as Fort Orleans, clearly intended as a trading post for the Missouris, appears to be mentioned by name, the probability is that these men were associated first with that post and later with the one that Joseph Deruisseau built among the Kansas Indians on the west bank of the Missouri River just above modern

Leavenworth, Kansas, sometime before 1747. The latter post, first called the Post of the Missouri and later named Fort de la Trinite, ultimately became known as Fort de Cavagnial.[25] The specifications for its construction are important in that so few details are available for contemporary forts along the Missouri River. De Cavagnial was to be

a fort of eighty feet on each side, surrounded by good posts, made of the best wood found in the place where the fort is located, with two bastions on the front side, and on the back side, according to the plan which has been made, twice as many stakes, and storied bastions.

There shall be in the said fort a house for the officer designated as commander; it shall be thirty feet long and twenty feet wide, with rooms distributed according to the plan, already made, with wooden separation walls, and upper and lower floors. It shall be built of posts covered with bark, with a kitchen contiguous to the building, built as a shed, covered also with bark, with a chimney as on the *boussilage*. . . . Also a guard house, twenty feet in length . . . built of posts covered with mud [*boussilage*] the whole structure covered with bark, and a chimney in said building made with mud with a high and low floor of split stakes, the upper being well coated with mud on its upper side. A square powder room, ten feet on each side, from post to post, covered with a high and a low floor of split stakes. Also a house to lodge the *fermiers* of the post, the size of which shall be determined at their convenience. Also another house for their men, the size of which will suit them.[26]

Detailed specifications notwithstanding, there is no reason to believe that the fort actually was built meeting these standards. Construction began in the spring of 1744, and it was probably abandoned, as were all French posts in Upper Louisiana, in 1764. Fort de Cavagnial was nevertheless an important center for French influence in the area for twenty years. It served as an outpost for French *voyageurs* who traded with the Kansa, Wichita, and Pawnee Indians, and even served as the origin of an ill-fated mission to Santa Fe (those who made the journey barely escaped execution by the Spanish).[27]

France ceded Louisiana to Spain in a secret treaty in 1762. This, it was hoped, would foil British designs on the region. The plan was partly successful, for the British ended up owning much of Louisiana east of the Mississippi while the Spanish retained control of the area west of the river. But the French and their activities continued as before, for it was not until 1769 that the Spanish governor—a man with the unlikely name of Don Alessandro O'Reilly—arrived in New Orleans to take control of his country's new possessions. It was not long before the Spanish began to suspect that the British also were interested in the west bank of the Mississippi, and that fear would dictate much of their national policy in Louisiana until Spain secretly ceded Louisiana back to France in the Treaty of San Ildefonso in 1800. That act was revealed only when the United States made the Louisiana Purchase three years later.

Bourgmont's monograph *L'Exacte description de la Louisianne* lists the tribes that lived along the Missouri River as far upstream as present-day South Dakota. There is no doubt that in his explorations he reached the mouth of the Platte River: the map of his journey drawn by Guillaume Delisle, dating to about 1714, ends abruptly at the mouth of that stream. Whereas Bourgmont's account of peoples living along the Platte and farther up the Missouri may be testaments to his interrogation skills among native Americans and the *couriers de bois* who knew them, they do not demonstrate that he penetrated above the Platte, nor does he claim to have done so. But he was the first European to present information on the Missouri River that far upstream to the French authorities. The Arikaras were the northernmost peoples he mentions along the Missouri, despite the renown of their upriver neighbors, the Mandans. Bourgmont is specific about Arikara contacts with Europeans in *L'Exacte description* when he writes, "They have seen the French and know them." At this time the Arikaras were living near the mouth of the Bad River in present-day central South Dakota; they did not move up the Missouri valley to villages near the mouth of the Cheyenne River until later.[28]

ST. LOUIS IN 1795

St. Louis was a town destined for greatness. The young community had been founded in 1764, by Pierre de Liguest Laclède and his thirteen-year-old stepson, Auguste Chouteau, only a few years after the end of the Seven Years' War. By the mid-1790s, Laclède's trading post had grown into a small town. It lay just north of the Des Peres River and about five miles south of the mouth of the Missouri River on a high flood-free bench of land that had the capacity for expansion. A large group of undisturbed prehistoric Indian mounds were north of town—structures that were slated for eventual destruction as St. Louis expanded over and beyond them. The Mississippi River here flowed from north to south, and its straight channel near the shore made it an ideal location for vessels to tie up to load and unload cargo.

From its beginning, St. Louis was a trading town: established as a trading post, it grew into a trading depot and point of departure for destinations hundreds of miles away. It was the major center for Upper Louisiana, lying about midway between New Orleans and the upper Mississippi and less than a day's travel from the mouth of the Missouri River, the gateway to the interior of what was to become the western United States. It would grow, as Laclède had predicted, into one of the finest cities in America.

The French had explored most of the valley of the Mississippi River between 1677 and 1687, but it was on April 7, 1782, that René Robert Cavalier de La Salle took formal possession of the basin of the Mississippi River "In the name of the most high, mighty, invincible and victorious Prince, Louis the Great, by the Grace of God, King of France and of Navarre, fourteenth of that name," and gave it the name "Louisiana" in his honor.[29] But it was not long before the area became a pawn in European politics, and its "possession" swung back and forth like a pendulum between France and Spain before it finally came to rest with the Americans.

The province, a vast tract of land embracing both sides of the Mississippi River, remained nominally French until the Treaty of Paris was signed on February 10, 1763. The treaty concluded the Seven Years War (fought on this continent as the French and Indian War). In it, France relinquished to Great Britain their North American possessions: all of Canada and Louisiana (but excluding New Orleans) became British territory, ending the French empire in North America. Because France had ceded the lands west of the Mississippi to Spain in 1762, this left the midcontinent divided between Spain and Great Britain, the Mississippi River providing the boundary between them. The Spanish were determined to monopolize the richness of this possession and to eliminate the encroachments that were being made in it by British merchants. This was to prove impossible.

The first swing of the pendulum came with the loss of the British colonies in the American Revolution. The consequence: the colonies that had been clustered along the Atlantic Coast now expanded west to the Mississippi River, a half-continent away. By the late eighteenth century, then, the Spanish monarchy faced the new republic across the Mississippi. It is perhaps appropriate here to anticipate future alterations in the region's government, for when Napoleon Bonaparte rearranged the map of Europe, he also manipulated that of North America. When Spain fell to Napoleon, he took back, in the secret treaty of San Ildefonso (October 1, 1800), the province of Louisiana, that is, the region west of the Mississippi. Needing money, and in a move designed to deny the region to any other European power (particularly Great Britain), Napoleon quickly sold Louisiana to the United States. The Louisiana Purchase, which defined the region as the basin of the Missouri River, was engineered by emissaries of Pres. Thomas Jefferson on April 30, 1803. Jefferson moved quickly to explore these new lands, dispatching Lewis and Clark to do so.

In 1795 St. Louis was still a small town, with a population of about twelve hundred people.[30] The town of Cahokia lay across the Mississippi and southeast of St. Louis, and for a time it rivaled the growing river port in size and population. The city may have had an impressive population for the frontier, but at the same time there were many Mandan, Hidatsa, and Arikara Indian villages on the upper Missouri River of equal and larger size, or at least there had been before smallpox epidemics decimated those settlements sometime in the mid-1700s and again in 1781.

The government of Spanish Louisiana was under the overall control of a governor general who presided over the area from New Orleans. Between 1783 and December 30, 1791, this man was Esteban Rodríguez Miró, but Don Francisco Luis Héctor, baron de Carondelet, took the reins of power on the last day of Miró's tenure and remained in office until August 5, 1797. He worked strenuously to extend Spanish control over the Mississippi valley and to insulate the commerce of Louisiana from the ever approaching American frontiersmen. His successor was Manuel Gayoso de Lemos, who was in office from 1797 to 1799; he died of malaria in New Orleans in the latter year. Two later governors (irrelevant to this narrative) enjoyed short tenures before the American purchase of Louisiana.

Upper Louisiana, or Spanish Illinois Country, was under the rule of the lieutenant governor, or commandant of Upper Louisiana, whose residence was in St. Louis, its capital. The lieutenant governor, one early observer said, "subsumes in his person all power—military, civil, fiscal, and judicial. [His capital] is the only town in Illinois with a garrison, which at some times has had as many as two hundred men, although usually has only forty to sixty at most."[31] Beginning in 1787, Manuel Pérez governed Upper Louisiana and was commandant of St. Louis. He was replaced by Zenon Trudeau in 1792, who in turn relinquished command to Charles (Carlos) Dehault Delassus in 1799. Delassus (1799–1803) was the last Spanish lieutenant governor before the territory became American.

Traders in St. Louis were not prepared to compete with the British. Not only were English goods superior in quality to those obtained by the Spanish— something the Indians readily recognized—but also the volume of British goods enabled them to monopolize the markets of the upper basin of the Mississippi River and indeed to trade with the distant Indians of the middle and upper Missouri River. Their numbers alone posed a threat to Spanish interests, for by 1792 no less than 150 British trading canoes were dispatched from their base at Michilimackinac. On May 31, 1794, Zenon Trudeau complained to Carondelet about "how small is the value of the commerce of Missouri, which yearly decreases more and more. The introduction of merchandise increases imperceptibly, but the amount of peltries taken out by traders grows less and less. They are satisfied now if they get twenty-five per cent when in times past they obtained as much as three or four hundred."[32]

Scholars are indebted to Nicolas de Finiels, an expatriate French engineer, for a description and a detailed map of St. Louis in 1797. He and his family had arrived and were in residence at St. Louis by June 1797, only one month after James Mackay returned from his upriver expedition. Finiels did not remain in St. Louis very long; by the early summer of 1798, he had left for New Orleans.[33] In that year he nevertheless produced his monumental 1797–98 map of the Mississippi River, showing its valley in minute detail from the mouth of the Ohio River to that of the Illinois River. Streets, roads, and individual houses all were shown on this giant chart, measuring nearly a yard wide and nine feet long. From it one can obtain a bird's-eye view of contemporary St. Louis and its environs.

THE ST. LOUIS AND CANADIAN FUR TRADE

St. Louis fur traders, like their Canadian brethren, based their livelihood on beaver fur; the pelts of these harmless animals were sought above all others. Many other kinds of pelts were taken in trade, but they were always subordinate to those of beavers, which were driven almost to extinction by the demand. It was not the outer fur of the beaver that was desired but the rich underfur, called "muffoon" by later mountain men. Because the quality of felt depends on the matting qualities of the fibers, the microscopic barbs on this layer of fur meant they could be shaved away and pounded into a fine felt that was then shaped into a soft, lustrous, and durable material. Beaver hats were not only popular with fashionable European men, but they also denoted status in a manner that other items of apparel did not. A gentleman could be identified as to his place in the social structure according to the style and material of his hat. There was even an etiquette for the ways one tipped or moved the hat.[34] Beaver pelts therefore demanded high prices.

The resulting hats were popular in Stuart England even before the founding of St. Louis, and they continued to be popular until the middle of the nineteenth century. The underfur was most luxurious on beavers in the far north, on the plains, and in the mountains, where winters were bitterly cold. Beaver pelts were so prized that they became money: a prime pelt, or "made-beaver," for decades was a standard of currency in the West. The first riches of the region thus were not minerals but animals: beavers' watery dens were as valuable then as the gold mines were later for prospectors.

By the end of the eighteenth century, fur traders from eastern Canada had worked their way deep into the Canadian West by way of the many lakes and the streams draining that land, nearly leveled by the repeated glaciations that swept south during the last ice age. The major nerve centers and depots of the competing French and British "North Traders," as they were often called, were in Montreal, on the banks of the St. Lawrence River, and at posts along the shores of Hudson Bay. Goods reached central Canada and then the Missouri River tribes by two routes. The French went up the Ottawa River to Lake Huron and along the northern shores of the Great Lakes to Grand Portage; then west through what is now called the "border waters," including Rainy Lake and Lake of the Woods, to Lake Winnipeg; and thence on into the western frontier. The British traders built supply posts along the western shore of Hudson Bay, principally Albany Factory, and took their goods inland up the Albany River, portaged to the headwaters of the English River, and went downstream to Lake Winnipeg—then like the French they went deeper into the interior by way of the intricate inland waterways.

The Canadian system was to come into contact and competition with the traders from St. Louis who began to reach the Mandans and their neighbors in the latter part of the eighteenth century. The southern traders began as a trickle. One of the first such visitors may have been a man called "Old Pinneshon." Peter Pond, who traded on the upper Mississippi River between 1775 and 1778, wrote that a former French soldier from the Illinois Country had told him that he had "Desorted His Post & toock his Boat up the Miseeurea among the Indians and Spant Maney years among them. . . . He [eventually] Got among the Mondans [Mandans] whare he found Sum french traders who Belongd to the french facterey at fort Lorain [La Reine] on the Read [Red] River this facterey Belong to the french traders of Cannaday." The date of Old Pinneshon's visit is unknown, though if we accept Pond's account, the trader would have had to reach Fort la Reine before 1763, when the French garrison there was withdrawn. Certainly, it was abandoned well before 1793, when Hudson's Bay Company trader John Macdonell referred to the site of "ancien Fort *de la Reine*." At that time its ruins were scarcely distinguishable.[35]

Consequently, whereas there may have been earlier visitors, the first Europeans firmly documented as having reached the Mandans from the mouth of the Missouri River were Jacques D'Eglise in 1792 and John Evans in 1796. Lewis and Clark reached the Mandans in the fall of 1804. On the heels of American possession of the river, the trickle of traders up the Missouri became a flood, so that by 1818 the trade from Canada was overwhelmed by establishing the international boundary and the influx of American traders.

At this time the Mandans and Hidatsas lived in five villages clustered near the mouth of the Knife River some fifteen miles south of the Big Bend. (The Big Bend, so named because here the Missouri River, after flowing across the present-day states of Montana and western North Dakota in an essentially eastern course, abruptly turns south for most of its course through the rest of North Dakota and South Dakota.) Here the Canadian-based and the St. Louis–based trade spheres overlapped at a profitable Indian intertribal trading center, a site that reached deep into the prehistoric past. Exchange with Indians from the south and east meant that small numbers of trade goods were reaching these villages at a time when the white traders, many hundreds of miles distant, had heard only rumors of the Mandans and Hidatsas. This, indeed, was the stimulus for the first Europeans to travel to the Mandans, and in 1738 the French trader and explorer Pierre Gaultier de Varennes, Sieur de La Vérendrye, reached them from Fort la Reine, his base along the Assiniboine River.

Of the five communities, three Hidatsa villages, known today as Amahami, Sakakawea, and Big Hidatsa, were clustered around the mouth of the Knife River. From south to north, they consisted of the Awaxawi Hidatsa (also known as the Amahami, Ahaharaway, Watasoon, or Shoe Indians) who lived in a village at the mouth of the Knife River called Mahawha (Amahami). The village has been all but destroyed by the construction of the town of Stanton; a single earth-lodge ruin remains today in the county courthouse lawn. This small but aggressive Hidatsa group usually was distinguished from the other Hidatsas because of their slightly different dialect and lifestyle. The middle village lay on the south bank of the Knife a mile from its confluence with the Missouri. It was occupied by Awatixa Hidatsa (also called the Minitarees) and was known as Metaharta (Sakakawea). Its modern name came from the fact it was at one time the home of Toussaint Charbonneau and his young

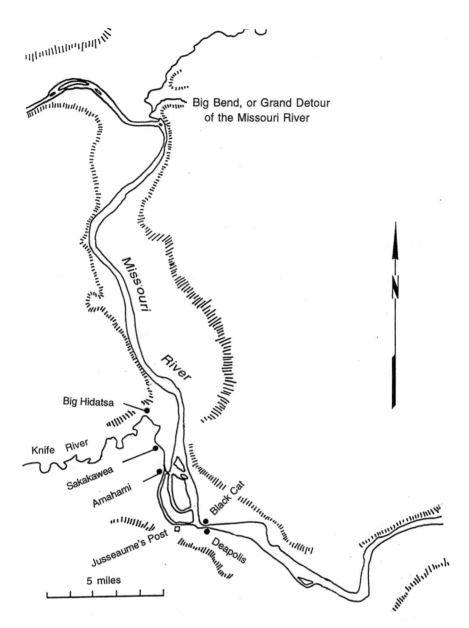

Big Bend, or Grand Detour
of the Missouri River

Missouri River

Big Hidatsa

Knife River

Sakakawea

Amahami

Black Cat

Jusseaume's Post

Deapolis

N

5 miles

Fig. 2. The five Mandan and Hidatsa villages at the mouth of the Knife River and the presumed location of Jusseaume's Post. (Adapted from Wood and Thiessen, *Early Fur Trade*, map 2)

Shoshone bride, Sacagawea, of Lewis and Clark fame. Menetarra (Big Hidatsa) was the most northern, and largest, village. It was occupied by the Hidatsa Proper and lay on the north bank of the Knife River in the "peninsula" between that river and the Missouri.

The two Mandan villages were just downstream from the mouth of the Knife, around a sharp bend in the Missouri River. One of them was on the north side of the river (Ruhptare) and the other was on its south bank opposite it (Mitutanka). Archaeologically, these villages are known today as Black Cat and Deapolis, respectively, and in Evans's and Lewis and Clark's day, they were under the leadership of two renowned chiefs, Black Cat and Big White (or Shehekea).[36]

During the late eighteenth century, the Canadian fur trade was dominated by two large companies: the Hudson's Bay Company and the North West Company. In 1795 North West controlled more than 93 percent of the total Canadian trade.[37] Both companies had built a series of posts along the Assiniboine River and its tributaries, in what is now southern Manitoba and Saskatchewan, north of Turtle Mountain, an uplift area that straddles the boundary between North Dakota and Manitoba. Personnel from two of these many posts became players in the conflict that arose when John Evans attempted to prohibit their trade with the village tribes. Both companies were involved in trade with the Mandans and Hidatsas.

The first British traders from Canada began their illegal entrada into Spanish territory about 1785. We know almost nothing about earlier visits to the villages, though it is likely the French had been visiting them, however rarely, since the time of La Vérendrye. A major smallpox epidemic swept across the northern plains in 1780–81, and because of massive population losses among the Indians, trade with the villages was sharply reduced. The outbreak's disruptive effects soon closed down the trade until about 1793, when two posts were built on the Assiniboine River by the competing fur companies.

The Hudson's Bay post, Brandon House, was built in October 1793, and in 1797 it was under the direction of factor James Sutherland. The competing North West post, also built in 1793, was Macdonell's House, whose chief factor was its namesake, John Macdonell (though it was also called Assiniboine House or Fort Assiniboine and, in the selected documents below, River La Souris). Both posts were on the north bank of the Assiniboine River a few miles above its confluence with the Souris (Mouse) River, separated by a distance of about three miles. Their principal trade was with the neighboring Assiniboine, Cree, and Ojibwa Indians, but the Missouri River trade was becoming increasingly important to both companies. Another North West post, River Tremblante, under the direction of Cuthbert Grant, was still farther up the Assiniboine. That great river there flowed through a broad, shallow valley cut into a gently rolling plain, having then only sparse timber along its banks.

Hudson's Bay and North West parties from these posts made frequent trips to the Missouri River. These parties—usually consisting of two to eight men—went to trade for furs on horseback during temperate weather and in winter with sleds drawn by dogs. They might remain for a few days or a few weeks in the villages, trading for the pelts offered by both the Indians and by the free European traders who lived with the Indians. Despite their often bitter competition, traders for the two companies sometimes made the trip together since small parties were often plundered, if not killed, by hostile Indians. Trading took place for the most part during the fall through spring months, when pelts were in prime condition.[38]

By the last decade of the eighteenth century, a well-developed trail linked the Assiniboine River posts with the Missouri River villagers. Much of the path followed the Souris River, a stream that begins in southeastern Saskatchewan, flows through present-day North Dakota, then makes a great arc back to the north, flowing into southwestern Manitoba and thence into the Assiniboine. Traders first went up the shallow valley of the Souris, then crossed the low, rolling terrain within the river's great bend, which once had been the floor of a glacial lake. South of the Souris was the Mandan Plain, the high ground (physiographically known as the Missouri Coteau) that separates the basin of the Souris from the Missouri valley. Consequently, this high ground was the east-west continental divide, separating the waters that flow north into the North Atlantic from those that drain south into the Caribbean Sea. When the travelers arrived at the Big Bend of the Missouri, near the present location of the Garrison Dam, they went down the east bank of the Missouri and crossed over at the mouth of the Knife, midway between the Mandan and Hidatsa villages. The two-hundred-mile journey usually took about two weeks.

THE AMERICAN INDIAN TRADE SYSTEM

Aboriginal North America was blanketed by a network of trading relationships that linked, to a greater or lesser degree, every tribe to one or more of its neighbors. The nature of that intertribal trade helps explain many aspects of the lives of the Plains Indians. These systems involved transactions that bound different tribes together in a complex economic system.

Knowledge of aboriginal trade in the northern plains, as first described by Joseph Jablow, was substantially augmented by the studies of John C. Ewers.[39] The scholarship on the nature of this trade is based on the journals of Lewis and Clark, their contemporaries, and their immediate successors that describe trading conditions in the area beginning about 1790. The surviving documentation reflects aboriginal trading patterns that were not fully destroyed until about 1850, when tribal economies finally were disrupted by Euro-American fur traders.

The trading system described by Ewers testifies to the presence of at least two major trading centers: the Arikara villages near the mouth of the Grand River in South Dakota and the Mandan and Hidatsa villages near the mouth of the Knife River in North Dakota. These tribes were sedentary gardeners, living in earth-covered dwellings in fortified villages along the Missouri. The Mandans, Hidatsas, and Arikaras were middlemen, acting as brokers between the nomadic hunters who lived on either side of the Missouri River. These centers capitalized on their location by harvesting garden crops and serving as centers of exchange with neighboring groups in the autumn.

Early accounts document the three routes by which goods came into the hands of the villagers. First, the Crows came to the villages from the upper Yellowstone River area with goods obtained from farther west at a gathering called the Shoshone Rendezvous. Another route ran between the American Southwest and the northern plains from the Cheyennes, Arapahoes, Comanches, and other nomads of the southern plains. Finally, the Mandans, Hidatsas, and Arikaras also exchanged goods with the nomadic Assiniboines and Crees in the northeastern plains as well as with the Tetons and Yankton Sioux.[40] The aboriginal trading pattern had been modified by the addition of horses, which began arriving in the northern plains during the early 1700s, although they did not become common until the end of the century.

The villagers exchanged corn, beans, and other garden produce with their nomadic neighbors for products of the hunt: dried meat, deer and bison robes, bows made from mountain sheep horns, and leather goods, such as decorated shirts and leggings. Exchange in the village centers was divided into individual trade and ceremonial trade.[41] Both men and women engaged in individual trade, each gender tending to exchange goods with individuals of the same sex. The women exchanged foodstuffs and items of apparel, while the most important goods that men exchanged were horses and guns.

The Shoshone Rendezvous took place every spring in the Great Basin. Its location cannot be pinpointed, although its most probable locale was in or near southwestern Wyoming. This gathering served as a link in the transmission of goods between the Pacific Coast and the Missouri River area. Crow Indians carried goods to this rendezvous from the northern plains; Utes brought goods to it from the Southwest; and Shoshones, Nez Perces, and Flatheads brought goods from the Great Basin and Plateau.

Many plains tribes were at war with one or more of their neighbors, yet they managed to maintain trading relations through an alternating pattern of economic dependence and social avoidance. The safety of traders was assured by a "market peace." For example, "when the Dakota saw a certain flower . . . blooming on the prairie, they knew that the corn was ripe, and went to the villages of the farming Indians to trade. From the time they came in sight of the village to the time they disappeared, there was a truce. When they had passed beyond the bluffs, they might steal an unguarded pony or lift a scalp, and were in turn liable to be attacked."[42]

Exchange with the very tribes with which the traders were currently at war was effected not only by a market peace but also by important rituals. After the calumet ceremony, even bitter enemies traded safely within the villages along the Missouri River: "A father-son adoption ceremony was the key mechanism . . . which enabled members of warring tribes to trade in peace. The Mandan were adopted by fictitious fathers, and in turn were adopted by sons in tribes with whom they dealt. . . . Plains Indian trade was accomplished by barter between fictitious relatives. From a larger perspective, a vast network of ritual kinship relationships extended throughout the entire Plains."[43]

Intertribal trade required its participants to communicate with groups having alien speech. George Catlin and others commented on the Mandans having been adept in learning foreign languages, and certainly it was mandatory in view of their role as middlemen. But there was another technique for overriding linguistic boundaries on the plains—its famous sign language. It surely is no coincidence that sign language was known by every group involved in the northern plains trade. Plains sign language is said to have been the most elaborate and most efficient form of nonverbal communication in the nonliterate world, and it permitted the ready transmission of complex messages between linguistically alien groups.[44]

Trade contributed to tribal specialization. Ewers points out that trade on the northern plains emphasized exchange between gardeners and nomadic hunters: nomads brought dried bison meat and other products of the chase to trade for corn and other produce from the villagers' gardens. This "had the effect of intensifying the labors of the nomads and the horticulturists in their own specialities," the nomads relying more on the chase and the villagers on their gardens in order to have the necessary surplus to trade.[45]

In addition to such staples, anything could change hands at trade fairs: tools, trinkets, folktales, songs and dances, and even brides. Gambling at these fairs was rampant and provided an avenue of exchange for many goods other than those brought for the express purpose of trade. In other words, the flow of goods and ideas—not to mention of persons and disease organisms—from one area to another was a simple matter and was often exceedingly rapid. The social interaction at these fairs facilitated the rapid dissemination of information and ideas over large parts of the continent. American Indians were in contact with one another over vast distances.

The villager's wealth and importance was a major problem, however, since the first European explorers were attracted to them precisely because of their renown as trading centers. White traders quickly insinuated themselves into the native trading network, establishing lines of communication far in advance of other white movements into the West. It is also not surprising that the villagers were decimated very early by epidemics carried by Indians moving along native trade routes—diseases unwittingly transmitted to them by Europeans who, anxious to intercept profits from exchanges at these trading centers, had attached themselves to the native exchange network.

American Indians were shrewd, experienced traders, and any suggestion that they were pawns of the Europeans is false.[46] They were skilled in bargaining, but more to the point, they recognized the threat to their system if they allowed Europeans to bypass them and eliminate their profits by trade with their neighbors. It was for this reason that they jealously guarded the Missouri and often halted trading parties going to their neighbors or enemies, if they did not kill them outright or steal their goods.

THE MISSOURI COMPANY

Traders had penetrated far up the Missouri River by the late 1780s. Those men, however, were licensed by the Spanish colonial government. "Theoretically, the trade was open to all Spanish subjects, but in practice the licensing requirements limited the actual number of participants to a favored few whom the Spaniards used as quasi-governmental agents."[47]

For example, Manuel Perez wrote to Governor General Miró in New Orleans on August 23, 1790, giving a roster of individuals who had been appointed to trade on the Missouri River. The list ignores the Osage Indians because of the Spaniards' "inability to send traders to the two Osage nations, which are the best of the Missouri nations for trade" (trade with them had been forbidden):

Kansas	to the commandant and to Auguste Chouteau
Missouri	to the commandant of Ste. Genevieve
Panis (Pawnee)	to Pedro de Volsey
Otos	to Don Bentura Collell
Republic (Republican Pawnee)	to Juan Bartélemy
Pani Maha (Skiri? Pawnee)	to Benito Vasquez
Mahas (Omaha)	to Juan Bautista Pratte[48]

In May 1794 Lt. Gov. Zenon Trudeau wrote to Governor General Carondelet listing the various Missouri River trading posts and providing the following estimates of the amounts of goods that would be taken to each of them:

Grands Eaux (Big Osage)	72,000 *livres*
Petits Eaux (Little Osage)	24,000
Kansa	24,000
Republique (Republican Pawnee)	6,000
Otoes	14,000
Panis Bon chef (Grand? Pawnee)	4,000
Panis Tapage (Tappage Pawnee)	5,000
Loups (Wolf or Skiri Pawnee)	5,000
Mahas (Omahas)	20,000
	175,000 *livres*[49]

No wonder that "The Indian trade is an issue of great urgency and competition among the inhabitants of Illinois," as Nicolas de Finiels said of contemporary St. Louis. He continued:

Hardly has the ice disappeared, freeing traffic on the streams, than large pirogues, light flat-bottomed barges, and birchbark canoes are made ready. Soon they are filled with trade goods, which have become indispensable to the Indians because of their contact with white men. *Engagés* press around these frail vessels; they stretch their arms, which are numb from six months of inactivity, but which soon recover their suppleness, elasticity, and vigor. Farewell songs ring out; paddles whip the waves into a froth, leaving behind a long wake that is quickly swallowed up by the next; din from the splashing paddles rises in the air to mingle with joyful shouts. The frail vessels finally triumph over the waters; they soon disappear in the winding river and lose themselves in the distance among the islands that intersect their course.[50]

These trips were not only economically oriented but also a social necessity:

In order to be respected, you must acquire the reputation of being a good boatman; to be a man you must have made three expeditions, paddle in hand—one to New Orleans, one to Michilimackinac, and one up either the Missouri or the Ohio. Then you can go a-courting, which would be contemptible if you had not shown the strength and the courage necessary to endure the hardships of these three trials.[51]

Jacques D'Eglise was among such men when he received a license to hunt on the Missouri in August 1790. There are no details of the voyage he was now to undertake. Even the date of his departure from St. Louis is unknown, and it is not even clear how far he planned to go upriver and with whom, for he most certainly did not go alone. Given the August date of his license, he probably left the following spring, in 1791. He reached the Mandans sometime in 1792, the first man that is soundly documented as having penetrated that far up the Missouri. He had succeeded in contacting the people that La Vérendrye, coming down from Canada, had met a half-century earlier. He could not have spent much time among them, for he returned to St. Louis the same year, in October, and was interrogated by Trudeau.

D'Eglise's return to St. Louis set the Spanish officials in a dither, but the garbled message with which he returned nonetheless told them of the magnitude of British commercial incursions into Spanish territory among the Mandans. Trudeau recorded that D'Eglise was "so simple and from a province in France of such a peculiar language [dialect] that nobody can understand it." Nevertheless, the lieutenant governor gleaned from him the fact that "although the commandant had forbidden all trading with the nations we know, he [D'Eglise] has dared to make his way in his hunting more than eight hundred leagues up the Missouri. There he found eight villages of a nation about which there was some knowledge under the name of Mandan, but to which no one had ever gone in this direction and by this river."[52]

A number of significant facts are embedded in D'Eglise's report. Eight Mandan villages of some four or five thousand persons had welcomed him, and they were provided with arms through direct trade with the British. A Frenchman (a man known only as Menard) had lived among them for fourteen years, and British traders were "established and fortified" about fifteen days from the villages (that is, at their posts along the Assiniboine River). The Mandans were "white like Europeans" and "have communication with the Spaniards, or with nations that know them, because they have saddles and bridles in Mexican style for their horses, as well as other articles which this same de la Iglesa saw." This was upsetting news, for Trudeau had been "strictly enjoined not to permit traders, even English ones, in territory subject to His Catholic Majesty."[53] Carondelet and Trudeau were united in one goal: to secretly discover a route west of the headwaters of the Missouri River across the Rocky Mountains to the Pacific Coast. They planned to reinforce and defend this route with a series of trading forts. D'Eglise's report spurred them into action.

The Missouri basin had been the preserve of independent fur traders and trappers for decades before the business became a corporate venture. The first company to be formed for this purpose, in 1794, was the Missouri Company, directed by Jacques Clamorgan, who had been elected to direct this "Syndic of commerce." This "syndic" was to control the profits to be made on the company's activities on the upper Missouri River. Clamorgan had a firm grip on the company and its associates. Part of that control included the fact that his associates were modest businessmen, not the richest and most influential merchants in St. Louis. For example, the Chouteau family, which was later to dominate the lower Missouri River trade, was conspicuous by its absence from this operation, and there is no doubt that the Spanish company would have profited by its business acumen. The consequent lack of expertise was one of the elements that eventually doomed the new company.

Clamorgan had bold plans for the company: they were even to penetrate to the Pacific Coast. On July 18, 1795, Governor General Carondelet had offered "in the name of the king three thousand *pesos* to the one who should succeed in first reaching the South Sea, [this I did] partly to arouse those people to a dangerous undertaking by greed and the reward, and partly in consideration of the fact that such a discovery was important to the state; for it would determine its boundaries in a permanent fashion by founding a settlement with all the necessary arrangements to prevent the English or the Russians from establishing themselves or extending themselves on those coasts, remote from the other Spanish possessions and near Nootka Sound."[54]

D'Eglise, accompanied by Joseph Garreau and three men, reascended the Missouri in two pirogues about March 1793 in an effort to return to the Mandans. His efforts were thwarted when they were stopped by either the Arikaras or the Sioux somewhere in central South Dakota. As a consequence, he suffered losses on the river. D'Eglise returned to St. Louis, but Garreau remained on the upper Missouri with the Arikaras for many years.[55] On June 19, 1794, D'Eglise petitioned Carondelet for the exclusive trade with the Mandan and the "Tayanne" Indians for a period of four years.[56] His request was denied. D'Eglise himself remained active in the Missouri River trade as late as 1803 or 1804. Prior to the Louisiana Purchase, he had hoped to reach the Pacific Ocean and win the three-thousand-peso reward that the Spanish government had offered. But like so many men of his era, this first St. Louis visitor to the Mandans ultimately met a violent death on the frontier. D'Eglise went to New Mexico, where he was "barbarously murdered" sometime before November 20, 1806. Three years later his accused murderers "were sentenced to death, shot, 'and their bodies hanged on the royal.'"[57]

THE FIRST SPANISH EXPEDITION: JEAN BAPTISTE TRUTEAU AND PONCA HOUSE

With D'Eglise's information in hand, the Missouri Company was not long in dispatching its first expedition up the Missouri. Jean Baptiste Truteau, a native of Montreal, had become a schoolmaster in St. Louis in 1774 and remained a teacher—save for his stint on the Missouri River—for more than forty years. The rationale for choosing him to lead a fur-trading expedition up the Missouri was never made clear, although the fact that Lieutenant Governor Trudeau had described the schoolmaster as his relative (a cousin) may be relevant, for Truteau's trip was made even before the governor general of Louisiana, baron de Carondelet, had sanctioned the company's charter.

Truteau left St. Louis on June 7, 1794, in a large pirogue with eight employees: Pierre Berger, second in command; Noel Charron, hunter; Joseph La Deroute; Joseph Chorette (who drowned on the trip); two men surnamed Quebec and Savoie; and two others. The schoolmaster had a clear set of directives: ascend the Missouri River to the Mandans, evict any British traders in residence there, and build a trading fort. He was to reserve his best goods for the Mandans and to trade only blue cloth or woolen blankets with the Omahas. From the Mandans he was then to find his way to the Pacific Ocean.

On August 6 Truteau was overtaken by Jacques D'Eglise. Despite Truteau's pleas that they continue together, D'Eglise and his four men, who were traveling lighter and could move more quickly, near the mouth of the Platte River moved on and soon left Truteau in their wake. His haste was his undoing, for a short time later D'Eglise was robbed by the Poncas of a great deal of his guns, ammunition, and other goods.[58]

It was fall before Truteau reached Omaha and Ponca country. He was able to avoid detection as he slipped by the Omaha village (known as Big Village) on August 24, and he continued to move cautiously to avoid the Poncas. Their village, he said, was "situated a league above [the Niobrara], near the Missouri." The Poncas probably were living at the time in a village known as Ponca Fort, near the mouth of Ponca Creek, a few miles upstream from the mouth of the Niobrara. Truteau drew near the mouth of the creek on September 14 and approached the village "with suspicion." The traders remained hidden on the river behind Ponca Island until dark, when they resumed their upriver trek to the Arikara villages. They did not try to travel during the day because Ponca Fort was very difficult to pass without being seen, "for besides there being prairie on both sides of the Missouri near their lodges, there rise up hills from the tops of which they can watch up and down the Missouri for three or four leagues." Their caution was well founded.[59]

Truteau continued up the Missouri River toward the Arikara villages in central South Dakota, but probably somewhere below the Grand Detour, a band of Teton or Yankton Sioux intercepted them. They relieved Truteau of part of his goods when they learned he was on his way to the Arikaras. Eventually, he was able to leave the Sioux, but the traders were shadowed as they moved upriver. Truteau therefore cached the remainder of his stock and hiked north, overland, to find the Arikara villages and seek their help. But their villages, on the west bank of the Missouri between the mouths of the Bad and Cheyenne Rivers, were empty. They may have fled to escape the Sioux, but perhaps they were on a fall bison hunt at the time. Whatever the case, the Arikaras were to move farther up the Missouri before Truteau's return the following year. Truteau had little choice but to return to his cache near the Grand Detour, empty it, and retrace his route downstream. Snow and bitter cold were imminent, and he was in the middle of Sioux country. Unless he could relocate farther downstream near more friendly Indians, he would not survive the winter. Upon entering Ponca country in October, he stopped and again buried his trade goods for safekeeping at some point opposite the Ponca village.

On November 11 his party began building a cabin for a winter post on the Missouri above the mouth of Ponca Creek—a cabin that has come to be known as Ponca House. (Its site was on the left bank of the Missouri in present-day Charles Mix County, South Dakota; the site was later obliterated by the changing channel of the river.) There he traded with the Dakotas, Omahas, and Poncas during the winter of 1794–95. But he was not alone in the area: rival traders Solomon Petit also wintered in the same vicinity, as he had earlier, as well as employees of Juan Meunier. Their trade reduced his profits. The French had in fact been very active in this area for a long time. Truteau commented that the natives were "very roused up against us . . . and particularly against Jacques d'Eglise, who hastens stealthily along the road every summer they say."[60]

Truteau had scarcely chosen the locale for Ponca House when Big Rabbit, second chief of the Omahas, arrived on the scene on November 12. A month later Blackbird himself arrived; he was indignant that Truteau had avoided the Omahas on his upriver trip, but the trader told him that he had stopped at Big Village and had found it deserted.

In the spring Truteau abandoned Ponca House. He sent a few of his men back to St. Louis with the few furs he had managed to obtain, and he went back up the Missouri River on March 25, 1795. He stopped briefly among the Poncas and later reached the Arikara villages near the mouth of the Grand River, where the Arikaras had relocated after leaving their homes near the mouth of the Cheyenne. He remained among them until the spring of 1796, apparently having made no contact whatsoever with the Mandans. He returned to St. Louis "before the summer of 1796 was a month old."[61]

On his return Truteau had a message for his superiors in St. Louis: cultivate the friendship of the Omahas, for they were crucial to further upriver exploration; build a post at their village; and send tribute to Blackbird: a medal, a great flag, and annual presents. The Omaha post was essential: "In order to pass above, this [post] is absolutely necessary, in order to place the great chief of the Omahas in our interest."[62] A post in northeastern Nebraska made eminent sense: it was about halfway to the Mandan villages and would provide an admirable location to provision traders.

In the long run Truteau's expedition was a failure, and the company learned little from it: they ignored his recommendations. The idea of an Omaha post was either premature for them or they were not yet prepared for the expense of such construction. Instead, they sponsored a second and more expensive campaign on the river, but with more limited goals.

THE SECOND SPANISH EXPEDITION:
LÉCUYER AND ANTONIO BREDA

The second expedition, larger than that of Truteau and carrying twice the amount of trade goods, was also a disappointment to the Missouri Company. It was dispatched upriver in April 1795 under the direction of a man named Lécuyer and "will be very fortunate if it reaches the Mandana nation at the end of fall, and before the severe cold, so as to be able to go overland to the Rocky Chain [Mountains] whither he has orders to go without delay in order to reach, if possible, by next spring, 1796, the shores of the Sea of the West." The party accomplished none of its goals: it never passed the Poncas, where it was plundered in the summer of 1795; James Mackay later reported that Lécuyer "has not had less than two wives since his arrival at the home of the Poncas, [and] has wasted a great deal of goods of the Company." The expedition was a total fiasco, and its losses had to be written off. When news of its misfortune reached St. Louis, the company sent Antonio Breda to its aid. He was too late, arriving after the expedition had been plundered. Six of Lécuyer and Breda's *engagés* later joined Mackay and Evans on October 27.[63]

This is about all we know of the second expedition, and much of Mackay's account of it has to do with denigrating Lécuyer's actions. His "infamous" actions are not specified beyond his acquisition of "two wives," but in an era when sexual fraternization with American Indians was a way of life, it is difficult to believe he chastised him solely on that account. The cost of the Missouri River expeditions, in any event, was deepening for the Missouri Company, for still another and more expensive third upriver effort was in the making even before what was left of Lécuyer's abortive party returned to St. Louis.

CHAPTER TWO

THE THIRD SPANISH
EXPEDITION TAKES FORM

"Marching with Long Strides upon Unknown Soil"

THE LEADER: JAMES MACKAY

The directors of the Missouri Company chose a new arrival in St. Louis to lead their expedition upriver. To one unfamiliar with the times, James Mackay was an unusual choice. A native of Scotland, Mackay was born around 1759 in Arrichliney, County Sutherland. The ruins of the town of Arichlinie lie not far from Loch Arichlinie, which itself is less than twenty miles south of the northernmost coast of Scotland. The gently rolling, treeless landscape surrounding the ruins and the loch are, in photographs, hauntingly reminiscent of the vast Great Plains landscapes of North America with which he was to become so familiar.

Mackay was one of several sons of a family descended, he claimed, from Irish royalty who had settled Scotland several centuries earlier. We know nothing of his education, although in his postexpeditionary years he is recorded as speaking French,[1] a language he also could write. It would be reasonable to assume that he acquired French as a consequence of his wide-ranging activities in French Canada.

Mackay left his highland home during a time of substantial change in Great Britain, a time that placed grievous hardships on poor country dwellers. The Enclosure Act had led to the subdivision of grazing lands into large private landholdings, and the means for ordinary people to make a living were becoming increasingly difficult to obtain. Young James came to North America sometime between 1774 and 1776 hard on the heels of an uncle and at least three of his brothers who had settled in the nascent United States. James, however, went to Canada. A few years later he had made the long journey

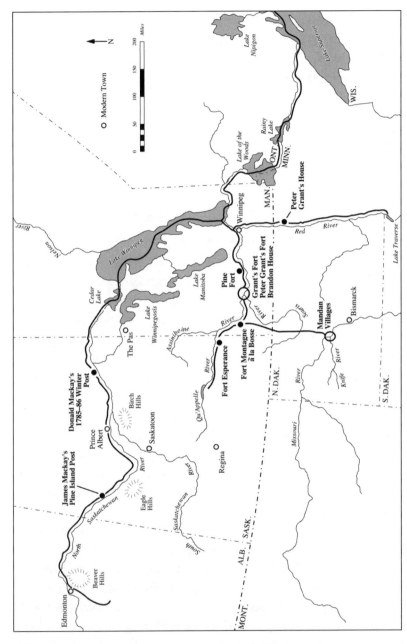

Fig. 3. James Mackay's 1786–88 travels through south-central and western Canada, superimposed on a modern map. (W. R. Wood, ©2001)

from Montreal to the *pays d'en haut*, the high country in western Canada, and had become engaged in the fur trade for the British North West Company.

Probably in May his brigade left the great stone buildings that housed North West's store of trade goods, upstream from Montreal at the great rapids at La Chine (they were on the road to the "China Sea"—the Pacific). The voyageur's canoes continued up the Ottawa River, then down the French River to Lake Huron, passing westward along the north shore to Sault St. Marie and pressing on to Grand Portage, the trading rendezvous on the northern shore of Lake Superior. The six-to-eight-week voyage on to central Canada consisted of eighteen-hour days of backbreaking labor for those who paddled, pulled, and poled the canoes upriver and who also carried the canoes and their contents over innumerable portages, where water travel was impossible.[2]

James Mackay's first known position in the fur trade was as a clerk in 1783 with Robert Grant on the upper Assiniboine River. In 1784 he traveled south along the Red River toward its headwaters, probably from Grant's North West Company post on the lower Red River in what is now northwestern Minnesota. A map made in 1791 by Edward Jarvis and Donald Mackay shows "Mr Peter Grant's House" at or near the mouth of Pembina River in present-day North Dakota. In 1800 Alexander Henry the Younger said that opposite the mouth of the Pembina, "On the east side of the Red River is the remains of an old Fort, built by Mr Peter Grant some years ago and was the first establishment [of the North West Company] ever built on the Red River."[3]

In 1785 Mackay changed allegiance and joined Hudson's Bay Company employee Donald Mackay as his assistant. The two men were not related, although James had been born only twenty miles north of Donald's home in Scotland. Donald became an independent, if not particularly successful, trader at an unnamed post on the upper Saskatchewan River between 1785 and 1787. All that we know of James's activities there is that in the spring of 1786 Donald sent him to the rendezvous at Grand Portage for a supply of trade goods. A dotted line on the 1795 Soulard map suggests that Mackay also went as far west as present-day Edmonton, just west of the Beaver Hills. Some scholars believe that he did not make this trip himself but based his claim of that excursion on information he obtained from Hudson's Bay employee James Gaddy. If, however, we are to credit Mackay's own words, he had met with Piegan Indians who were living several hundred miles west of the Mandan and Hidatsa villages not far from the location shown on the Soulard map.[4]

James's employment with Donald was a brief one, for he left his employer in 1786 and once again went to trade on the Assiniboine River for Robert

Grant. According to information he later provided Antoine Soulard in St. Louis, and which Soulard incorporated on his 1795 map, Mackay wintered on the Saskatchewan River in 1786–87. Grant then sent him to Fort Espérance, which Grant had founded on the Catepoi (the modern Qu'Appelle) River. It was from this post that Mackay said he made his visit to the Mandans in 1787.[5] There the Canadian traders obtained pelts, buffalo robes, and corn.

Mackay wrote his own account of his visit to the Mandans, which he says took place in "the Beginning of the Year 1787," probably in January. Since Soulard shows him spending the previous winter (1786–87) on the Saskatchewan, it is possible that Mackay is one year off in the date of his visit and that he actually went to the Mandans in 1786. Whatever the date, his description of the visit provides no reason to believe that any part of it is a fabrication.

Leaving Fort Espérance, Mackay's most probable course was to travel down the valley of the Assiniboine River to Fort Montagne à la Bosse, then walk overland to the valley of the Souris River. He arrived at the Mandan villages after a seventeen-day trek across a height of land between the Assiniboine and Souris River drainage and the Missouri valley, a land he said was "inhabited by a Savage nation that they call Assiniboines, those Indians generally keep or have their residence near Turtle Mountain." His arrival was an impressive one, particularly for a man who had just walked across the snowy northern plains for more than two weeks. Word somehow reached the Mandans well in advance of his coming, for "many of their Chiefs Came to Meet me, at some distance from their village, and would not permit me to enter their Village on foot, they carried me between four men in a Buffaloe Robe, to the Chiefs tents." This had been a Mandan custom for greeting incoming Europeans as early as the 1738 visit by Pierre Gaultier de Varennes, the Sieur de La Vérendrye. The elder La Vérendrye, after being met by the Mandan chief many leagues from their village, said that they "would not allow me to walk, but insisted on carrying me. I had to consent, being urged by the Assiniboines, who said that it would cause much dissatisfaction if I refused."[6]

Mackay's hosts quickly prepared a feast for him and his party, and the few trade goods his group had brought along were soon exchanged. The Mandans, he said, "offered me in Exchange the best of what they had in Possession" for his merchandise, "to which they appeared to set a great value." Mackay saw evidence of other, though indirect, trade with Europeans, for the Mandans had guns and balls they had obtained in intertribal trade. Indeed, the La Vérendryes had seen goods imported from the Spanish southwest fifty years earlier, for "The chief showed them a Spanish bridle."[7] The brief account of

Mackay's visit generally is silent concerning his activities during this ten-day visit, but his departure was marked by regret on the part of his hosts, for whom Mackay had a high opinion. They "are in general people as good as they are mild who lay a great value on the friendship of the Whites."

The young Scottish trader was the second visitor to the Mandans to say anything of significance about them and about their neighbors, the Hidatsas. "The Mandaines, jointly with the Manitouris [Minitarees] and Wattasoons [Amahamis] live in five Villages, which are almost in sight of one another, three of those Villages are on the South of the Missouri and two on the North Side. The Situation of those five Villages is charming they are built on an Elevated plaine, even and fertile, which extends on either Side to a considerable distance. Those Nations cultivate the Ground round about their Villages and sow Corn Beans, Pumpkins and Gourds; they also make earthen pots in which they Boil their Meats, these Pots resist to fire as well as if they were iron." Although Mackay did not specify the locations of these villages, it is clear that they were at the mouth of the Knife River—a location and a village count confirmed later by the narrative and map that David Thompson prepared when he arrived seven months after John Evans's departure in 1797.[8]

Things did not go well with Donald Mackay's enterprise on the Saskatchewan. In 1787, when his frustrations caught up with him, he returned to London. There, in 1788, he set up an agreement with eight partners (including his former clerk, James Mackay) to conduct trade in western Canada for seven years. The enterprise, unfortunately, rapidly disintegrated, and some of his partners began to attach his property. The relations between Donald and James also soured, for James brought suit against his former employer in 1789 for wages for the time he had spent on the Saskatchewan.

Not long after, James Mackay left Canada for the United States. His activities for the next several years are not well documented, but about this time he met in New York Don Diego Maria de Gardoqui, the Spanish minister to the United States.[9] On June 25, 1789, Gardoqui wrote a letter to Don José de Monino Redondo, conde de Floridablanca, the first foreign minister to Great Britain's King George III, in New York. Gardoqui wrote:

> One of the many enthusiastic Englishmen who roam [corren] these western countries of the King's dominions inhabited only by Indians has arrived here.
>
> This person, although a young man, says he has traveled for nearly five years from the English establishment of Hudson Bay towards the

west among various Indian nations, crossed the Mississippi and the Missouri and arrived at the cordillera of mountains which divide the waters [*arrojando por sus faldas*], some to this ocean and others to the Pacific.

He reports that the furthest nation he reached assured him that about 100 miles from that place there was a river which empties into the Pacific Ocean, and he adds that the distance to it was short.

He has made a map, *a su modo* [in his manner], which I have seen and I have furnished means in order to obtain a copy.[10]

Who was the man that had just arrived in New York? Surely it was Mackay, then only twenty-eight years old, who had indeed traveled through British territory west of Hudson Bay for "nearly five years" and had been affiliated with the Hudson's Bay Company. This brief itinerary matched his Canadian travels, for he had traveled west of the Mississippi, visited the Missouri River, and come very near the Rocky Mountains and the headwaters of rivers that flow into the Pacific. A copy of the map that Gardoqui obtained from the "enthusiastic Englishman" would be exceedingly informative regardless of the man's identity. In any event, Gardoqui apparently did meet James Mackay in New York and was responsible for introducing him to the Spaniards in St. Louis as one knowledgeable about the country they were about to explore.

Mackay's introduction to the notion that there were Welsh-speaking Indians in the West is illuminated in notes that he probably penned sometime between 1799 and 1803:

> On my way from New York to Louisiana in 1794 I met a worthy Gentleman, Doctr. Jn. Rees [Morgan John Rhys], who, after informing him of my intended expedition, furnished me with a small vocabulary of the Welch Language written by himself and informed me respecting a Mr. John Evans from Wales who was gone to the Illinois with the intention of traveling westward to see the supposed Welch tribe.
>
> Having arrived in Louisiana, I got ready for my voyage to the West. I sent for, & engaged for my assistant, Mr. Evans who spoke & wrote the Welch Language with facility, and during Our Tour had a sufficient opportunity to prove that neither the Paducas nor any other tribe in that part of the continent could speak one word of Welch nor anything simular thereto.[11]

These notes reveal that Mackay's duties as an expeditionary leader in Louisiana probably had been prearranged in the East and that he had already heard of

Evans, who had preceded him to the Illinois Country. In any case, he eventually "sent for & engaged" Evans as his assistant, a man that, as Bernard DeVoto has written, "was straight out of fantasy."[12]

Mackay arrived in Cahokia in 1791 and by October was already listed as a merchant. He became a Spanish subject in late 1793. His acquaintance with Lt. Gov. Zenon Trudeau dates to this period, and on May 20, 1793, Trudeau wrote to Carondelet that he hoped "to see within a few days a well informed Canadian mozo who has been in the said [Mandan] nation on discovery." Trudeau would transmit whatever information he obtained from the mozo— Mackay—to Carondelet. Trudeau obviously told Carondelet a great deal about the Scotsman, for when Mackay was retained in 1795 to lead the Spanish expedition upriver, Carondelet wrote that he had been employed by the British with "great success in the explorations of the countries, located north of the Missouri, with the intent of opening communication with the South Sea."[13] This was the exact mission that Mackay was now to undertake for his new employers. An additional reason for employing him was the knowledge that in 1787 Mackay had traveled from Fort Espérance on the Qu'Appelle River to visit the Mandan villages. These villages were one of the principal goals of the Spanish expedition, for the North West and Hudson's Bay posts in Canada were the bases from which traders made their way to these Missouri River gardeners.

Why did Mackay leave Canada eventually become a Spanish citizen? In 1798 Manual Gayoso de Lemos said, without elaboration, that James had been "displeased with the Canadian companies." Whatever his motives, Mackay went to New York City and was in Upper Louisiana in 1791. Given the fact that the purpose of his expedition was to expel the British and their illegal trade from the upper Missouri, he obviously left the Canada with a grudge and ill feelings against his fellow traders. A man with his experience would have been priceless to the St. Louis Spanish, for no one in that city could match his knowledge of the northern limits of Spanish territory. These qualifications led to his replacement of the Missouri Company's manager, Jean Baptiste Truteau, for Mackay was highly regarded before, as well as after, his return from the upper Missouri. "James Mackay was uniformly characterized by the officials of Spanish Louisiana as a man of ability, intelligence, prudence, loyalty and honesty, a man 'of knowledge, zealous and punctual.'"[14]

Lieutenant Governor Trudeau was the man responsible for engaging Mackay as the "principal explorer and director of the Company's affairs in the Indian Country." He was "to open a commerce with those distant and Unknown

Nations in the upper parts of the Missouri and to discover all of the unknown parts of his Catholic Majesty's Dominions through that continent as far as the Pacific Ocean."[15] His reimbursement for undertaking the hazardous upriver expedition was modest—only four hundred pesos a year—but he was richly rewarded with praise and, more importantly, lavish land grants upon his return to St. Louis.

THE LIEUTENANT: JOHN THOMAS EVANS

Had enthusiastic Welsh nationalists not become wedded to the idea of a legendary medieval prince and his colonizing of the New World, James Mackay would have picked another man as his partner for the 1795 expedition. A London literary society, the Gwyneddigion, came to believe the myth that the Welsh had discovered the New World in 1170. Prince Madoc, son of Oswain Gwynedd, a prince of North Wales, supposedly had led a group to the New World, which eventually resulted in a tribe of Welsh-speaking Indians. The Gwyneddigions determined to seek out these elusive expatriates of their homeland and decided to send John Thomas Evans to America to find them. Evans was to accompany a man named Iolo Morganwg, but as things turned out he traveled to the New World alone; Morganwg was more interested in forging ancient mythology, including the story of Madoc, than he was in pursuing his literary creations. Evans was to pursue the myth of Madoc, a legend reinforced by the book *An Enquiry into the Truth of the Tradition Concerning the Discovery of America by Prince Madog ab Owen Gwynedd about the Year 1170*. This volume, published in London in 1791 by John Williams, supported the idea that the Madoc Indians were living in the interior of North America. That same year in London, William Jones "circulated an address, To All Indigenous Cambro-Britons, announcing the brave news that the Madoc Indians had been found on the far Missouri." During the closing years of the eighteenth century, the idea of the Madoc Indians was widespread not only in Great Britain but also in the United States, a phenomenon that often was called "Madoc fever."[16]

John Evans was a native of North Wales, having been born sometime before April 14, 1770, in Waunfawr, a few miles from the town of Caernarfon, on the northwesternmost coast of mainland Wales opposite Holy Island. He came from a poor family of Methodist ministers, but little of his early life is known beyond the names of his parents, Thomas and Anne Evans. At the age of twenty-one, he went to London to seek his fortune, and through his contacts with nationalist Welsh, he became attached to the idea of seeking the Madoc Indians, the "Lost Brothers in America." Setting sail for the New World, he arrived in Baltimore on October 10, 1792. His original plan of going to Upper Louisiana and ascending the Missouri River was a deeply entrenched one, although Welsh friends in and around Baltimore and Philadelphia tried to persuade him not to undertake such a hazardous voyage. But Evans was determined, for as he said in a letter to his brother, "God Almighty had laid [this mission] on his conscience" and nothing was to dissuade him. That he eventually reached the Mandans—fruitlessly, as it turned out, for his original purpose—is little short of miraculous, but it was because of his single-minded, almost religious dedication to locate the Madocs.

Evans left his position as a clerk in a countinghouse in the East in February 1793 and headed west, going first down the Ohio River and then up the Mississippi to New Madrid, arriving there a little later that year.[17] The fact that he arrived at all is astonishing: he had begun his journey with only $1.75 in his pocket. Eventually crossing into what is now Missouri at New Madrid, Evans was required to swear an oath of loyalty to Spain, its king, and to Spanish national interests, "in whose defense [he was] ready to take up arms." Some oaths of allegiance taken at New Madrid from 1793 to 1795 are preserved in the General Archives of the Indies in Seville. Although Evans is not specifically mentioned in those documents, a copy of the text for April 7, 1793, reads:

> We, the undersigned, swear, on the Holy Gospels, complete faith, homage, and loyalty to His Majesty. We wish voluntarily to live under his laws, and promise not to violate directly or indirectly His royal interests, to give immediate advice to our Commandants of whatever comes to our knowledge and which can in any way prejudice the general welfare of Spain and the special welfare of this province, in whose defense we are ready to take up arms on the first requisition of our leaders, especially in favor of this district, whenever forces should come by way of the upper part of the river or overland to invade it. In order that this may stand forth as our free and spontaneous will we sign the present oath of allegiance before the undersigned Commandant, and David Gray and Don Antonio Gamelin, witnesses present in Fort Celeste at New Madrid, April 7, 1793.[18]

Evans took the oath seriously, as he demonstrated a few years later on the upper Missouri.

Evans had an awful journey after arriving in New Madrid. "Now begins my life of misery and hardships. In 10 days after my arrival was taken by a violent and Intermiting fever succeeded by a delirium. Thank God for friends, for I was paid the greatest attention to in my Sickness by my kind land lady and all the Great People of the place, otherwise I should have died in the greatest poverty." In two months his fever abated, and, though still feeble, he unwisely departed for Kaskaskia. Losing his way on the road the first day, he was "lost in the infinite wilderness of America. Oh unsufferable thirst and hunger is an amusement in Comparison to this. The parent sun . . . threatens to bake my brains like a cake and withdraw from me my Pressuous Eye Sight." On the third day, his fever returned, but he continued on through a swamp with water up to his armpits, hardly able to walk a hundred yards without resting. Evans's "violent and Intermiting fever succeeded by a delirium" surely was malaria, the illness that eventually would kill him. No equally severe illness would be noted until the year of his death; if any medical problem afflicted him on his voyage to the Mandans, no record remains. En route to St. Louis, Evans stopped at Kaskaskia, where without explanation, he spent the next eighteen months. When he did leave, around Christmas 1794, it was due to having heard "of a gent. at St. Louis who was engaged to go up the [Missouri] River for three years."[19]

The Welsh Indian mythology held that the people most likely to be the Madocs were either the Padoucas (that is, Apaches), sometimes even alluded to as the "White Padoucas," or the Mandans. Both tribes were to be found west of St. Louis, but Evans was to decide that the Mandans were more likely to be those whom he sought.

When Evans arrived, St. Louis was in turmoil: at least its merchants and Spanish rulers were upset. Jacques D'Eglise had returned to the city in October 1792 with the disquieting news that the British were trading with the Mandans and other Indians on the upper Missouri—thus intruding into the domains of His Catholic Majesty, King Carlos IV. Already suspicious of the British, particularly since war between Great Britain and Spain seemed imminent, Evans at first was "taken for a Spy, Imprisoned, loaded with iron and put in the Stoks besides, in the dead of winter. Here I suffered very much for several days till my friends from the American side came and proved to the Contrary and I was released."[20]

One of the men who helped Evans escape prison was George Turner, the U.S. judge in the Northwest Territory at Kaskaskia, some sixty miles downriver from St. Louis. Evans had come to Turner's attention when Zenon Trudeau had visited the judge in Kaskaskia and mentioned his suspicions concerning Evans's plans. Turner, having earlier heard of Evans, urged Trudeau that he be allowed to continue his journey; perhaps Evans would make some valuable discoveries. And since the Spanish were sending an expedition to the Mandans, it would make sense to send along a man who could communicate with them—that is, if the tales circulating in the Illinois Country were correct about the Welsh origin of that tribe. Turner later wrote Evans from Kaskaskia on March 10, 1795, describing a strange animal that lived on the upper Missouri (probably the mountain sheep, *Ovis canadensis*) and asking him to seek out and return to him its skin.[21]

James Mackay was by now a seasoned traveler and explorer. What could have been his rationale for choosing Evans, a man who had spent two years on the frontier but who knew little as an explorer and had never been a leader of men, as the deputy of an expedition to explore new and savage country, a man who, by his own admission, *did not know one word of French*? First, Evans was already known to Mackay from conversations with Morgan John Rhys, a Welsh Baptist minister in Cincinnati. Evans's urge to explore the Missouri for Welsh Indians was well known, and his potential ability to communicate with the Mandans clearly would be of value. We also know, from Mackay's own hand, that he "was determined to use all means in my Power to unvail the mystery" of the Welsh-speaking Indians. Finally, Mackay may have wanted an English-speaking companion on a long wilderness journey that otherwise would be dominated by voyageurs having alien languages and backgrounds. On his arrival in St. Louis, Mackay "sent for, and engaged for [his] assistant Mr Evans."[22] It was a sound choice: Evans was to prove a capable and resourceful associate, and he took his new role as a Spanish agent seriously.

The information the Spanish had obtained from D'Eglise in 1792 about British activities among the Mandans had been distressing enough. But when D'Eglise returned on July 4, 1795, from yet another trip up the Missouri River, he brought with him two Canadian Frenchmen who had deserted a North West Company expedition to the Mandans, Juan Fotman (or Jean Tremont) and Chrysostom Joncquard (or Chrisosthomo Jonca). John Macdonell, the director of the North West Company's River La Souris Post, had sent René Jusseaume in mid-1794 to the Missouri River, where his party built a small fort between the Mandan and Hidatsa villages, a fort that, to the chagrin of the Spanish, was weekly capped with a British flag.

Fotman and Joncquard had been members of Jusseaume's party, so their stories provided a final straw for Spanish patience. No mention is made of information that could have been obtained from another man who had accompanied the two deserters to St. Louis. Joseph Garreau, trading at the Arikara villages, had sent this man, a bondservant named Loison, to the Hidatsa villages, where he arrived in early April 1794. Loison returned to St. Louis with D'Eglise and the two deserters, both of whom D'Eglise had found living among the Pawnee Indians.[23]

There were other worrisome political elements in the air. Spain and France signed the Treaty of Basel in the summer of 1795, bringing peace to the two nations. While this alleviated some tensions, it did not relieve the suspicion that the French were still interested in regaining Louisiana. There were other nagging problems. In making peace with France, Spain had severed its alliance with Great Britain and thereby cast more fuel on the Anglo-Spanish rivalry in Upper Louisiana.[24] The strained relations between Spain and Great Britain did not long resist war: the two nations clashed in October 1796. These events were not known in Upper Louisiana at the time the Mackay and Evans expedition left St. Louis, nor for most of the time the expedition was gone. Still, it is not hard to imagine the sense of urgency that the unsettled politics of Europe, as they were known in St. Louis, plus the news of the blatant British economic imperialism in the north—news that was scarcely two months old—provided the backers of the Missouri Company as their third expedition left the St. Louis waterfront.

THE CARTOGRAPHIC BACKGROUND: THE 1795 SOULARD MAP

Mackay and Evans were not exploring terrain previously untrodden by white Europeans. The land and the Missouri River as far as the Mandans had been visited, repeatedly, by traders either ascending the Missouri River or going overland from bases along the Mississippi River. Some of the information that such men obtained concerning the upper Missouri was available, at least orally, in St. Louis, but as far as we know there were no graphic representations of the area above the Omaha Indians that would have surpassed what was known on Guillaume Delisle's great map of 1718. An expedition as costly and groundbreaking as that of Mackay and Evans would have been provided with every resource available. Since no good map was at hand, it is reasonable to believe one would have been made for them. One likely made expressly for this expedition is one created by the Spanish surveyor general in St. Louis, Antoine Pierre Soulard. The chart bears the very month and year that Mackay and Evans are believed to have left St. Louis: August 1795.

By 1795, a great deal was known of more than fifteen hundred miles of the course of the Missouri as far upstream as the Mandan Indians, living near the mouth of the Knife River above modern present-day Bismarck, North Dakota. Cartographic details of its upper reaches, however, often were severely distorted if not in outrageous error. But Soulard's map, created nearly a decade before Lewis and Clark's transcontinental journey, most closely approximates reality. An equivalent map, at least in terms of the general terrain it portrayed, was one prepared by Gen. Georges-Victor Collot, a French engineer and spy. Collot had come to Louisiana to covertly examine the boundary between Spanish Louisiana and the territory of the United States. Not long after his 1796 arrival in St. Louis, however, Spanish officials became suspicious of his mission, and they arrested and quietly expelled him. The map he managed to prepare of the Missouri basin, based on information then available in St. Louis, was probably engraved before Collot's death in 1805, but the report containing it was suppressed and did not appear in print until 1826.[25] The improvement in Collot's representation of the upper Missouri over that of Soulard undoubtedly derived from information he obtained after his expulsion from St. Louis in 1796. In any event, by 1826, his map was wholly obsolete, for William Clark's map of the West was widely known and used.

The visiting Collot and the resident Soulard had access to the same general sources in St. Louis, and one might suspect they would have created roughly equivalent maps. But for whatever reason, the general's map of the course of the Missouri and the upper Mississippi was vastly superior in detail and configuration to that of his countryman, officially employed by the Spanish government. The two charts, of course, contain many of the same details— for example, both of them confuse part of the lower reaches of the Platte River with that of the Loup River, and both show the forks of the Platte—but Collot's version, nevertheless, was the better representation. He portrayed the Grand Detour of central South Dakota in its proper proportion, although its orientation is reversed exactly 180 degrees. It was historian Aubrey Diller's belief that Collot's account and his map of the Missouri River were based in part on Soulard's map and in part on the upriver voyage by Jean Baptiste Truteau in 1794.[26] Certainly, the text for Collot's description of the Missouri was taken from Truteau's own statements about the river, but that description was also available to Soulard and the Missouri Company, which had dispatched Truteau.

The Soulard map has a tangled history, in part because the original chart disappeared for nearly two centuries: it only recently surfaced in a private collection in Spain. It is difficult to overestimate the importance of this map,

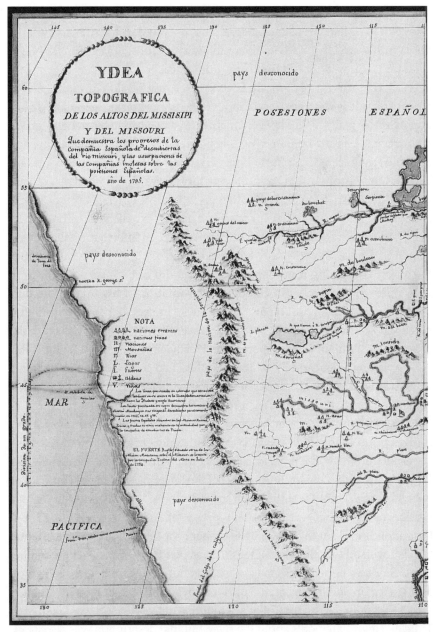

Fig. 4. Antoine Soulard's 1795 map of the Missouri River. (From Wood, "Missouri River Basin," fig. 1, courtesy of the Karpeles Manuscript Library, San Diego)

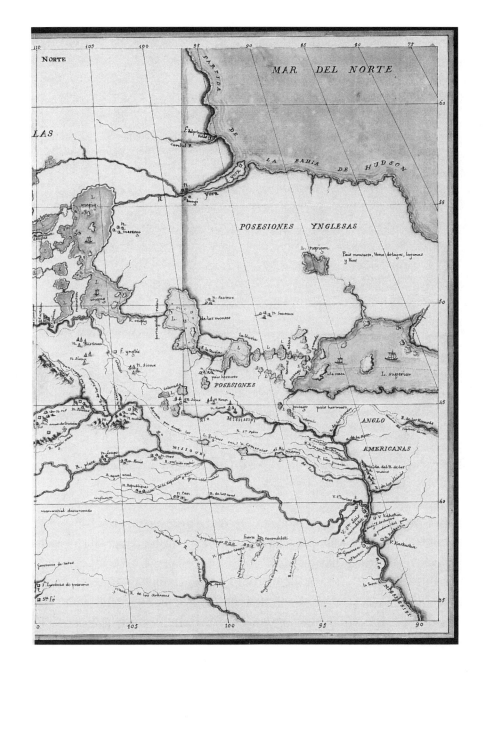

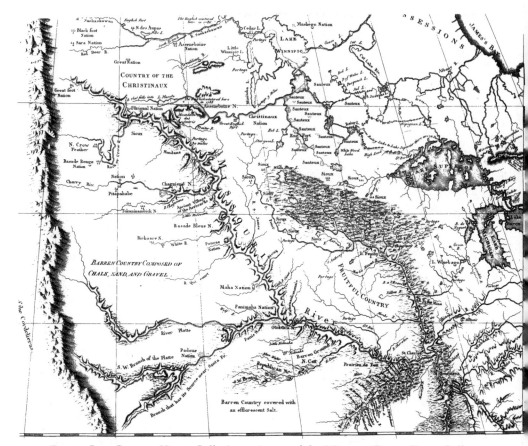

Fig. 5. Gen. Georges-Victor Collot's 1796 map of the Missouri River. (From Collot, *Journey in North America*, atlas, plate 29)

for it was acclaimed by Aubrey Diller, one of the most distinguished historical cartographers of the Missouri valley, as "virtually the first original and independent map of the [Missouri] river since Delisle's famous *Carte de la Louisiane* of 1718."[27] Soulard's chart is an important representation of the Great Plains of North America and their environs at the close of the eighteenth century, a view that extended from the southern plains deep into western Canada. Who was the man that compiled this miniature atlas of the midcontinent? It is worthwhile to devote some time to a discussion of both the cartographer and his map.

Antoine Pierre Soulard was appointed surveyor general of Spanish Louisiana by Lieutenant Governor Trudeau on February 3, 1795. He had been highly

Fig. 6. Antoine Pierre Soulard. (From Stevens, *Missouri the Center State*, opposite p. 108)

recommended for the post by Manuel Gayoso de Lemos, the governor general of Louisiana, as early as May 16 of the previous year. Soulard was born in Rochefort, France, in 1766 and served for a time as a second lieutenant in the French navy. Perhaps it was in this capacity that he gained his knowledge of surveying and cartography. He apparently came to New Orleans about the time of the French Revolution. Leaving New Orleans, he arrived in Ste. Genevieve, Missouri, in February 1794 and helped build a fort. He moved on to St. Louis a little later that year. In his own words, "Shortly after [visiting Ste. Genevieve], my good friend M. Zenon [Trudeau] took me in hand, and since then I have lived in St. Louis." This assertion makes it likely that he was in the city as early as March 1794. The twenty-eight-year-old Frenchman was appointed to the post of surveyor general early the following year, a position he retained until Louisiana passed into American hands in 1803. Soulard was also captain of the militia, adjutant to the lieutenant governor of Upper Louisiana, and surveyor for St. Louis and Ste. Genevieve. He became a well-known and respected figure in contemporary St. Louis, and the city today commemorates his name with a street, place, and playground, for example, in a district of downtown St. Louis that also carries his name.[28]

Five versions exist of the 1795 Soulard map: one unfinished prototype sketch, the "original" finished map, and no less than three extant copies, one each in Spanish, French, and English. The prototype sketch is unimportant, and with the original map now available, the Spanish copy is redundant, and the French and English copies simply illustrate its later history.

The most easily recognized feature of the Soulard map and its derivatives is the depiction of the Big Bend, or "Grand Detour," of the Missouri River in central South Dakota as a grotesquely exaggerated U-shaped bend between the Mandan and Arikara villages. On his map it is as large as the southern part of Lake Winnipeg, whereas on the ground it is only 25 river miles around. A person, however, could walk across its neck in an hour and a half, for it was only 1.75 miles from bank to bank. The presence of the great meander had long been known—indeed, a Frenchman had been "settled" in its vicinity a full half-century earlier—but prior to Soulard's map, there was no cartographic representation of it.[29]

Soulard depicted features both above and below the Grand Detour with relative accuracy, although the river's course is sadly in error below the Arikaras. The configuration of the Missouri above the Mandans is remarkably accurate, although the Yellowstone River is conspicuously absent. The chart nonetheless is a "cartographic milestone," surpassing in detail and accuracy all other contemporary maps showing the same terrain. Firsts on the document include the earliest representation of the Grand Detour, and it is perhaps the earliest to show the forks of the Platte River. Although he is not known to have had firsthand familiarity with any part of the map other than the Mississippi

Fig. 7. Typical view of the Missouri River valley in central South Dakota before its inundation in 1963 by the Big Bend Dam and its impoundment, Lake Sharpe. (Photo courtesy of the National Anthropological Archives, Washington, D.C., MRBS Negative 3900-172)

River below St. Louis, Soulard once claimed to have ascended the Missouri River for about five hundred leagues, a distance that would have carried him to or near the Mandan villages.[30] Unfortunately, he did not reveal when or how he made the trip, although it is obvious that if he had done so, it was after he had produced his 1795 map. As a resident of St. Louis, he no doubt traveled the Missouri, perhaps as far as St. Charles, but no scholar has any reason to believe that he ever made a trip as far as the Mandans.

Truteau's trading expedition up the Missouri for the Missouri Company in the spring of 1794 is the first such venture for which any substantial record survives. A St. Louis schoolmaster, Truteau was engaged to lead the expedition to the Mandans. What did he know of his destination? Very little it seems, for there were no useful maps in St. Louis at that time for the area upstream from the present-day Nebraska–South Dakota boundary. Jacques D'Eglise had been to visit the Mandans two years earlier and to the Arikara Indians in 1793, but neither he nor his companions or colleagues are known to have produced a map.[31]

A chart of some description was nevertheless provided for Truteau's travels, for in his instructions to him, Jacques Clamorgan mentions "the plan which I deliver to him in order that he may know his whereabouts, and to change or correct the location of the nations and rivers, adding those that are found and not yet on the plan." When Truteau reached the then-deserted Arikara villages in early October 1794, he penned an entry in his journal that also intimates he may have had with him a primitive chart of the river between the mouths of the Platte and Cheyenne Rivers: "Besides, according to the indications which Jacques d'Eglise and Quenneville had given me, and which I had traced on a piece of paper, concerning the size of the rivers which discharge into the Missouri from the mouth of the River Platte up to the village of the Arikaras, and other notable places."[32]

Truteau left for the upper Missouri on June 7, 1794, and did not return to St. Louis until about June 1796.[33] No map that he may have carried, nor any chart directly resulting from that expedition, is known. Furthermore, there is nothing certain about the "plan" that Clamorgan provided him or about the "indications" that D'Eglise and Pierre Quenneville supplied. Neither document is identifiable today, although Clamorgan's "plan" was perhaps an early draft or the prototype of the 1795 Soulard map.

Knowledge in St. Louis of the upper Missouri was cripplingly poor. In fact, no maps of what was to become the Louisiana Territory were transmitted to the new Spanish governor by his French predecessor, for as late as 1785, Esteban

Miró, Carondelet's predecessor as governor general of Louisiana, possessed no such document. The French, indeed, had none to pass along, and Miró justly complained about the fact: "the French governor did not leave any map in this office, when he gave up this province, except those of the course of the Mississippi with the settlements that nation had made, but without any depth or explanation of the land on either sides, particularly on the west, which might have given information concerning the nations that border on the *Provincias Internas.*" It was pointless to complain in any case, for "about all the French governor could have done at the time of his departure would have been to leave Delisle's map of 1718, or some of the many later maps embodying its basic features." Guillaume Delisle's 1718 "Carte de la Louisiane" was without question the most important and influential map of the French period. It was plagiarized and reproduced in only slightly modified form from the date it appeared until the 1790s, although its recognizable, if somewhat garbled, characterization of the Missouri valley ends in the territory of the Omaha Indians.[34]

Five months after Truteau's departure, in his military report on the state of matters in Louisiana on November 24, 1794, Governor General Carondelet reported to his superior in Havana, Capt. Gen. Luis de Casas: "I have ordered the accompanying map prepared, which has been drawn from the most trustworthy plans that could be obtained since I have taken possession of their government. For all maps printed both in England and in the United States and in France are absolutely false, especially in regard to the course of the Mississippi and Missouri Rivers; besides which the settlements, both Spanish and American, which have grown up since the printing of those maps, could not be noted therein."[35]

The map that Carondelet "ordered prepared" is no longer with the original document in Seville, and there is no evidence that it has survived.[36] When was it drafted, and by whom? Almost certainly it was not by Soulard, although it was probably known to him and may have provided some of the information for his 1795 map. Soulard by this time had been in St. Louis for about eight months, though he was not appointed surveyor general until February 3, 1795, about two months after Carondelet wrote his 1794 report to Casas.

Carondelet's report was submitted to Havana nearly six months after Truteau left St. Louis. As Carl Wheat interprets this document, Governor Carondelet had "ordered a wholly new map prepared for the information of Jean Baptiste Truteau's 1794 expedition up the Missouri."[37] A map clearly was prepared for Truteau, but it does not appear to be the finished map that

Wheat suggests, a conclusion other authors have accepted.[38] Why not? It is because Truteau left St. Louis on June 7, 1794. If Soulard was the author of the map Carondelet ordered, he would have prepared the chart for Truteau, unofficially, at least nine months before his appointment as surveyor general—a plausible but altogether speculative scenario.

Fourteen months after Truteau left St. Louis, and before his return, the Missouri Company dispatched its third and largest expedition to the upper Missouri River. The Mackay and Evans expedition left St. Louis in late August 1795, the exact month and year specified on the French copy of Soulard's map, by which time Soulard had been surveyor general for about seven months. The extant documents do not mention Mackay and Evans having been supplied with a map. It was, however, a large expedition "composed of thirty-three men, well provisioned. These expenses are considerable."[39] It would have been unreasonable to invest in and dispatch such an expedition, nearly as large as that of the American Corps of Discovery, without the best preparation St. Louis officials could provide. For these reasons, we can be reasonably sure that the final form of the 1795 Soulard map was prepared for this expedition: it is dated the month of their departure, and it was drawn by a cartographer who had been appointed surveyor general by a partner in the company that sponsored the expedition.

The Prototype Spanish Copy

Carondelet's message of January 8, 1796, to his superiors in Spain referred to "a topographical map" illustrating the "usurpations" of the British and their designs on the northern frontier of Spanish Louisiana.[40] The map accompanying this report illustrated "the path the English follow and the line of forts built by them from Lake Superior to the Mountains of Black Rock [Rocky Mountains]." Abraham Nasatir was unable to find this chart in Madrid, but he did find a rough draft, or prototype, of the map.[41] It is not in the file containing Carondelet's report, but that file contains a sheet of paper that states, "No. 4 era un mapa que no ha a parecido [No. 4, a map that goes under separate cover]." Nasatir found a map in Seville he believed to be this one (or a facsimile of it) in the French copy of the instructions given to Truteau governing his trip up the Missouri. It bears the title (in translation), "Topographical Sketch of the Upper Mississippi and Missouri, Showing the Expeditions of the Spanish Company for Exploration of the Missouri River and the Encroachments of the British Companies on Spanish Territory, 1795."

The title and notes appended to the cartouche are identical to those on the finished Spanish original of the Soulard 1795 map (and its Spanish copy), and therefore this draft appears to be a prototype for it. The map carries no topographic detail, bearing nothing more than eleven labels for features ranging from the Gulf of California in the southwest to the camino del capitain carver ("the route of Captain Carver") in the northeast.

The often repeated statement that the Soulard 1795 map was prepared for Truteau's ascent of the Missouri appears to be based on the discovery of this prototype map in Carondelet's instructions to him, despite the fact that the French copy of the finished Spanish original is dated August 1795. Truteau had left St. Louis in mid-1794, more than six months earlier. If Truteau did carry a map, perhaps it was this nearly blank prototype chart on which he was expected to fill in the details.

The Spanish Original

The original Spanish map drawn by Soulard, once believed lost, was recently discovered in a collection of late-eighteenth-century Spanish manuscript maps that had been in private hands in Spain. The chart first came to light when it was auctioned by Sotheby's of London in 1984. It was purchased by W. Graham Arader III of Philadelphia and subsequently sold to the Karpeles Manuscript Library in Santa Barbara, California. Its identity is assured by the signature, verified to be that of baron de Carondelet, in the lower left margin below the neatline. "In no contemporary document does Carondelet give the name of the cartographer of his map, and on no copy of the Soulard map does Carondelet's name appear. With the discovery of [this] copy the connection between the maps is positively affirmed."[42] The chart is entitled (in translation), "Topographical Sketch of the Upper Mississippi and Missouri, Demonstrating the Progress of the Spanish Company in the Discovery of the Missouri River, and the Encroachments of the English Companies in the Spanish Possessions, 1795."

Carondelet attached this map to his report of January 8, 1796, which he forwarded to Spain, describing the "encroachments of the English" in Spanish territory. Its reappearance gives us the original map, endorsed by Carondelet, and the chart from which, in turn, the Spanish, French, and English copies derive.

The Spanish Copy

The Spanish copy of the Soulard 1795 map at Harvard University Library is a beautifully executed and faithful replica of the original, carrying the same cartouche, topographical features, and accompanying legends.[43] The title (in translation) reads, "Topographical Sketch of the Upper Mississippi and Missouri, Demonstrating the Progress of the Spanish Company in the Discovery of the Missouri River, and the Encroachments of the English Companies in the Spanish Possessions. 1785. [Endorsed] This is a copy made from the original held in the archive of this ministry—Chief of the Section, Manuel del Palacio."

Although the unknown copyist misdated it 1785, the title and its contents are otherwise identical to those on the Spanish original. The map was given to Harvard in 1895 by Clarence W. Bowen, who is identified in a manuscript note accompanying the map as being from or attached to the "Independent Office, New York City." No other information on the original provenance of the map is available. Wheat believes the ministry alluded to in the cartouche was the Ministerio de Estado (Ministry of State).[44] Soulard's name does not appear on either of the Spanish charts; he is identified as the draftsman only on the French version.

The French Copy

Aubrey Diller, in his article that accompanied the first publication and identification of this version of the map, provides a detailed essay outlining the history and importance of the chart, which may be from Soulard's own hand.[45] This copy was preserved in the former Bibliothèque du Service Hydrographique, Paris (now disbanded), catalog number C4040(33). Its cartouche is much the same as that on the Spanish original except that it goes on to provide important details on the map's history. Its title (in translation) reads, "Topographical Sketch of the Upper Mississippi and Missouri, Exhibiting Part of the Savage Tribes that Dwell There, According to Information Given by Various Traders. Drawn by Mr. Soulard, former sublieutenant in the Royal Navy of France and captain of the militia of His Catholic Majesty in Illinois, for Monsieur Bouligny, colonel of the Permanent Regiment of Louisiana. August 1795. [Brought back from Louisiana in 1804 by Mr. de Laussat, colonial prefect.]"

The cartouche asserts that it was drawn by Soulard in August 1795 for Francisco Bouligny, the founder of a prominent Creole family in New Orleans. The map, however, reached the naval archives in Paris through the offices of Pierre-Clément de Laussat, "the head of the French régime in New Orleans which, after a tenure of twenty days, officially transferred the authority to the United States on 20 December 1803."[46] The date, genesis, and disposition of the map, therefore, are well documented.

With rare exceptions, the legends for all topographic features on the Spanish-language versions are duplicated in translation on this copy. Missing, however, are the comments concluding the "Notes" that allude to Spanish forts among the Omaha, Ponca, and Arikara Indians along the Missouri and refer to a British fort, identified as what is today called Jusseaume's Post at the Mandans.

The English Copy

The English copy was found by Reuben Gold Thwaites among William Clark's expeditionary papers. It is now in the Coe Collection at Yale University. The "Note" in the lower left-hand corner and another note below the neatline of the sheet are in William Clark's hand.[47] This copy is entitled, "A Topographical Sketch of the Missouri and Upper Mississippi; Exhibiting the Various Nations and Tribes of Indians Who Inhabit the Country: Copied from the Original Spanish MS. Map."

Where did Lewis and Clark get their version of the Soulard 1795 map? No one knows, nor does anyone know who drafted it. Aubrey Diller speculated that it came to them from the U.S. territorial judge for Illinois, George Turner. Judge Turner held court at Kaskaskia during the winter of 1794–95, but he left Illinois Territory in May 1795, and no known relationship between him and Lewis and Clark has yet been discovered. Meriwether Lewis met with Soulard in December 1803 and did obtain a map from him, but Lewis says nothing about a chart that corresponds to the Soulard 1795 map.[48] Despite the lack of documentation, the most plausible source for the map is Soulard himself, although who made the copy and translated it into English remains problematic. Labels on the body of the map are not in the hand of either Lewis or Clark.

Carl Wheat quite reasonably concluded from its cartouche that this version was copied from the original Spanish map.[49] Its legends, however, most closely correspond to those on the version in Paris, although the notes on it were updated to reflect political changes by Lewis and Clark's time and many of the names for geographic features are omitted. More significant, the course of the Columbia River, labeled "Oregan, or R. of the West," which is lacking on all other versions, has been added. (The mouth of the Columbia had been entered on May 11, 1792, by Boston explorer Robert Gray, who named the great stream after his ship *Columbia*.) Other minor changes include deletion of the track and reference to Jonathan Carver's travels and omission of references that identify James Mackey's route in Canada, although the dotted line denoting it remains.

John L. Allen notes the influence that this version of Soulard's chart may have had on the perceptions that Lewis and Clark held of western geography, especially concerning the distance from the upper reaches of the Missouri River to the mouth of the Columbia River, although they did not long entertain his views of that distance. As one of the numerous travel maps that Lewis and Clark carried in their expeditionary "glove compartment," the Soulard 1795 map was decidedly inferior to those they also carried produced by James Mackay and John Evans. The Corps of Discovery's journals mention several observations made by Mackay and Evans along the banks of the Missouri. For example, in central South Dakota, Clark notes that "Mr. Evins" called a western tributary opposite the present site of Pierre, South Dakota, the "Little Missouri."[50] Lewis and Clark renamed the stream the Teton River after their hostile confrontation with a group of Teton Dakotas near its mouth. (Still later it was given its modern name, Bad River, when a raging flood drowned many Sioux who were camped along its banks.) The captain's dependence on Evans's route map is evident: Soulard's chart, however, is never mentioned; its drawbacks were obvious.

The Missouri River "Forts"

Among the many details on the two Spanish-language versions of the 1795 Soulard map deserving attention are the symbols for four European forts or posts between the Omaha and the Mandan Indians. They are depicted by small national flags along or near the banks of the Missouri River. Not one of them is named, but their locations are shown by the same symbol as that used for Fort Carondelet (also not labeled), built in August 1795 by the Spanish for the Osage Indian trade in what is now southwestern Missouri, and for Pine Fort (labeled *F. lepinette*), built in 1785 by the North West Company along the lower reaches of the Assiniboine River in Canada.

A Spanish flag depicted just below the Omaha (Maha) Indians is in the appropriate position to represent Fort Charles, the post built by James Mackay and John Evans in mid-November 1795. A second Spanish flag just above the Ponca Indians is in a position corresponding to that of Ponca House (although it is on the wrong side of the river), the modest trading post built by Jean Baptiste Truteau in November 1794. A third Spanish flag is below the Grand Detour among the Arikara (Ris) Indians and may plausibly represent either D'Eglise's Arikara post during the winter of 1794–95 or Truteau's stay among those Indians during the spring of 1795. The fourth flag, a British ensign carrying the cross of St. George, is among the Mandan Indians; it is an appropriate symbol for Jusseaume's Post, built in October–November 1794 by a North West Company party from Canada under the direction of René Jusseaume.[51] Curiously enough, not one of these four flags appears on either the French or the English version of the map. Did their copyists delete them because he knew they had been abandoned?

Two enigmatic symbols appear on the two Spanish-language versions between what seem to be the lower reaches of the Niobrara River and the Missouri: a fleur-de-lis labeled *"armas de Francia"* and an unidentified square to its left. No one has yet provided an explanation for them, for no French post, battle, or other structure or event is known to have been anywhere nearby. The most likely explanation is that these symbols are so badly misplaced as to be unidentifiable. On the French copy of the map, the fleur-de-lis is labeled *"Armes de Frances"* and the square simply as "Ft." On the derivative English copy, the term "French Arms" labels the fleur-de-lis, and the unidentified square is labeled "English Fort." Needless to say, no British establishment is known that could provide an identity for this feature, although there is an allusion in Mackay's account to a British fort that was to have been built nearby but was not (a post considered below). Curiously, *"Armas de Francia"* also appears on a Spanish derivative of the Mackay and Evans charts, but here the label marks a locality on the west bank of the Missouri immediately below the mouth of the Cheyenne River, where the Arikara villages were about this time. This information provides no further clues to its identity unless it alludes to French traders among that tribe.

Sources for the Soulard Map

What sources did Soulard consult in constructing his chart? As we have seen, Aubrey Diller described it as virtually the first original and independent map of the Missouri River since the time of Guillaume Delisle earlier that same century. His assessment is correct, for no part of the Missouri River on the map appears to be derived directly from existing charts. Details of the Mississippi River above St. Louis, for example, are vastly inferior to those shown on Delisle's 1718 map, and although the configuration of the Missouri basin has been improved, its lower reaches were much better known than Soulard would lead us to believe. His placement of Santa Fe and the upper Rio Grande, which were better depicted on earlier charts, were shifted much too far to the east to a point not very far south of the forks of the Platte.

Although the map is a product of Spanish St. Louis, it leans heavily on British sources for the northern part of the area it depicts. Since James Mackay arrived in St. Louis in 1791, it seems clear that Soulard obtained from him much of the information regarding the northern rivers and British fur-trading posts included on the chart. Diller's observation that "the map shows Central Canada even more fully and correctly than the Missouri Valley" demands that a knowledgeable Canadian source be available to Soulard. That man was James Mackay, and the information he passed along to Soulard is reflected by the configuration of the central Canadian lake system between Lake Winnipeg and Lake Superior as it was drawn by British mapmakers such as Peter Pond in 1785.[52] There are, however, major problems in his depiction of the Saskatchewan and Assiniboine river systems: the Souris River is not shown at all, nor is the South Saskatchewan River, although its upper reaches may be confused with what is shown of the upper Assiniboine River. An analysis of the Canadian half of the map, however, is a topic for another study—one by a Canadian specialist. Here the focus is on the southern half of the map, that area within the present-day United States.

Soulard shows Jonathan Carver's route between September 1766 and August 1767, probably from that Connecticut Yankee's account of his explorations through Wisconsin to the headwaters of the Mississippi and to Lake Superior. After serving in the French and Indian War, Carver had decided that he would find a land passage across the continent, publishing his three years' travel through the upper Midwest in 1771; the book surely was available to residents of St. Louis by 1795. Carver appears to have been the first Briton to winter on the St. Peters River, and the presence of he and his successors along the upper Mississippi surely contributed to Spanish insecurity, for at the St. Peters River, they were illegally in Spanish territory. British traders moving west from Minnesota during the period 1770–1800 continued on to the Missouri River. When this came to the attention of Spanish authorities, they became concerned and contemplated the construction of military forts to halt this intrusion. The mouth of the Des Moines River and other localities were chosen, though no construction ever took place. Another failed measure was to send row galleys up the Mississippi to stop British traders as they crossed that river at the mouth of the Wisconsin River.[53]

General knowledge among the residents of St. Louis also provided information for four important traders' routes shown on Soulard's map as dotted lines. One, a very early route beginning at the juncture of the Wisconsin River with the Mississippi (near what was to become Prairie du Chien), was shown as early as 1718 on Guillaume Delisle's "Carte de la Louisiane," labeled as the "Chemin des Voyageurs." This trail continued to be an important avenue of overland trade until the time of Lewis and Clark. Another, a very old route, led westward overland from the junction of the Des Moines River with the Mississippi across what is now northern Iowa, ending at the Big Sioux River and serving the Omaha and Ponca Indians. The Soulard map labels this track, in Spanish, "route the English take to trade on the Missouri River." A third route led from the mouth of the Little Nemaha River (near present-day Brownville, Nebraska) overland across the Big Nemaha and Big Blue Rivers to the Republican Pawnee villages along the Republican River in present-day north-central Kansas. One of these villages may well be the Kansas monument site, which dates from approximately the last quarter of the eighteenth century.[54] Soulard's depiction of the geography of this route is quite precise. (See these routes in figure 1.)

The fourth route, also shown on numerous later maps, led from North West Company and Hudson's Bay Company posts along the Assiniboine River in southern Canada overland to the Mandan villages. The encroachments of these "North Traders," as such merchants often were called, were of course the stimulus for the Spanish exploration of the river that led to developing the Soulard map and dispatching the Mackay and Evans expedition. This fourth route was, indeed, "the path the English follow," accompanied on the chart by "the line of forts built by them from Lake Superior to the Mountains of Black Rock [Rocky Mountains]," about which Carondelet had complained in his report to his superiors in Spain on January 8, 1796.

The publication in 1814 of Nicholas Biddle's edition of William Clark's 1810 map shouldered aside Soulard's older conception of the Missouri valley and became, in turn, the standard chart for several decades. Although cartographic information and a few manuscript maps did, indeed, benefit from the dual explorations by Truteau and by Mackay and Evans, they had very limited influence on printed maps. Some version of the 1795 Soulard was, however, the base for most of the maps of Louisiana published by Samuel Lewis in Aaron Arrowsmith and Lewis's *A New and Elegant Atlas* (1804) and in a few editions of Sgt. Patrick Gass's account of the Lewis and Clark expedition (first published in 1807). These depictions enjoyed only brief popularity, however, probably because Soulard's original map was never published; it was only copied in part.

The publication of the original, finished 1795 Soulard map puts to rest speculation as to its contents and its relation to the three known copies made of it. We now know that the Spanish copy at Harvard is a faithful replica and that the French copy and English copy follow, in that order, in conforming to the original. Questions concerning the date of the original chart, however, remain, although there is little question that it was composed and its basic content was completed in August 1795, as the French copy asserts. Since Fort Charles appears on the map, it is obvious that the copy in hand either post-dates Mackey's return in 1797 or was altered to include that post's location, for its position was not known before the expedition left St. Louis. In any event, with Carondelet's copy now in hand, we now know what the Spanish of St. Louis knew of their ethereal domains in the northern plains during the last five years of the eighteenth century. We conclude that, because his hand is so obvious in the map, James Mackay worked closely with Soulard to produce a chart for his own exploration of the river and that the map was finished only a few days before he and Evans left St. Louis.

CHAPTER THREE

FROM ST. LOUIS TO
FORT CHARLES

"An Expensive Enterprise"

Thirty-six-year-old James Mackay and twenty-five-year-old John Thomas Evans left St. Louis for the Mandan villages with a thirty-man crew in late August or early September 1795. One would have thought that the departure of a party this large and important would have been carefully noted, but there is little agreement as to the actual date. In his journal Mackay states that they left about the end of August, but when he wrote Jacques Clamorgan announcing his arrival at the mouth of the Platte River, he told him it had been "a forty-four days' march," implying a departure around the first of September. Still other documents suggest dates as early as late July. Some of the confusion may come from the fact that the expedition may have left later than they had planned.[1]

Their mission was an exploratory and scientific one analogous to that of Lewis and Clark in almost every respect save one: the Americans were to open the area for trade, but unlike Mackay and Evans they did not engage in trade themselves nor were they told to build trading forts anywhere along their route. But Mackay and Evans's directions were astonishingly similar to those Pres. Thomas Jefferson provided his two captains.

Except for the leaders, the Spanish expedition was an anonymous assortment: only one man's full name is known of the crew that left St. Louis, a Frenchman named John Lafleur. Three other men are mentioned in a letter that Mackay wrote to Evans at Fort Charles on February 19, 1796: one is designated only by his initial (I. or J.), another is called Scarlet, and a third is named Tollibois (or Jollibois).[2] In all probability the rest of the crew—at least the majority of them—also would have been French. St. Louis was founded by the French, and despite Spanish political and military dominance from 1764 to 1803, the town had never lost its essentially French culture and orientation. The lifeblood of the town, its population, and the rivermen who brought the furs down the Missouri was dominated by them.

About 75 percent of St. Louis's male population in 1780 were either boatmen or hunters. Most of them had emigrated from Canada (59 percent) or had come from the Illinois Country (11 percent), "America" (4 percent), or New Orleans (3 percent).[3] Consequently, it is reasonable to suspect that the only "outsiders" on the trip were its leaders. It would be interesting to know if anyone from the crew later served on the Lewis and Clark expedition; if not, they undoubtedly knew some of the men who did serve the American Corps of Discovery.

The small flotilla consisted of four boats packed with merchandise. The report by Clamorgan and Antonio Reihle on July 8, 1795, states that one boat's cargo was for the Arikaras; one contained goods to ransom their way past the Sioux; one was for the Mandans; and the last held goods they hoped would carry the expedition to the Rocky Mountains and on to the Pacific.[4] On October 14 Mackay's journal relates that he unloaded his "berchas and pirogues" at the Omaha village, suggesting that two different kinds of vessels were used on the expedition. This would not be unusual; after all, Lewis and Clark moved their expedition upriver using a keelboat and two "pirogues" that, in their case, were not dugouts but substantial, planked, canoe-shaped river craft.

Dugouts were among the most sensible ways to travel the Missouri River (keelboats per se would not be used until Manuel Lisa introduced them in 1811). Birchbark canoes were impractical because the local birch could not support the building of canoes of any size, which would have been sunk quickly by the countless snags in the river anyway. Such craft apparently were only rarely used on the Missouri, for only one source (of which I am aware), Nicolas de Finiels writing in 1803, alludes to their use on that river.[5]

Did they use wooden dugout canoes? Such craft could be paddled upstream against the constant current of the Mississippi and Missouri, but they were heavy and hard to manage. They were hewn from single large tree trunks, usually cottonwood or cypress; the latter was preferred because of its light weight when dry. One side of the trunk was flattened, and its core was hollowed out using adzes and, perhaps, fire to leave a thin wooden shell. Bulkheads commonly were left at intervals to strengthen the hull and provide compartments for the cargo, and the pointed or rounded prow was pierced for attaching a mooring rope. Sometimes their upper surfaces were planked over to protect the cargo. Their size depended on the height and girth of the tree selected, but could be as much as six feet wide and forty to fifty feet long. Dugouts large enough to have carried thirty men, their two leaders, and all their goods would have been very large indeed. Depending on the number of men who may have accompanied the expedition upriver on shore to hunt for food, each of the four pirogues would have been propelled by no less than six men.

The expedition also used barges. *Berchas* were essentially barges, favored by merchants of the time. The French cognate for this term, *berge*, appears in varying accounts for riverboats of varying size and shape. The description left us of a barge that William Dunbar described on the Washita River in 1804 may be representative: "She is upwards of 50 feet long & 8 1/2 feet in breadth built tolerably flat, her bottom being still a little convex & being pretty well formed for running. This boat with some improvements is probably the best form for penetrating up shallow rivers." A *bercha* was built on a keel with its ribs covered with planks, though it might be flat bottomed, and differed little from the later keelboats used on the Missouri, having a cabin and cleated footways along the gunwales and usually propelled by poles. *Berchas* were wider and heavier than keelboats and might have one or two masts fitted with square sails.[6]

Because of the imprecision of contemporary terminology and the fact that there are no descriptions of Mackay's vessels from which one can infer anything of their construction, we are left with the speculation that he probably employed both *berchas* and pirogues. His *berchas* likely would have been among the larger forms, for smaller versions usually were called *berchitas*. The crew of riverboats were called *voyageurs* (properly translated as "boatmen," not "travelers") and were given two allotments of hard liquor two or three times a day by the *patron* (the navigating officer or steersman) of the vessel.[7]

Mackay and Evans undoubtedly were the *patrons* of two of the four vessels; the names of any other leaders are not known. The goods packed into their small flotilla amounted to 50,000 pesos in value. Armaments for the four vessels cost 15,000 pesos, and the salaries of the thirty men amounted to 30,000 pesos. "Things necessary to furnish them setting out, 3,000"; and for the salaries of those employees who would not return by the end of the year, an additional 6,000, for a grand total of 104,000 pesos. We have no roster of the trade goods, but archaeological findings in a Ponca Indian village site of the same era, Nánza, or the Ponca Fort, illustrate the kinds of things that were being

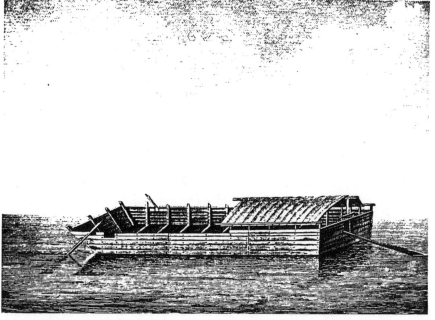

Fig. 8. Sketch of a flat-bottomed boat, a *bercha*, such as were used on the Ohio and Mississippi Rivers in 1796. (From Collot, *Journey in North America*, atlas, plate 7)

imported into local American Indian inventories at the time.[8] Additionally, the inventory that Jean Baptiste Truteau took with him in 1794 probably is representative:

guns	awls
ells of cloth	packets of large and small knives
tobacco by the carrot	white blankets
powder by the barrel	pickaxes and hatchets
musket balls	sacks of vermillion
gunflints	cooking kettles
wormscrews	hammers
medals	flags
combs	

Later writers testify to the problems that faced expeditions that left frontier settlements for western waters. Henry Brackenridge, for instance, notes that in 1811, when Manuel Lisa left for the upper Missouri, their party proceeded only a few miles upriver from St. Charles, then camped. The reason was that some of the men had consumed too much alcohol in their farewell celebration

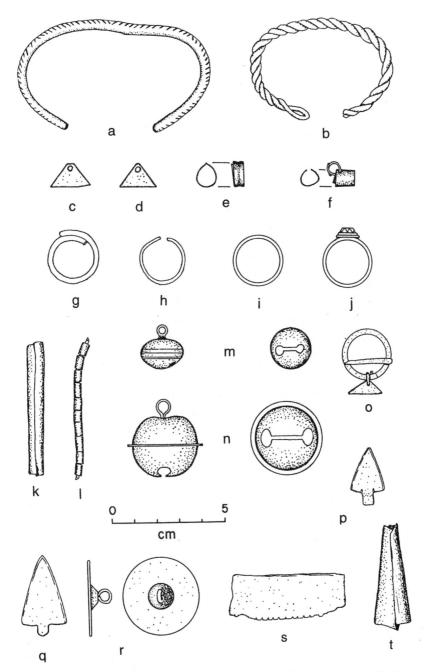

Fig. 9. European trade goods from the 1937 archaeological investigations at the Ponca Fort village site. They probably are a mixture of items from Spanish and English sources. (From Wood, *Náⁿza*, figs. 9–11, 13)

and had missed the departure, and they straggled into camp the next day. Others were simply in no condition for the labor of getting upstream.[9] Time was needed to rejuvenate their ravished constitutions. This must have been standard practice, for Lewis and Clark had done the same thing in May 1804.

Moving any vessel up the Missouri by paddling or any other means was brutal work. The days were long, and the food that was not obtained from game killed en route was poor. The food that Manuel Lisa provided his keelboat crew in 1811 probably was representative: a breakfast of hominy and a lunch of hard bread or biscuits with a slice of pork fat or sowbelly (hence the term for a laborer *mangeur du lard*, or "pork eater"). Dinner was a pot of mush with a pound of tallow melted in it. Hunters customarily ranged the banks ahead and alongside the river party, bringing in all manner of game to supplement that dreary diet. It probably was not difficult to do so. Pierre-Antoine Tabeau, speaking of 1803, said: "Game is very abundant at low water. From the river of the Osages to the River Platte the roebuck [white-tailed deer] is seen everywhere, bounding over the flats; turkey hens abound on the points; wild cats are common; and bears are met with quite often."[10]

Prince Maximilian said that the men, or *engagés*, who later towed keelboats up the Missouri usually were French Canadians or were descended from early French settlers, for few Anglo-Americans would contemplate or accept such labor. Engagés were accustomed to the bitterly heavy, bone-breaking work, and they provided much of the workforce of the fur companies from the earliest times. Indeed, the workers of the inland waters of North America had been and continued to be dominated by French, from the frozen wastes of northern Canada to the Great Lakes and in the basin of the entire Missouri and Mississippi Rivers. François Marie Perrin du Lac was deeply impressed with the severity of their life. "On long voyages they suffer indescribably. They wear no clothes except those necessary to provide decency, and their skins, burned by the sun, peel off several times. . . . It is not unusual for them to succumb to fatigue and die oar in hand."[11]

In later years trips up the Missouri were undertaken principally in June, the time when the river level is highest because of the runoff of spring snowmelt from the Rocky Mountains. The "June rise" began in mid-May and lasted through the middle of July. Steamboats and keelboats needed the deeper water to maneuver, but pirogues could manage with the shallow water and slower current. Still, the rapidity of the Missouri's waters made upriver travel difficult at any time of the year.

The little flotilla probably left from the landings below the rocky ledge that supported the village of St. Louis, moving upriver toward the mouth of the Missouri River. It is not difficult to envision the scene: cursing men loading and maneuvering the boats, the shore crowded with friends and relatives saying farewells, and officials of the Missouri Company giving last-minute instructions and encouragement, among them the director of the Missouri Company, Jacques Clamorgan, and the lieutenant governor of Upper Louisiana, Zenon Trudeau. Contemporary accounts provide a sense of the nature of the trip to St. Charles, the first settlement to develop on the Missouri River: "You can travel from St. Louis to St. Charles by water in two or two and a half days, and sometimes even in a day and a half. You can rather easily ascend the Mississippi, in which you find Isle à Cabaret and Grande Isle before arriving at the mouth of the Missouri. At that point, the work increases. More effort is required to overcome the force of the current; snags multiply; a dozen islands and vast sandbars compel you to make considerable detours in the short stretch of river that you must ascend."[12]

One might also make a good case for the idea that Mackay and Evans left not from the riverfront at St. Louis but from the town of St. Charles. This alternative is based on the fact that the first landmark on the Indian Office map, which was made under the expedition's leader after his return, does not show St. Louis, or even the mouth of the Missouri River, but commences abruptly at St. Charles, the westernmost settlement on the Missouri at the time. Founded in 1769 by a French Canadian trader, Louis Blanchette, the town quickly became a center for hunters and traders. Beginning the expedition at this western outpost would have eliminated the need to ascend the first difficult miles of the Missouri. The little town of La Charette, which was the westernmost settlement when Lewis and Clark went upriver, was not built until 1797, either when Mackay and Evans were upriver or just after their return.[13]

Mackay had little comment to make concerning the trip upriver except that "the bad weather and one of the pirogues of my convoy, which has continually filled with water, delayed me."[14] His silence on the matter suggests that the voyage otherwise was uneventful. He nevertheless had to have been plagued with a number of problems that he did not mention, for later voyagers were sufficiently impressed by the difficulty of traveling the Missouri River that it is not hard to guess what Mackay's party had to endure. The riverbed was littered with partially submerged trees, and the turbulent current sweeping over and past these hazards made travel perilous by any kind of watercraft.

The constantly changing channel meant that any previous experience one might have had on the river meant little in navigating its channel the following year. On occasion, sails could be used when the wind was obliging, but these times were rare, and because of its meandering course, the river might well flow in all four directions in a matter of only a few miles. There were always problems. Pierre-Antoine Tabeau, who ascended the Missouri in 1803, provides a graphic account of other matters that plagued the rivermen:

> of all the inconveniences and sufferings of the voyage, mosquitoes should be put down as the worst, and nowhere can more be seen. During the whole day the boats were enveloped as in a cloud and the engagés, who were compelled by the extreme heat to keep the body naked, were covered with blood and swellings. Often our hunters, not being able to endure them, returned at full speed to throw themselves into the boats. What is more they could not aim their weapons when covered with these insects. In short, the mosquitos, not leaving the crew at liberty to take their food in the evening or their rest at night, exhausted them as much as did all the work of the day.[15]

Lewis and Clark also experienced difficulties, and not just with mosquitoes. At a point above St. Charles that they called "retragrade bend," the current was so strong they were swept back downstream for two miles.[16] The current was swift even in autumn, when the river level was low, when Mackay and Evans were traveling. Nevertheless, they made the trip to the mouth of the Platte River in eastern Nebraska in forty-four days (or about fifteen miles a day), a good pace, assuming that they left St. Louis or St. Charles on August 31. The fact the expedition made such good time and experienced so few difficulties meant they were traveling with experienced voyageurs who were already familiar with the problems of travel on the Missouri River. The first Indians they met were the Oto Indians at the mouth of the Platte; there is no mention of their meeting the Kansa Indians, living near the mouth of the Kansas River, nor of the powerful Osages, who were living south of the Missouri in present-day southwestern Missouri.

The trip upriver, indeed, appears to have been devoid of adventure. They experienced only the rigors of the voyage through a near pristine wilderness. Fourteen years later a Dr. Thomas, accompanying Manuel Lisa's expedition up the Missouri, reported, "The face of the country on each side of the river, is so monotonous up [to] the river Flat [Platte] that one day's journey would nearly give the history of every thing worthy of notice."[17] The valley varied

Fig. 10. An Oto Indian warrior (left) and an Omaha warrior (right). (From Catlin, *Letters and Notes*, vol. 2, plates 143, 146)

in width, but everywhere its floodplain generally was lined by cottonwood and elm, with the forests on the uplands gradually diminishing into rolling prairies.

They reached a point on the Missouri River a league below the mouth of the Platte on October 14. It later took Lewis and Clark sixty days to reach the same point, the Corps of Discovery making only about eleven miles a day. But by the time Mackay and Evans reached the Platte River, winter was coming on, and it was bitter cold and snowing. Despite the weather, they stopped on the following day just above the mouth of the Platte and spent several days holding discussions with the Oto Indians and acquiring "fresh provisions"— meaning that the hunters needed to obtain fresh meat.

There is no record that they celebrated their arrival at the Platte. It is not known when the custom began, but by the time Manuel Lisa and Theodore Hunt made their way upriver in 1811, passing the mouth of the Platte had assumed for rivermen what crossing the equator was to sailors: a time to celebrate and an excuse to initiate newcomers to the river. Henry M. Brackenridge, a member of Lisa's party, said that those who navigated the Missouri regarded the Platte as "the equinoctial line amongst mariners. All those who had not passed it before, were required to be shaved, unless they could compromise the matter by a treat. Much merriment was indulged on the occasion."[18] The Platte marked the boundary between the lower Missouri and the upper Missouri, and for many later travelers it meant their journey was half over.

THE OTO INDIANS AND THEIR NEIGHBORS

The Siouan-speaking Oto Indians were linguistically and culturally related to the Ioway and Missouri Indians, all of whom shared the same general lifeways and traditions. These groups were also somewhat more distantly related to the Omahas and Poncas. At the time of Mackay's visit, the Otos were living near the mouth of the Platte River together with remnants of the Missouris. In 1798 Trudeau gave their number as 400 men, but although Lewis and Clark described them in 1804 as once having been a powerful nation, disease and warfare had reduced them—and their relatives the Missouris—to only 250 men. At that time, and probably also in Mackay's day, the two groups lived in an earth-lodge village on the south side of the Platte not far from its mouth; they hunted between the mouth of the Big Nemaha River and the Boyer River (near Omaha, Nebraska). The Ioway Indians were on friendly terms with the Oto-Missouris, and their 250 men lived farther north along the Missouri River, principally on its east bank.[19]

When sixty of the principal men of the Oto tribe arrived, Mackay assembled their chiefs and, speaking through an interpreter, berated them for their "evil conduct" with Spanish traders who had come to them with "the goods that they needed." The Indians responded, he said, with "weak excuses." Mackay pointed out the consequences that would follow if they did not change their conduct immediately, and the Otos agreed to be more cordial to traders if he kept his word with them. The chiefs told him that the traders who had come to them in the past had lied to obtain their furs and made promises that they never kept. At this Mackay responded that a company had been formed to supply their needs and that it would fulfill its promises only if the Otos behaved well. For his part, he promised that the Missouri Company would build a fort for them the next autumn (he did not say where) to protect them and supply their needs without their having to go to British traders.

Mackay was satisfied with this conference. Although in the past the Otos had pillaged traders' boats bound up the Missouri, they touched nothing that he did not offer as a gift and stayed clear of the pirogues laden with goods for the Mandans and others upriver. Mackay, only another trader as far as the Otos were concerned, had made his own promises, and in his report to Carondelet he begged that they be honored. He remained with the Indians eleven days, continuing his talks and attempting to "attract them by means of mildness to our side."

The Spanish party left the Otos eleven days after their arrival, on October 25. Mackay left behind some men to run a small trading post he had ordered built on the twentieth, a modest establishment he called the "Post of the Otos." It clearly had been built to mollify the villagers for the past sins of earlier traders, but he believed that the post was a necessary prelude to controlling the upriver trade.

THE POST OF THE OTOS

The documents Mackay left us provide three separate locations for the Oto post: above, below, and opposite the mouth of the Platte. In his journal he says that he "reached a place one-half league above the said river, in order to construct a house for the wintering of the traders whom I left there on the 20th." It is impossible to reconcile this statement with another in his "Table of Distances" that describes landmarks along the Missouri River. In that table he lists the "First building, or fort, belonging to the Company of the upper Missouri" as being on the south (or west) bank of the Missouri River two leagues below the mouth of the Platte.[20]

To complicate matters, the Indian Office map, which Mackay drew in St. Louis upon his return, has a diamond-shaped symbol representing the "Premier Poste de la Compagnie du Missouri" on the east bank of the Missouri just below the mouth of the Platte (see fig. 19).[21] Which location is correct? Mackay is our only chronicler, and there is no independent corroboration for any of these three potential locations. Consequently, the Oto post could have been built anywhere within an area of some fifteen square miles on either side of the Missouri River, although a west-bank location seems most plausible since the Otos lived on that side of the river.

A few years later a French *engagé*, Pierre Cruzatte, built and operated a post for the Omaha Indian trade at the mouth of Mill Creek near the town of Blair, above modern Omaha. Cruzatte later was one of the permanent members of the Lewis and Clark expedition, and his unnamed "old Trading House" is shown on the west bank of the Missouri on William Clark's map of the expedition's course for August 3–8, 1804. Clark says that it was "the remains of an old Tradeing establishment" where Pierre Cruzatte spent two years trading with the Omaha Indians.[22] Cruzatte's knowledge of their language, derived from his Omaha mother, would have made him ideal for that business. Unfortunately, Clark does not mention the dates that Cruzatte either built or operated this post. We know little of Cruzatte: was he one of Mackay's men who returned upriver after the expedition to build or staff this post, only to abandon it before Lewis and Clark engaged him for their expedition?

We know nothing of the operation or fate of the short-lived Post of the Otos, but one would suspect that it was abandoned and its occupants returned to St. Louis when Mackay aborted the expedition in the spring of 1797.

"MR. MACKEY'S TRADING HOUSE"

After an eleven-day stay with the Otos, the expedition resumed its way upriver on October 25. On the twenty-seventh, eight leagues above the mouth of the Platte, their small fleet met, and was joined by, six members of the Missouri Company who had been part of a trading party to the Ponca Indians. They had come upriver either with Lécuyer's mission (that is, with the second expedition of April 1795) or with a later *pirogue* commanded by Antonio Breda, whose adventures already have been related. By this means, the men left behind at the Post of the Otos were replaced. Among those who returned upriver with Mackay was Breda himself—about whom Mackay was to have good words, for he became his "commissioner"—and apparently Pierre Antoine Tabeau. Mackay later called him, for reasons that are not entirely clear, "an infamous rascal."[23]

News of the expedition traveled up the Missouri with great speed. On November 3, only two weeks after arriving at the mouth of the Platte, they were met by a party from the Omaha village. That delegation was led by the son of Blackbird, the despotic chief of that village. The son was no stranger to Europeans: he had been in St. Louis only the preceding summer. Blackbird sent his son with a band of young men—that is, warriors—to protect Mackay's party from any problems that he might encounter on his way to the Omahas. Mackay accompanied them overland, he said, for a two-day march to the village. His journal, however, says that it was not until November 11 when he reached a point where he met Blackbird "a day's journey" from the village. Blackbird and the lesser chiefs with him greeted Mackay with "affection and friendship."

For whatever reason, the two-day march had stretched into more than a week, perhaps because of erroneously recorded dates or perhaps because of miserable weather, for he commented that the "cold and snow have been so great that my voyage has been retarded considerably." Since one of Blackbird's first acts was to place an overnight guard on the Scotsman's boats to prevent theft, he must have awaited the slower upriver pace of the rest of his party so that they could enter the Omaha village as a complete unit. Providing the guard was in Blackbird's own best interest, and Mackay was not to realize until later that this surface friendship masked the chief's greed, for future events made it clear that Blackbird wanted most of the goods for himself.

Blackbird habitually confiscated for his own use the greater part of the goods that any trader brought to his village, providing only token and often nearly worthless hides in exchange. The nearly impoverished trader then tried to make do with what remained of his inventory. Furthermore, in the years before Mackay's arrival, Blackbird had effectively blockaded the Missouri River, preventing traders from going upriver to trade with the Poncas and their neighbors. Mackay expressed the displeasure of the Spanish with the indignities that their traders had suffered at the hands of the Omahas, and he told Blackbird that the Spanish were prepared to meet all of their needs for trade goods. Blackbird, in return, was to sponsor the Missouri Company and help them in getting their boats upriver past the Ponca villages.

THE OMAHA INDIANS

The Omahas at this time were the power brokers on the Missouri River between the Platte River and the Dakota Sioux, who dominated the region north of them. They were, however, relatively recent arrivals in the area. Earlier in the century they had lived, together with the Poncas, on the Big Sioux River north of present-day Sioux City, Iowa. Around 1715 they moved to the mouth of the White River in central South Dakota, where traditions say the Poncas split away and moved to the Black Hills. This split may have found expression on Delisle's 1718 map, on which two "Maha" groups are shown. The Poncas later returned to the mouth of the White River, and around 1735 the Omahas moved to Bow Creek near present-day Wynot, Nebraska, location of the "Bad Village."[24] The village on Bow Creek was so named because it was the scene of a schism in the tribe, and it might have been here that the Poncas made their final break with the Omahas. The latter moved farther down the Missouri River, leaving the Poncas behind. The new group occupied the valley of Ponca Creek and its vicinity from their first known contacts with Euro-Americans until 1877, when most of the Ponca were forcibly removed to

Indian Territory in what is now Oklahoma. (After a special investigation, about 75 percent of them elected to remain where they were, but the others returned from Indian Territory and continue to live in northeastern Nebraska.)

The Omahas moved to the vicinity of modern-day Sioux City and eventually settled at Big Village, or Tonwontonga, where they lived for most of the seventy years between about 1775 and 1845. Big Village was in Dakota County, Nebraska, in a locale that today is bisected by U.S. Highway 77/73, about two miles northeast of the town of Homer, on the banks of the now-channeled Omaha Creek and Pigeon Creek Ditch.[25]

At the time Fort Charles was built, Big Village was ruled by Blackbird (Washinga-sabe, or as the Spanish called him, El Pájaro Negro). British traders had provided Blackbird and his followers with the guns and wealth that permitted them to dominate their neighbors. Blackbird was without doubt the most renowned Omaha chief in their history, although the Omahas do not think highly of him today. He came from a family without particular distinction, but he became a successful warrior and a "medicine man," and his ambitious nature led him to the chiefdom, a position that most sources agree was maintained by the unscrupulous use of poison (arsenic), provided by traders, to remove his rivals and enemies. His end came in 1800–1801, when he perished in a smallpox epidemic that also carried away two-thirds of his people, ending both his rule and Omaha domination of the Missouri trade. His son, also named Blackbird, survived him and, because he also later became a chief, has often been confused with his father.[26]

In the 1770s the Spanish knew little of the Omahas, but the two traders among them produced five thousand pounds of furs annually. Big Village was in a prairie in the wide alluvial Missouri valley, well suited for the Indians' garden crops; the region had abundant game; and it was ideally situated to benefit from not only from intertribal trade but also exchange with British traders. The latter came overland from either Prairie du Chien, up the Des Moines River from its mouth, or up the Missouri River from Spanish St. Louis (see figs. 1, 4). "The archaeological evidence from Big Village," however, "attests to the Omaha preference for English goods; almost nothing Spanish can be identified. The Omahas had been completely swayed to the English; the Omahas 'robbed, maltreated and ridiculed' Spanish traders, financially ruining 'a great number.'"[27] This is understandable enough, given the fact that Chief Blackbird had become enmeshed with the British traders at Prairie du Chien. By 1795, however, the Spanish were ready to do something about this state of affairs and intercept the British incursions. Earlier Spanish expeditions had not been successful in obtaining the Omaha trade, but now a major post was to be built near them, and James Mackay was to be its founder.

A neglected comment in Mackay's journal tells us of the introduction to Indians along the Missouri River of a number of plants that were alien to the New World. There is no way to tell whether watermelons and peaches, for example, were introduced to American Indians in the upper Missouri valley by way of early French or Spanish contacts via the Mississippi valley or whether they reached them through contacts with Spanish settlements in the southwest, perhaps from Santa Fe. Watermelons had been introduced into Florida as early as 1576 and may have reached the Great Plains by the late seventeenth century. Watermelon seeds and a peach pit have been found archaeologically in the King Hill Oneota village site, probably a Kansas Indian village predating 1714, in St. Joseph in northwestern Missouri. Watermelon seeds also have been identified at the Utz site, a prehistoric to early historic Missouri Indian village near the confluence of the Grand River and the Missouri River in central Missouri.[28]

James Mackay's statement that he had taken "several kinds of seed, such as Water and Musk Melon and of other Vegetables" with him on the Missouri River expedition is perhaps the only written documentation we have concerning the introduction of such plants to the tribes of the Missouri valley. When he said that he had "sowed them and they succeeded very well," we may suppose he had done so during his stay at Fort Charles, the only time he would have had the opportunity to do so during the expedition. Unfortunately, he does not say which Indian groups he had "made a present of those Seeds." In any case, the Indians "succeeded and reaped a harvest of them as in the Illinois and they preserve the seed with great care." What "other Vegetables" he took with him is unknown, although garden peas are a good possibility; the Mandans called them *omeniasamakeri*.[29]

On August 2, 1804, William Clark noted that the Otos and Missouris had sent the Corps of Discovery some "Water Millions." These conjoined tribes were living along the Platte River just above the mouth of Elkhorn River. It is entirely possible that watermelons had reached them via the Omahas, who lived only a short distance up the Missouri and who "cultivated corn, beans, and melons." By 1804, watermelons were even present among the Arikaras, for Sgt. John Ordway wrote, on October 10, 1804, that they "Raise considerable of Indian corn, beans pumkins Squasshes water millions a kind of Tobacco &.C.&.C."[30]

The watermelon (*Citrullus lanatus*) is a native of Africa, but the pioneer botanist Melvin R. Gilmore was so impressed by its early appearance on the

Great Plains that he advocated the idea that there had been an undescribed native North American species, probably derived by intertribal trade from Mexico.[31] The muskmelon (*Cucumis melo*), like the watermelon, is a member of the *Cucurbitacae*, a family comprising squashes, pumpkins, gourds, and watermelons.

THE PONCA INDIANS

The Poncas enter recorded history in documents prepared in St. Louis by Spanish officials. An unsigned 1785 letter, probably from Esteban Rodriquez Miró, governor general of Louisiana, to Antonio Rengel, commandant of the Interior Provinces of Louisiana, states, "the Poncas have a village on the small river below the River-that-Runs," or the Niobrara; the reference goes on to say, however, that "nevertheless they are nomadic."[32] This reference, the first to mention the Poncas by name, places the group downstream from the mouth of the Niobrara, probably on Bazille Creek. The latter stream enters the Missouri about five miles below the "River-that-Runs."

Eight years later, in 1793, the trader Jean Baptiste Meunier (or Monier) claimed that in 1789 he had been the first European to visit and "discover" the Ponca. He petitioned for and obtained the right of exclusive trade with them, although his claim later was disallowed when its falseness was exposed. He and his partner, Jacques Rolland, nevertheless dealt with them from a trading house that they established near the Ponca village. He did not have the market to himself, for Solomon Petit, another St. Louis trader, ignored Meunier's monopoly and built a house for the Ponca trade for the winter of 1794–95. Trade with the Poncas had certainly preceded Meunier's monopoly by many years, but the documented beginnings of exchange specifically with them are dated to his claim. Meunier and his competitors continued to trade with the Ponca until about 1795. Clamorgan commented in April 1794 on "the events that gave rise not to the discovery of the Ponca nation [by Meunier] but in the first trading that was done at the village of that nation. . . . These same Poncas usually come to trade their furs with the trader assigned to the Mahas' village without his having the trouble of going any farther. . . . Since this time a separate trade has been made of them."[33]

As Joseph Jablow notes, "as far as the St. Louis fur trade is concerned," 1789 or 1790 was the first time "that trading was done in a purely Ponca community." The "separate trade" with the Omahas and Poncas about which Clamorgan spoke is confirmed in the instructions that Truteau was given on his departure up the Missouri River in 1794: he was to "arrange with the dealer of the Mahas, or of Poncas in whatever of these stations he may stay."[34]

The earliest chart on which the Poncas appear in their traditional territory is the 1795 Soulard map. It depicts with three dots the "N[ation] Poncas" on the right bank of the Missouri River just above the "R Apueard," or Niobrara River. Just above these symbols is a rectangle marked by a Spanish flag that represents Ponca House, occupied by Truteau between November 11, 1794, and March 1795 (although it is shown on the wrong bank of the river). The Ponca village on the Soulard map may be the archaeological site today known as Ponca Fort. The first known reference to a village that can be plausibly identified as Ponca Fort is in the journal of Truteau, who headed the first trading expedition of the Missouri Company up the Missouri River.

Ponca House is shown on the charts resulting from the explorations of Mackay and Evans and on the William Clark 1804 route map for September 4–9. It was on the left bank of the Missouri River some twenty-seven air miles above the mouth of Ponca Creek (see fig. 20), about opposite the mouth of Scalp Creek. It was built on the floodplain of the river some one to two miles below the site of the modern Fort Randall Dam in present Charles Mix County, South Dakota. About eleven miles downstream from the post was a prominent landmark, "The Tower," that was to be mentioned by many river travelers in the years to follow. Sometime after 1839, the Missouri shifted and carried away the bottomland on which Ponca House was built. Since at least 1856 the channel of the river has flowed over its former location, brushing against the base of the bluffs on the left bank behind the site, so that the post's remains have been scattered downstream.[35]

Four months after he built Ponca House, Truteau went to visit an unspecified Ponca community—probably Ponca Fort, their only known contemporary village site. Arriving on March 26, 1795, he wrote, "their lodges are built about half a league from the Missouri." In his 1796 "Description of the Upper Missouri," however, he is more specific: "The Ponca nation has its habitations placed at two leagues higher than [the Niobrara's] mouth. Their huts are built upon a hill on the edge of a great plain about a league from the Missouri. The buffalo, the deer, and beaver are common in this place."[36]

The mouth of Ponca Creek today is six miles up the Missouri from the mouth of the Niobrara, and Ponca Fort is on the south side of Ponca Creek about 1.25 miles from the Missouri. Using a figure of 3 miles to the league,[37] these figures compare very closely with the distances given by Truteau. Modern maps show that the channel of the Missouri River here—unlike its channel in so many other areas—has not changed appreciably since Truteau's time. Differences in the distances from the Missouri to the Ponca village may be the result of calculating the distance from the Missouri River along the channel of Ponca Creek rather than overland from the channel of the Missouri.

Truteau returned to St. Louis in the early summer of 1796, where he reported to Zenon Trudeau, lieutenant governor of Spanish Illinois and commandant at St. Louis, sometime before July 3.[38]

Beginning in the 1790s, if not earlier, the Poncas began the practice of stopping and raiding trading craft as they made their way up the Missouri River. This caused delay in the development of trade on the upper Missouri, not to mention considerable financial loss to the companies owning the vessels. Zenon Trudeau reported that the Ponca pillage of one trading expedition resulted in the loss of merchandise valued at seven thousand pesos.[39] While Mackay and Evans began their journey up the Missouri in 1795, Truteau was still on the upper Missouri, and the Otos told him that the Poncas had pillaged a pirogue under the supervision of a man named Lécuyer; the loss amounted to eight thousand *piastres*. Goods also passed into Ponca hands through other, informal channels; it was said that Lécuyer had no less than two wives while he was with the Ponca and had wasted a good deal of Missouri Company merchandise while he was with the tribe.

On the Beinecke Library map, showing Evans's travels in 1796–97, the "Ponca R. & Village" is indicated by three triangular symbols on the north side of Ponca Creek a short distance above its confluence with the Missouri. Although the word "village" is singular, triangular symbols of this nature depict individual villages elsewhere on the map. Ponca Fort is shown on the south side of Ponca Creek, consistent with the occupation of the fort in 1796–97. On the Indian Office map, two triangular symbols are shown between the Niobrara and Ponca Creek in about the same location for Ponca Fort, labeled "village des panis—Panis Village."

The first map to show Ponca country in near-modern detail was published in France by François Marie Perrin du Lac in 1805 (an English edition followed in 1807), although the map carries the date 1802. This chart was derived from the Mackay and Evans maps produced in 1796–97, and the information in Perrin du Lac's narrative likewise derives from Jean Baptiste Truteau and Jacques D'Eglise.[40] Since Mackay and Evans are documented eyewitnesses, and since Mackay himself explored the lower Niobrara River valley, the Perrin du Lac 1802 map and other copies of the Mackay and Evans charts reflect with reasonable accuracy the features observed by these two travelers in 1795–97.

Documents relating to the journey of James Mackay in 1795–97 show that the Ponca village visited by Truteau in 1795 had not moved. Mackay's "Table of Distances" documents the "River & village of the Ponca . . . Upon the south bank, at a league and a half from the Missouri. There is a large island in front of the village."[41] This description corresponds in most particulars to that of Truteau's Ponca village of 1795. A large island, "Ponca Island," is at the mouth of Ponca Creek today, exactly as it is shown on the Beinecke Library map and on William Clark's 1804 map, documenting that the major features of the Missouri River channel, at least in this locality, have not changed significantly since the turn of the eighteenth century.

The Poncas were seriously affected by smallpox during their residence at Ponca Fort. This may well account for the many graves placed in low hummocks outside the fortification ditch there. Lewis and Clark are not specific about dates, but the Ponca's reduction by smallpox and Dakota attacks led them to take up a nomadic life about this time. According to Perrin du Lac's sources, in 1802 the villagers had "three hundred and fifty warriors, notwithstanding the ravages of the smallpox." The Poncas, with the Omahas, Ioways, Otos, and others, suffered heavily in 1800–1801 from that disease, and traders returning from their villages were quarantined under guard before being permitted to reenter St. Louis.[42]

FORT CHARLES

When the party reached a point a few miles below the Omaha Indian village on November 11, Blackbird came to meet the expedition "a day's journey distant" from the village. This locale was almost exactly halfway to the Mandans, about 760 miles from the mouth of the Missouri. Because it was so late in the year, Mackay decided to build a post here and resume his explorations in the spring. The establishment was called Fort Carlos, after the reigning king of Spain, Carlos IV, but is best known as Fort Charles. While Mackay was building this post, his colleague Jean Baptiste Truteau was far upriver, trading with the Arikaras.[43]

The expedition unloaded their supplies on November 14 and began construction. Mackay's journal provides a clear description of the fort's surroundings:

> On the 29th, the Prince came to visit the fort which was being built in a plain located between the very village of the Mahas and the Missouri River, on the shore of a small river which flows into the latter, and is fairly navigable. This plain is very extensive, the land excellent, and

never inundated by the waters. The location of the fort seems to have been prepared by nature. It is in a commanding district, which rises for a circumference of about one thousand feet. It looks on the shore of this river, as if to command the rest of the area. I have established my settlement and my fort there, although at a distance from the woods; however, the horses of the Prince are at my service.[44]

Fort Charles was built about five miles southeast of Big Village, the principal village of the Omahas, at a point near the south boundary of present-day Dakota County, Nebraska, some twenty-five air miles below Sioux City. The fort's exact location is unknown, but it must have been somewhere near modern Blyburg Lake, an old cutoff meander of the Missouri River. Several attempts have been made to find Fort Charles, but all have been unsuccessful despite the fact that there are three primary maps showing its location. Unfortunately, two of these are small-scale charts and are of little use in pinpointing its location. One is the Indian Office map, and the other, found in the Beinecke Library, illustrates John Evans's 1796–97 travels. More helpful is the larger-scale map drawn by William Clark illustrating the expedition's route for August 13–21, 1804. This detailed chart depicts both the Omaha village and "Mr. Mackey's trading House" in relation to the river and the bluff line.[45]

The Missouri River in this part of its valley was subject to wild variation before it was channelized, explaining why the location of Fort Charles is so uncertain today. Although the position of "Mr. Mackey's trading House" is clearly shown on Clark's map, the many changes in the river's course since that time render it impossible to determine the post's former location with any confidence. On August 11, 1804, in fact, Clark had written that "the river is verry Crooked. . . . I have observed a number of places where the river has Changd its Bead at different times."[46]

It is probably no coincidence that it was an issue of the *Sioux City Register* in 1868 that introduced the timeworn quotation, "Of all the variable things in creation, the most uncertain are—the action of a jury, the state of a woman's mind, and the condition of the Missouri River." The Missouri valley near Sioux City and the Fort Charles site is eleven miles wide, giving the river more than ample room in which to meander, and it did so often—and capriciously.

The most recent investigations seeking the site of Fort Charles were in June and July 1987 and in October 1990 by Gayle F. Carlson, an archaeologist with the Nebraska State Historical Society, assisted by Rolfe D. Mandel, a geomorphologist. Mackay's description of the fort's setting is consistent with a location along the bank of modern Omaha Creek on an alluvial terrace above the elevation of seasonal flooding. It is, however, possible that the site fell into the Missouri River during one of its many channel changes.[47]

Carlson concludes that the points best resembling the fort's setting, as described by Mackay, are on a low terrace on the west side of the Missouri at a height of about four meters above the modern floodplain as seen on the U.S. Geological Survey's 7.5 minute Homer, Nebraska-Iowa, quadrangle. Only a few locations in this area seem to correspond to Mackay's description and to Clark's map. The quest for the fort's remains was abandoned, however, when the tests Carlson and Mandel made at these locations found nothing.

What did this post look like? The only honest answer is, we have no idea. We do not know what specifications, if any, Mackay may have been given for its construction, and he says nothing in his journal that provides a clue to its appearance. Was he given some latitude in its size and design? If so, he may have drawn on his experiences and recollections of fur-trade posts in Canada for its plan. In this case we can say little, for our knowledge of even those establishments is limited, and having only limited archaeological investigations, existing reconstructions of eighteenth-century posts are heavily infused with speculation. We know only that Fort Charles's defenses were planned to include cannon, which were to be brought to the post the coming summer.[48]

Because the post was hurriedly built, it could not have been very large or substantial. Mackay originally had with him a party nearly as large as that of the Lewis and Clark expedition, so manpower was not a problem, at least initially. Although Mackay began building the fort about November 15, he nevertheless recorded on November 21 that the "scarcity of food retards a trifle the construction of the fort which I am building, but will not prevent me from finishing it soon."[49] Because there was so little to eat, he had sent some of his men to accompany an Omaha bison-hunting party that day. Whatever its scale, the post was certainly a more modest establishment than the one Truteau had been directed to build among the Mandans.

Because both Truteau and Mackay were employees of the same fur company, some of the specifications of Truteau's unnamed Mandan post (it was never built, much less begun) may be relevant to Fort Charles. Truteau was to "cause to be constructed . . . a building [*cabaña*] thirty feet long and fifteen feet wide, built of logs placed one upon another in English fashion, the corners joined and fitted by a kind of mortise; on the inside he shall have a partition made in order that one part may serve as a storeroom and the other as a lodging." The directions continue: "He shall cause to be constructed another building,

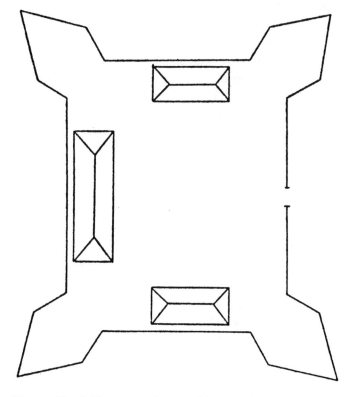

Fig. 11. Sketch illustrating the specifications of the fort that Jean Baptiste Truteau was to build for the Mandan trade. (From Nasatir, *Before Lewis and Clark*, 1:244)

or *cabaña* in the same manner, for his men, opposite the first, with a distance of fifty feet between them. He shall have the doors and the windows of the two *cabañas* made exactly opposite each other and only on the sides facing each other, but no opening must be made on any of the other three sides." The buildings of Truteau's proposed Mandan fort were to be surrounded later by an elaborate bastioned palisade. There is an astonishing disparity between the magnitude of this proposed post and the eight-man crew Truteau had with him. He had been asked to do the impossible. When he did build Ponca House just above the mouth of the Niobrara River in November 1794, it was a structure that he merely called a "winter cabin."[50]

We might imagine that Mackay built two buildings such as those that Truteau was to erect but defended by a more simple stockade. This idea, however, is speculation, however plausible it might be in terms of the architecture of the period and the length of time that Mackay's men had to do the work. Still, housing nearly thirty men would require more than one structure, and there would have to be room for their trade goods and other supplies.

Construction after December 18, by which time the Missouri was completely frozen, would have been possible but uncomfortable, so the men had four and a half weeks to make the buildings secure for the winter between beginning construction and the onset of bitter cold weather.[51] Mackay said the fort was "at a distance from the woods," so building material had to be moved some distance to the construction site. However, help in hauling logs apparently was provided by the Omahas, judging from Mackay's comment that "the horses of the Prince are at my service." The snow and cold that had "retarded considerably" his last few days' travel to the Omahas also slowed construction.

Adding to the delay was a slow but steady erosion of the work force before and during the fort's construction. The thirty-man crew with which Mackay left St. Louis had been reduced a month earlier when some men were left near the mouth of the Platte River to build and maintain a house for the Oto trade. The party had, of course, been augmented by the six company men they had met and retained above the mouth of the Platte, so their numbers remained about the same up to that point.

How many men were left behind to operate the Post of the Otos? We do not know. In one sentence in his journals, Mackay speaks in the plural, for a single man would surely not have survived long in this setting, even though he also speaks of "The agent that I have placed there for the trade."[52] Nor do we know how many men Mackay sent with the Omaha hunting party on November 21, which did not return for some twenty-five days. Furthermore, we are ignorant of the number of men in the detachment that Mackay sent upriver to visit the Arikaras on November 24 while construction of the fort was still in progress. The latter group was forced back by an encounter with a Sioux bison-hunting party, however, and returned to Fort Charles on January 6, 1797. They traveled homeward by the same route but arrived after the fort's construction was essentially completed.

Mackay's contacts with Blackbird were cordial, for the men had interlocking agendas. The Scot promoted Spanish interests; conferred several medals on the chiefs and distributed gifts generously; and made an alliance with Blackbird, who promised to avenge the injuries that the Poncas had perpetrated against Spanish traders. Blackbird also offered to send emissaries to the Sioux and other tribes upriver to induce their chiefs to visit Fort Charles in the spring with a view to securing peace and free passage on the river. He also promised to escort Mackay to the Arikaras personally, a pledge that he never fulfilled.

Blackbird continued to give promises as Mackay continued to harangue him and distribute gifts to the chief and his subjects. This attempt to gain friendship cost Mackay the greater part of his supplies, and he soon sent a boat to St. Louis for reinforcements and resupply, a move that simultaneously reduced his existing manpower and diminishing supplies. On April 10, 1796, Clamorgan wrote to Carondelet: "Not satisfied with the presents which Mr. Mackay brought to him last fall, he has just caused the aforesaid Mackay to send us a boat to get the things which he needed. Consequently, eight days ago [April 2, 1796], we sent a *voiture* armed [i.e., manned] with nine men for the fulfillment of his *mémoire* [with what he asked for]." Clamorgan added, "This expedition, which is pure loss to us, adds a very cruel sum to our expenses." The voiture surely alludes to a small boat, although usually the term would be glossed as a cart, carriage, or caisson. It is unlikely that a cart, even "armed with nine men," would have survived such an overland trip, much less its escort. We presume that the boat reached Fort Charles, but no further mention is made of it or its contents. Whatever the case, the company dispatched another party up the Missouri on August 24, 1796, under twenty-four-year-old Francisco Derouin that did succeed in reaching its destination. He was in charge of goods destined for the Oto tribe, probably for trade at the Post of the Otos. Derouin (also known as Don Frederico Autman) carried "an outfit of goods sufficient for the use of that nation." He also may have carried supplies upriver that reached Mackay at Fort Charles, although no mention is made of it.[53]

Derouin's report to Zenon Trudeau on his return in May 1797 gives us a skeleton outline of his trip. The voyage to the Otos took eight and a half weeks, for he arrived among them on October 22, and he remained with them all winter. His trade with them was a disappointment, for much of it was dispensed to assure their continued good will, and the remainder was sold on credit. The trip to the Otos, he told Trudeau, was reckoned "by all travelers" as two hundred leagues, taking "about fifty days unless one meets with bad weather or has sickness among the rowers." (Derouin may have carried with him a commission from Governor Carondelet to Blackbird's son dated May 12, 1796.)[54]

EVANS'S ABORTIVE FIRST MISSION

Mackay was worried about his progress to the Mandan villages and feared that he would not reach them before the following summer. As a result, one of his first acts after halting among the Omahas was to send a party upriver to contact Truteau, who by this time was to have built a fort among the Mandans. The party, "a well-accompanied detachment" under Evans's command, set out overland on November 24, 1796, to find out what was happening upriver. There were reports of hostilities between the Poncas and the Arikaras and between the Arikaras and the Sioux—events, if true, that would be detrimental to the Spanish party's continued upriver advance.

Evans took with him several experienced men, two of whom Mackay names (Scarlet and Tollibois, or Jollibois), men in whose conduct and perseverance Mackay had confidence.[55] This reconnaissance team (for it can hardly be referred to in more flattering terms) aborted its mission abruptly when they encountered a Sioux bison-hunting party. Fearing for their lives, they reversed course, with the Sioux in hot pursuit, and returned to Fort Charles on January 6. They had managed to reach the vicinity of the White River, about eighty leagues above the Omahas, where they met the *Sious of the Grand Détour*. This midwinter excursion, consuming forty-four days, must have been a painful experience, combining miserable traveling conditions and the humiliation of being driven back. On their return Blackbird again promised to accompany the expedition upriver, but as events were to prove, his promise again proved empty.

Hoping to make his way upriver more pleasant and less stressful, the "preceding winter" Mackay had sent the Sioux a "parole," or message, suggesting that they meet, but they refused to come visit him. Some prominent Sioux chiefs later visited Fort Charles, however, and between his talks and the generosity with which he gave them gifts, the Scot succeeded in smoothing over their past misunderstandings.

Mackay and Evans had been warned about the Sioux. The Indians were well known for their haughty, vexing actions against traders on the Missouri, especially their tendency to pilfer or loot merchandise or to demand ransom for traders to pass up the river. Truteau was especially vocal in his denunciation of the Sioux, writing that Mackay and Evans should avoid these people "as much for the safety of their goods as for their lives." Only a bold and potentially explosive military confrontation allowed Lewis and Clark to bypass the Teton Sioux at the mouth of the Bad River in 1804. Yet the Sioux were the powerbrokers along the Missouri between the Poncas and the Arikaras, constituting both a military and an economic presence that the Spanish emissaries simultaneously wished not only to exploit and befriend but also to wean away from the British traders who supplied them from posts along the Minnesota and Des Moines Rivers.[56]

THE BRITISH PRESENCE

Fort Charles and the Post of the Otos were the first and only Spanish fur-trading posts known to have been built along the Missouri in the present states of Nebraska or Iowa. They may not, however, have been the first Euro-American posts in the area, for Mackay's journal leaves little doubt that a British "fort" was built, or was to have been built, somewhere near the Omaha village. In January 1796 he wrote: "The English of the river of San Pedro [the St. Peter's, or Minnesota River] had concluded among this tribe last autumn [apparently in 1795] the construction of a fort for them on the shore of the Missouri, which they were resolved to maintain against all resistance. My arrival here changed all their projects."[57]

The wording leaves one with the impression that a post was indeed built along the Missouri among the Omahas but that Mackay's arrival led to its abandonment. If it was actually built—a dubious notion—it was short lived, for neither Mackay nor anyone else subsequently alludes to it nor does Mackay speak of dispossessing any alien traders. Truteau makes no mention of any such establishment when he wintered at Ponca House in 1794–95. The British had, of course, been trading with the Omahas and their neighbors for many years, and Truteau said of Chief Blackbird that "the nation situated on the Mississippi . . . brings him every spring in exchange, scarlet cloth, china ware and unwrought silver, and some little brandy for which he has a great passion."[58] The solitary reference to this ephemeral, nameless post gives no clue to where the British had planned to build it.

Baron Carondelet alluded to a similarly elusive post when he wrote in May 1796 that the English had a fort "on the Chato [Platte] River . . . where they have erected a blockhouse [*casa fuerte*]."[59] Yet the British are never known to have planned, much less built, any such "fortified post" anywhere along the Platte River. The Spanish, fearing the worst, appear to have been turning the anxiety of British competition into rumor. Whatever the case, the elusive posts were never built, and their traders continued to travel to the Missouri overland from the Mississippi valley.

By Mackay's time, this trade between the Missouri River tribes and Europeans in the upper Mississippi valley had been going on for nearly a century. The first trading post in the region had been built in 1700 by French trader Pierre-Charles Le Sueur for trade with the local Sioux. Fort l'Huillier (or Fort Vert) was established on the Minnesota River near the mouth of the Blue Earth River near present-day Mankato, Minnesota. At this time the Ioways and Otos were living near Spirit Lake, or Lake Okibojo, Iowa, but they soon moved to the Missouri and established residence along that river, the Ioways living in the general area of the mouth of the Big Sioux River and the Otos near the Platte River.[60]

Some of the Euro-American goods reaching the Omahas and Poncas around the turn of the eighteenth century came to them by way of Spanish-sponsored traders based in St. Louis. There was, nevertheless, significant competition for the Missouri River trade by the British, whose goods annually reached the Missouri valley by a variety of routes and in greater volume. The principal trails were overland from Prairie du Chien, some four miles above the mouth of the Wisconsin River, and up the Des Moines River from its confluence with the Mississippi River. The Des Moines valley was a direct route to the villagers living near the mouth of the Big Sioux River: the Omahas, Poncas, Otos, and Ioways.

These routes are illustrated on several early maps. By 1703, the trade was illustrated on Guillaume Delisle's "Carte du Mexique et de la Floride" by an unlabeled trail between the mouth of the Wisconsin River and a location just below the mouth of the Little Sioux River. A more prominent *Chemin des Voyageurs"* is shown on Delisle's 1718 map between the mouth of the Wisconsin River and the "Aiaouez" and the "Maha," whose villages appear to be along the Little Sioux and Big Sioux Rivers in present-day northwestern Iowa.[61] Furthermore, the original and each of the three copies of the much later 1795 Soulard map carries a dashed line beginning at the confluence of the Des Moines and Mississippi Rivers, and the northern branch of that route reaches the Missouri River in Omaha and Ponca country. It is reasonable to assume that trade goods from the Mississippi valley had been reaching the Omaha-Poncas via such routes as early as 1700 and probably earlier.

This trade continued into Spanish times, including two well-documented incursions into Spanish territory from Prairie du Chien by British traders Jonathan Carver in 1766–67 and Peter Pond in 1773.[62] These men were trading along the Minnesota River with the Santee Dakotas, Teton Dakotas, and the Cheyennes, all of whom were in contact with tribes of the Missouri River.

Abraham Nasatir has documented the extent of Spanish distress at these incursions: they planned to build forts on the Mississippi to intercept this trade. A fort at the mouth of the Des Moines River was especially desirable, for British traders went up that river to reach the Missouri tribes.[63] They probably took canoes to the head of navigation. Here it is reasonable to suppose that the British built a few small cabins for storage and to house canoes for the return downstream. The U.S. Army later built Fort Des Moines at the base of a fourteen-mile-long rapids, an obstacle to river travel that may have constituted the head of navigation.[64] If the traders initially went by canoe, they continued on to the Missouri on foot from such an obstacle; if not, they probably went the full route by horseback, for the *voyageurs* were moving against river currents on the way west.

Spanish governors tried to stop the trade several times by sending galleys to "cruise in the channels of the Mississippi," but the Indians were so hostile to them that after several visits these ventures were abandoned. The reason for the popularity of the British traders was clear to everyone. Truteau's letter to Carondelet dated October 2, 1793, states it simply: the "Canadians and English of Michilmaquinac . . . by the cheapness of their merchandise attract all the savages who would come to us. They give them bad counsel as they have always done and take away from us the best furs."[65]

It was not simply the "cheapness of their merchandise" that the Indian customers appreciated. The superiority of British products is an oft-repeated theme in documents of the time, which combined with the scarcity of Spanish goods meant real trouble for the Spanish St. Louis merchants. There is an abundance of documentation on the British penetration of the upper Mississippi River area, and although the details are sketchy, it is obvious that they openly and aggressively sought to insinuate themselves into the Indian trade in the prairies and plains west of the Mississippi. Not only did British traders go to the Missouri to trade, but also some of the Missouri valley tribes themselves went to the Mississippi.

In 1791 Manuel Pérez, lieutenant governor of Spanish Illinois, recommended that the Spanish build forts at the mouths of the Des Moines and Minnesota Rivers to prevent British smugglers from trespassing into Spanish territory. Although this theme is repeatedly voiced in Spanish documents, the forts never were built, and the Spaniards had little success in restraining the illegal Anglo traders on the Missouri River. One recorded exception occurred in 1777 when Spanish traders to the Oto Indians confiscated the goods of two British traders. The men themselves escaped, but the Spanish took 1,473 *libras* of deer skins the trespassers had obtained from the Otos.[66]

These British traders were reaching the Otos via the Ioway Indians and penetrating even deeper into Spanish territory, visiting and trading with the "Panis and Loups" along the Platte River. In his journal entry for January 18, 1796, James Mackay notes that traders from the Des Moines had "sent twelve horses, laden with goods, to trade with the Panis and the Loups [Lobos, or

Wolves] on the Chato [Platte] River. The caravan crossed the Missouri in the month of last December. I would be glad to be able to deal them a blow on their return." The British had indeed entered "the villages of the Panis" as early as 1773 and 1777.[67] His last sentence above further reinforces the hostility that Mackay felt toward his fellow countrymen and the depth of his loyalty to the Spanish. Whatever his feelings, he does not mention English traders to the Pawnees again.

These British trips were successful and effectively excluded the Spaniards from the trans-Mississippi area. Truteau, in fact, says that "some *coureurs de bois* formerly made great profits." Duchêne Perrot, a Spanish trader in the Des Moines River area, registered a bitter complaint with Zenon Trudeau in St. Louis about British wrongs against him: "They have already indoctrinated the savages so well that one cannot any longer, without risk, go to the Mahas, Hotos, and Poncas, from where they have been removing all the beaver and otter, as well as, the other fine furs."[68]

As late as December 1801, a trader named Thomas G. Anderson wintered with the Ioways about fifty miles above the mouth of the Des Moines River. Still he found it necessary to carry goods to the Missouri River, where the tribe was hunting. Anderson and several companions packed trade goods to the Missouri in six days and carried out a good exchange with them.[69]

In 1804 Meriwether Lewis concluded that the Spaniards did not successfully compete with British traders because Spanish traders were "shackeled with the pecuniary impositions of their governors" and the British could "enter without the necessity of a Spanish passport, or the fear of being detected by them." For this reason, "all the country west of the Mississippi nearly to the Missouri, was exclusively enjoyed by the British merchants."[70]

Writing at Fort Mandan during the winter of 1804–5, Meriwether Lewis commented that "the Yanktons of the North, and the Sissitons" obtained trade goods from Murdock Cameron at the head of the St. Peters (Minnesota) River. In turn, they bartered these goods to the "4 bands of *Tetons* and the *Yanktons Ahnah*" at the annual Indian trade fair along the James River in what is now east-central South Dakota. These groups lived along the Missouri River and upper reaches of the Des Moines River. Lewis's solution to barring the British from the trans-Mississippi trade was the same as that of the Spaniards: build military posts along the upper Mississippi to intercept these interlopers.[71]

We need not rely entirely on written records to document the early presence of Europeans in the Arikara villages. In the 1990s the remains of a forty-to-fifty-year-old Caucasian male were discovered by forensic anthropologists while studying the interments from an Arikara cemetery at a village near the mouth of Swan Creek, South Dakota. The village, investigated by a University of South Dakota archaeological team during the mid-1950s, was estimated by its excavator to have been occupied between about 1675 and 1725.[72] The site is on a high terrace on the left bank of the Missouri River nearly seventy river miles above the mouth of the Cheyenne River. The man is presumed to have been a Spaniard or a Frenchman—the most likely traders along this part of the Missouri River at the time—although we cannot dismiss the possibility that he may have been British. A forensic sculptor has partially resuscitated him, composing a computer-generated image of what his skull can tell us of his facial appearance.

This unknown trader had lived a rough life: three healed depression fractures on his skull testify to his familiarity with violence, although there is no indication as to how he met his death. Most likely he had been a resident trader living at the village on good terms with his hosts, for upon his death he had been interred in the same manner as his former customers. Only modern forensic techniques permitted his identification from among the remains of the Arikaras with whom he had lived.[73] Many such men, perpetually nameless, met death among strangers thousands of miles from their homes, but the Swan Creek *coureur de bois* has attained a far more public identity than any of his colleagues.

CHAPTER FOUR

THE MISSOURI RIVER
BASIN EXPLORED

"Those Remarkable Things Mentioned by Evens"

T
he commercial center of the upper Missouri River consisted of the five Mandan and Hidatsa villages that lay clustered near the mouth of the Knife River. Here the two groups acted as middlemen in a far-flung trade network with contacts as far west as the Pacific Coast. The first white to visit them and leave an account of doing so was Pierre Gaultier de Varennes, the Sieur de La Vérendrye, in December 1738. He was drawn to their villages by accounts of their importance as tradesmen on the northern plains. After a short visit, La Vérendrye returned to Fort La Reine, his post along the Assiniboine River, leaving behind two men who were to learn their language; the following summer the men also returned to Fort La Reine. The Mandans, then as later, proved to be a magnet for Euro-American fur traders from both Canada and later St. Louis.[1]

THE MANDAN INDIANS AND THEIR NEIGHBORS

Some twenty years before John Thomas Evans's arrival, the Mandans had been living in strongly fortified villages farther down the Missouri River near the mouth of the Heart River. At that time they lived in perhaps nine villages with a population of about nine thousand individuals. Their nearest and most amiable neighbors were the Hidatsas, who lived upstream at the same villages they occupied when the Welshman arrived. The two tribes were similar in so many ways that their names are often, and appropriately, hyphenated together. Mandan relations with nearby nomadic tribes usually were hostile despite their middleman role in the regional Indian trade system.

The Mandans and Hidatsas were living in a rapidly changing world during the closing years of the eighteenth century. In 1780 a smallpox epidemic, perhaps beginning among the Sioux in the upper Mississippi valley, had swept across the plains to infect the Missouri River villagers. Smallpox also was raging among Indians in the American Southwest, and perhaps the disease reached the villages from that direction. Regardless of its origin, it had devastating effects on all of the sedentary and nomadic groups of the northern plains. Arriving among the Mandans and Hidatsas sometime between late April and the summer of 1781, the virus quickly spread to other groups. The best information on the epidemic's expansion concerns its move to the north, where the Assiniboines were infected in October and the Blackfoot about the same time; it then passed on to the north to the Crees in early to midwinter. At this time the Mandans were living near the mouth of the Heart River in several large settlements such as Double Ditch, a heavily fortified community twelve miles north of present-day Bismarck. This village and others nearby were abandoned about this time; William Clark wrote on one of his route maps in 1804 that one such site was "destroyed by the Soux and Small Pox."[2] Depopulation led the surviving Mandans to abandon their villages and move north, where they built two new villages near the Hidatsas at the mouth of the Knife River. Smallpox also spread south and west to the Shoshone (the Gens du Serpent, or Snake Indians) and others, though this is less well undocumented.

The Shoshones, better known as the Snakes, probably have been residents on the northwestern plains since late prehistoric times. They had been pedestrian bison-hunting nomads between about 1500 and 1700, during which time they became a highly aggressive bison-hunting people. After they obtained horses, their raiding lifestyle through the northwestern plains in the period 1700–80 became legendary.[3]

In short, the Shoshones once occupied and dominated much of the trans-Missouri country between Wyoming and Montana, their power extending east almost to the Missouri River west of the Mandans. If we credit the cartographic evidence, they remained in control of this territory at least until 1780, but by the late eighteenth century, their numbers too had been reduced by disease, a circumstance that permitted the Blackfoot and other tribes, with more ready access to firearms, to drive them to the west. By the time of Lewis and Clark, they were living in the foothills of the Rocky Mountains and beyond.[4] Their demise, and the reduced number of Mandans and Hidatsas, left a power vacuum in the northern plains that permitted the Lakota Tetons to expand their control of the region on both sides of the Missouri. These nomads had been less affected by the epidemics, and they now surrounded the villagers and outnumbered them.

The first traders from Canada to visit the Mandans had been the La Véren-dryes in 1738 and 1743. In all probability, there had been individual traders among the Mandans in the years between 1743 and 1785, but they have gone largely unrecorded. In 1785, however, North West Company traders based in Montreal built Pine Fort on the Assiniboine River and established regular trade with the village Indians. It was not long before competing posts were established and traders from the Hudson's Bay Company vied for the villagers' furs.[5] It was into this setting that John Evans arrived, planning to deny the Canadian traders the right to exploit resources on soil claimed by the Spanish crown.

The Mandan villages were established along the Missouri River bank a few miles below the mouth of the Knife River. One of them, known today as Deapolis, occupied a high terrace overlooking the river channel; the other community, known today as Black Cat, which was the name of its chief, lay on the river bank in the bottomlands on the north side of the Missouri, nearly opposite Deapolis. The three Hidatsa villages, today known as Big Hidatsa, Sakakawea, and Amahami, were on terrace rims along the Missouri valley along the lowermost reaches of the Knife. The Mandan towns were stoutly defended by a dry moat and post palisades, sometimes reinforced by bastions or strong points. Their homes were circular, earth-covered structures with a covered entryway on one side.

Physically, the Mandans were like most of their neighbors except that there seems to have been an unusually high incidence (about 10 percent) of pre-mature graying of the hair, a trait also known in other tribes, including the Cheyennes. This condition (achromotrichia) frequently was confused with "blondism." Light skins, dark brown hair, and blue eyes also were said by early explorers to be common among the Mandans. Whereas these features (not including the blue eyes) clearly are the result of biological variation in pigmentation and facial features, their presence lent false fuel to the early romantic theory of Welsh origins.[6]

The Mandans became better known than many American Indian groups, thanks largely to three circumstances. First, they figured prominently in the journals of Lewis and Clark, for the Mandan villages were only a short dis-tance from Fort Mandan, the expeditions' wintering post for 1804–5. Second, the Okipa ceremony and its spectacular torture features attracted much atten-tion when George Catlin first brought this elaborate ritual to public attention. And third, the myth linking them with Welsh Indians brought them perpetual notoriety.

The richness and affluence of Mandan social and ceremonial life was such that they, together with the Hidatsas, provided a cultural climax for the northern plains despite their location, so marginal for an agrarian society. Their power and reputation, based as it was on a population of many thousands of individuals, was shattered by the epidemics that swept the plains, leaving them at the time of Evans's visit with perhaps only about 10 percent of their early eighteenth-century population.

EVANS'S JOURNEY UPRIVER

A detailed, six-part map of Evans's excursion from Fort Charles to the Mandans, here called the Beinecke Library map, permits us to use these charts as a surrogate for the journal, most of which is now lost, that he was instructed to keep during the voyage.[7] Most of the charts were annotated by William Clark during the voyage of the Corps of Discovery. Consequently, the charts must be used with care to avoid conflating details on the original map with those placed on it by Clark. (These additions and emendations are discussed in chapter 5.)

Mackay gave Evans an elaborate, seven-point set of instructions upon his departure up the Missouri. It is sometimes said that Pres. Thomas Jefferson copied these instructions for Lewis and Clark.[8] Comparisons, however, reveal no close similarities, nor is there any evidence that either Jefferson or Lewis ever laid eyes on Mackay's instructions. Nevertheless both Mackay's and Jefferson's documents provided meticulous directions for the conduct of their respective subordinates.

Evans was instructed, "From the time of your departure from this fort until your return to the place where I will be living on the Missouri, you will keep a journal of each day and month of the year."[9] He was to make copious notes on the Indian tribes he met, including their language and religion; on the geography and its resources; and his latitude and longitude. He was also to prepare a chart of the route, for no reliable map of the upper Missouri existed. Evans was also to proclaim to the Indians that Carlos IV of Spain was "the protector of all white and red men," just as Lewis and Clark later proclaimed American sovereignty over the land.

Mackay anticipated that Evans would go, as article 3 specified, "by land," though this point seems to have been disregarded. Even day-to-day conduct was specified: "You will take for provisions on your route some well-skinned dried meat," and "You will never fire any guns except in case of necessity; you will never cut wood except with a knife unless it should be strictly necessary; you will never build a fire without a true need, and you will avoid having the smoke seen from afar, camping if it is possible in the valleys. You will not camp too early and will always leave before daybreak." He was asked to bring back with him, if possible, live animals unknown to the Spanish as well as "vegetables, minerals, and other curious things that you can find."

After he reached and had crossed the Rockies, Evans was to "build some canoes to descend these rivers" to the Pacific Ocean. He was to mark his "route in all places where there will be a portage to pass from one river to another or from one water-fall to another by cutting or notching some trees or by some piles of stones engraved and cut; and take care to place in large letters Charles IV King of Spain and below [that] Company of the Missouri, the day, the month, and the year when you do this in order to serve as unquestionable proof of the journey that you are going to make." He was to return from the Pacific immediately, with specimens to prove his arrival on an ocean shore, and was directed to report directly to Mackay. If this was not possible, Evans was to go immediately to St. Louis to "deliver all your papers, plans, charts, and journals to *Monsieur* Clamorgan, Director of the Company," or to Zenon Trudeau, "keeping in your possession a copy of each thing to be delivered and sent to the said *Monsieur* Zenon Trudeau by a safe means." Evans was to comply only minimally with these and a multitude of other instructions. Still, the map that he prepared of his voyage to the Mandans from Fort Charles and the surviving fragments of his journal reveal that he took his instructions as seriously as was practical on the trip.

The journey to the Mandans ultimately took Evans nearly four months, although he was denied travel for perhaps six weeks by an enforced stay among the Arikaras. The same route took Lewis and Clark sixty-eight days, a little over two months, despite their own contacts with the Sioux and the Arikara Indians.

Despite his directions to go by land, the journey surely was undertaken by boat. Evans's map shows the river and its islands in rich and precise detail, a feat that would have been impossible had he followed any practical over-land route. Virtually every major island in the Missouri River is shown—islands that are duplicated in every instance on Clark's more detailed route maps. Yet, certain details on the map assure us that Evans, like Clark, spent some time onshore, following the party on foot as they made their way upriver.

There are few details on the nature of the Mandan expeditionary party that left Fort Charles on June 8. Evans recorded, "After having received from Mr.

James McKay Agent of the Missouri Company the necessary Instructions, as well as men, Provisions and Merchandizes, I sat off from the Company's Establishment at the Maha Village." His mode of transport, personnel numbers, and what merchandise he took with him are all ignored in the opening extracts from Evans's journal. Mackay is equally sparse with information about his colleague, saying only that Evans left "with picked men, who occasion us great expense." We can be assured that all or most of them were French; indeed, René Jusseaume, a Canadian trader who corresponded with Evans while the latter was at the Mandan villages, expressed in a letter to him, "My compliments to the French."

Only after "a long and fatiguing voyage" did Evans arrive among the Arikaras on August 8. By this time, two of the four months it would take him to reach the Mandans had passed. Despite their "softer and better Character," the Arikaras detained him in their villages for several weeks. They did not want the upriver tribes to have Evans's goods but wanted them themselves. He spent his enforced stay there, in part, meeting some Cheyennes and other Rocky Mountain Indians who in all probability had come to the Arikaras for a late-summer trading rendezvous. Somehow he convinced the Arikaras to release him with "a few Goods" and continued his trip. The figures he provided for the trip, however, do not add up: his journal tells us that he arrived among the Arikaras on August 8 and among the Mandans on September 23. Since it took Lewis and Clark forty-seven days (a little less than seven weeks) to make the latter trip, he could have spent only a few days among the Arikaras. It is reasonable to conclude that he moved more quickly than did the Corps of Discovery. Was this because he had a smaller contingent of men with him?

There is no surviving record of Evans's adventures and hardships on the way to the Arikaras or of the journey from their villages to those of the Mandans. What can we deduce of this expedition in the absence of a narrative? Some of the answers lie embedded in the legends, sometimes cryptic, on the map he produced of his trip.

The Beinecke Library map is strikingly accurate, and its six sheets conjoin to form a single image. Overlaying this chart on a modern map reveals that it deviates very little from reality. There are no direct statements as to how it was made, although references on the chart to a compass and sextant make it obvious, as one would expect, that Evans used these instruments, together with a chronometer, to compose his map. At five points on the Missouri River there are notations to "Latitude by Observation" usually accompanied by the legend "Latitude by Chart" or "by the Quadrant." Some of these notations deviate surprisingly little from their modern equivalents.

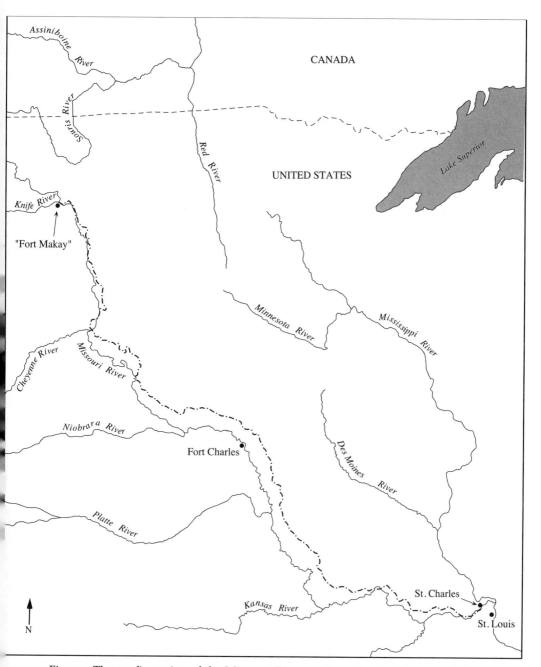

Fig. 12. The configuration of the Missouri River on the Beinecke Library and the Indian Office maps (dashed line) compared with a modern base map. Endpoints of the maps are juxtaposed, ignoring latitude and longitude. (W. R. Wood, ©2001)

Determining latitude was a relatively simple matter. A sextant, usually made of brass, was used to observe the altitude of the sun or a star above the horizon. Latitude was then ascertained using the resulting readings together with a book of astronomical tables.[10] Determining longitude, however, was another matter entirely. Evans would have to know the precise Greenwich time at the sun's meridian passage at the position he was attempting to determine. Probably for this reason, he determined the longitude of only two points on his map: Fort Charles, and the distance west of Fort Charles and St. Louis of a point a few miles downstream from the Mandan villages. Lewis and Clark had equal difficulty in obtaining correct longitude during their expedition: indeed, their readings are no better than those of Evans, in part because of the difficulties they had in keeping their chronometer working.

Beinecke Library Map, Sheet 1

The approximately 255 river miles from Fort Charles to Island au Parish (present-day Hamilton Island) contain notations on a number of islands in and tributaries of the Missouri (see fig. 21).[11] The predominance of French terms for rivers and islands on the map continues all the way to the Mandans. It is no mystery how these features were named, for there had been constant, if spasmodic, French penetration of the stream for decades. But who transmitted these named features to Evans? One of Truteau's men might have given him information for the geography as far north as the Arikaras, near the mouth of the Cheyenne River, but above there it meant that Evans probably had to have obtained information from perhaps Jacques D'Eglise or one of the *engagés* who accompanied him on his way to the Mandans between 1790 and 1792.

Although Truteau's Ponca House probably was in ruins by this time, its remains may have been obvious from the river, for the site is shown on Evans's map by an open square symbol directly on the left bank of the Missouri. Such structures rarely survived abandonment very long, usually being destroyed either deliberately by Indians or accidentally by prairie fires.

Beinecke Library Map, Sheet 2

That part of the trip from Island au Vase (present-day Mud Island) to the mouth of Island au Biche (probably modern Fort George Island) just east of present-day Pierre, South Dakota, must have been well known to French rivermen, for most of these legends are in their language (see fig. 22). A conspicuous exception is the name applied to modern Medicine Creek: Tylers River (it is spelled "Tylors River" on Clark's 1804 route map). The Indian Office map labels a small river and island in the same area as the "R. du vieux Langlois," meaning "Old Langlois's River." This legend was misinterpreted in the English translation on the map to read "Old Englishmans Island." The name "Old Langlois" seems to imply that the locality was named for a family of French extraction. Assuming that both terms were applied to the same locality, how did the French surname become transformed into an English one? An English name stands out among the others on this sheet, but who was he? No one named Tyler or Tylor is identifiable at the time. Perhaps he was an adventurous British trader from Prairie du Chien or some other post along the upper Mississippi River, the most likely source for someone with an English name. This area became a favorite of later traders, for about 1800 Régis Loisel built a post on an island in the Missouri a few miles above the Grand Detour nearly opposite the mouth of Tylers River.[12]

Other traders had been here long before Evans. La Vérendrye's son, the Chevalier de La Vérendrye, visiting the Arikara villages near the mouth of the Bad River in 1743, says that "three days' journey from where we were, there was a Frenchman who had been settled there for several years."[13] The younger La Vérendrye is silent as to the man's location, but he must have been stationed downriver, perhaps near the Grand Detour of the Missouri. If so, this would place him not far from Tylers River, where the mysterious French (or English?) trader later resided. Since the chevalier wished to see him but did not, and because the explorer returned to Canada by going north, one may assume the trader was not living upriver.

La Vérendrye's entry gives us a further clue to a source for information on the Missouri River. When the chevalier arrived at the Arikara village in March 1743, the Indians were just returning from their winter quarters, and he met a "man among them who had been brought up among the Spanish and spoke their language like his own." The wording of this statement may identify this man as a member of a tribe other than Arikara. It is possible that Evans met someone comparable during his enforced stay with the Arikaras during his own journey. News of the outside world, often distorted, to be sure, trickled into the villages along the Missouri River throughout the Dakotas through intertribal trade with the Spanish Southwest. But there is abundant evidence of Spanish goods in the upper Missouri villages, for the La Vérendryes mention a Spanish bridle they saw among the Arikaras.[14]

One enigmatic feature of sheet 2 is the legend that was scratched out at a point on the southern bank of the Missouri River below the mouth of the

White River, east of what is today called Landing Creek in northern Gregory County. The wording cannot be deciphered even by a close inspection of the original, but it must have had some special interest because the legend is highlighted by the sketch of a hand with the forefinger pointed at the deleted wording. Its identity, however, is revealed by an inspection of the Indian Office map. On that chart the only words near this location are "Vieu Volcano," or "old volcano."

The Lewis and Clark expedition passed this locale on September 14, 1804, and Clark noted the "high Land" on their left, or larboard, side. He goes on to say: "I walked on Shore with a view to find an old Vulcanio, Said to be in this neighbourhood by Mr. J. McKey of St. Charles. I walked on Shore the whole day without Seeing any appearance of the Villcanoe." Nothing in the landscape in this vicinity has the slightest resemblance to a volcano, and the origin of the inscription on Evans's and Mackay's maps remains a mystery. It would be reasonable to suppose that this lack of evidence led a disappointed Clark to scratch out the legend on Evans's map. It was a common belief of the time that there were volcanoes on the upper Missouri. A light, frothy rock resembling pumice often was found floating down the river, a stone described by the captains and believed to be volcanic in origin. Instead, the stones are nothing more than clinkers, derived from the burning of lignite coal beds along the present-day boundary between Montana and North Dakota.[15]

How did the idea of a volcano in central South Dakota come about in the first place? Mackay had never been this far up the Missouri, so whatever he told William Clark about it had been hearsay—information that he could only have obtained from D'Eglise, Truteau, Evans, or one of his men. Surely the scratched-out legend on Evans's map did indeed allude to such a feature, one that also came to appear on the Indian Office map. In any case, with the return of the Lewis and Clark expedition, all allusions to volcanoes on the upper Missouri River disappear from charts.

Beinecke Library Map, Sheet 3

The major features of interest between "R au high water" (modern Antelope Creek) and Diamond Island (modern Fishermans Island) are the "uper Villages" and the "Lower Ricara Villages & Island" shown on the right bank below the mouth of the Cheyenne River (see fig. 23). These are the only Arikara villages mentioned by name on the map, and they may well have been the villages that Truteau had visited two years earlier in October 1794 and the ones that Evans reached on August 8. Here Evans spent perhaps six weeks before continuing upriver to the Mandans. The long, high set of terraces along the west bank of the Missouri River in this area once were crowded with the ruins of earth-lodge villages.[16] Many of these sites are of Arikara origin of the time. Several of them were excavated by Smithsonian Institution field parties before the area was flooded by the Oahe Reservoir, but the resultant reports remain unpublished. Which of these villages hosted Truteau and delayed Evans on his upriver trip is a matter for speculation.

It is likely that Evans met Joseph Gravelines in one of these Arikara villages, although there is no hint of it in any of the narratives or on the maps by Mackay or Evans. Gravelines, a Frenchman who was employed a decade later by Régis Loisel, is probably the man who was reputed in 1811 to have lived among the Arikaras "more than twenty years," that is, since about 1790.[17] Had he accompanied D'Eglise or some unnamed voyageur upriver about that time and chose to remain? Whatever the case, remain he did, for he did not leave the Arikaras until 1806, when he accompanied Lewis and Clark's entourage back to St. Louis.

Beinecke Library Map, Sheet 4

Spring Creek enters the Missouri River from the east near present-day Pollock, South Dakota. On Evans's map it is labeled "Stone Idol C[reek]," in William Clark's hand, and is shown entering the Missouri at "I[sland] au Cock," having originated in a lake and in "Several litle Swamps" (see fig. 24). Before the arrival of Euro-American settlers, Spring Creek (once also known as Hermaphrodite Creek) was a perennial stream, fed by innumerable springs along its course. The origin of the name "Stone Idol" derives from William Clark, who named the stream on October 13, 1804, because of "a Stone to which the Indians asscribe great Virtue &c. &c."[18]

Clark's reason for giving the stream its name may be found in the modern town of Fort Yates, North Dakota, headquarters of the Standing Rock Indian Reservation. On a street paralleling the former riverbank, now the shoreline of Lake Oahe, stands a yellow brick monument surmounted by a gray stone alien to the locality but identifiable as an igneous or metamorphic rock carried to the area by glacial action. The monument bears a brass plaque that reads:

Standing Rock
Inyan Woslata

A famous sacred stone which many years ago came into possession of the Sioux. According to Dakota legend it is a body of a young Indian

Fig. 13. The Standing Rock memorial on the Lake Oahe shoreline at Fort Yates, North Dakota. (W. R. Wood, ©2000)

woman with her child on her back who were left in camp when she refused to accompany the tribe as they moved south. When others were sent back to find her, she was found to have turned to stone. The stone is held in reverence by the Sioux and is placed here overlooking the waters and the empire once held by the mighty Sioux nation.

Sponsored by

Local Lions Club

American Legion

Tribal Council

1983

A brief history of this stone, called *Inyan Woslata* by the Dakotas, is given by James McLaughlin, an early Indian agent at Standing Rock. The stone was the common property of the Teton Lakotas, but it lay for many years in a region occupied by the Lower Yanktonais, and that group served as protector of the rock. Allegedly, the rock was carried by the group and occupied a position in the center of each village in which they lived. When McLaughlin first came to Standing Rock, the stone was located about five miles north of Fort Yates near the mouth of Porcupine Creek, but following his suggestion, it was brought to the agency and erected on Proposal Hill, a flat-topped butte just north of the agency, so named because of its popularity among local young couples. A prominent Dakota Indian was chosen to direct the elaborate ceremony that accompanied its dedication.

A more romantic story of its origin is told in *North Dakota: A Guide to the Northern Prairie State*, compiled during the Great Depression by workers of the Federal Writers' Project of the Works Progress Administration. According to an undocumented Dakota legend, a young Indian woman, angered by her husband having taken a second wife, refused to leave camp when her community moved. The people nevertheless broke camp and moved on, believing she would relent and follow them. She was last seen sitting by a campfire with her child on her back. But the woman never appeared, and when the husband's brother returned for her, he found that she and the child had turned to stone, as had the woman's dog. The stone representing the woman and child later was moved from Proposal Hill to its present location. It is said that the woman's dog, in the form of a smaller stone, was misplaced and became embedded in the foundation of one of the agency residences.[19] Viewed from an appropriate perspective in the proper light, *Inyan Woslata* does resemble a seated woman with a shawl pulled over her head.

The veneration of the stone may, however, date to times before the arrival of the Dakotas along the Missouri River. George F. Will writes that it "appears to have been an Arikara 'medicine' long before the Dakota came to the Missouri." Stones often were venerated by the Arikaras and placed by the doors of dance lodges and earth lodges. Drawing on commentary by Lewis and Clark and perhaps on observations of his own, Will notes, "In 1804 it was located on the east side of the river, on the upper course of Spring Creek." This was not its location as reported by McLaughlin, and Will's reference may well be to another stone. When Robert C. Farrell interviewed Judge Francis B. Zahn in 1952, this Hunkpapa Dakota stated that the term "Standing Rock" was a mistranslation of a tribally unspecified Indian term, which properly means "upright rock."[20]

Beinecke Library Map, Sheet 5

Evans's sheet 5 begins near the modern North Dakota–South Dakota boundary with two legends reading "W. Jacques" and "W. Jacques wintering ground with the Riccaras" (see fig. 25). The notations appear just downstream from two village symbols in the area between the now-deserted town of (old) Kenel and present-day Fort Yates, North Dakota. The identity of "W. Jacques" is unknown, but he certainly was an independent French trader: was he plying the Arikara trade from St. Louis or from the upper Mississippi River? We may presume that Evans visited with the man, though no records of such a meeting remain. The date that such traders entered into the upper Missouri River trade is unknown, but rare individuals were on the river even as the first French were exploring south from Canada.

The "old Village Cheyen," just to the north of present-day Fort Yates, alludes to a long-abandoned Cheyenne Indian village documented by William Clark and John Ordway at the mouth of Porcupine Creek. The village was also mentioned in George Grinnell's studies of the Cheyenne Indians. Grinnell recorded Teton Lakota traditions of a Cheyenne Indian village built along the Missouri on the south bank, a community that was abandoned, however, before the great smallpox epidemic of 1780.[21]

The next feature north of the old Cheyenne village is "Carp river & Island," now known as Beaver Creek, in Emmons County. These were waters that no one from St. Louis except D'Eglise or his companions are known to have traveled, yet there are clues on Evans's map that someone was giving him information that he could not have had without outside assistance. How did he know that the Cheyennes had occupied the village he calls the "old Village Cheyen"? Its identity certainly would not have been obvious from its abandoned remains. For this reason we must assume that an individual knowledgeable about the area, either French, associated perhaps with Truteau or D'Eglise, or an Indian who accompanied him on either his ascent of the river or his return. Otherwise, such elements could not have found their way onto the chart Evans prepared of his expedition.

The silence of Evans's journals on the scenes that daily unfolded on his trip deprives us of what he must have thought of the ascent of a river larger than any in all of Europe. He must have been awestruck. The lighting on the landscape along the Missouri is flat and lifeless at midday, but as the evening shadows begin to spill into the rolling depressions along the river, the grasslands assume sharp contrast along the chokecherry- and buffaloberry-studded breaks. The evening squadrons of white pelicans patrolling high over the valley add an unreal dimension to such scenes. At dawn, the land is bathed in a golden hue as sunlight erases the shadows as it flows down the bluffsides to the water.

Between Beaver Creek and the Cannonball River, there is a sequence of small named and unnamed islands and tributary streams. Evans called the Cannonball River the "Bomb River," a name we also may presume to derive from his hypothesized companion. (In this instance, we may speculate on a French origin, for an Indian identification of the individual is improbable.) "Bomb" is an appropriate name, for the banks and valley of this stream once were home to uncounted spherical sandstone concretions that ranged from a few inches to several feet in diameter. Some of them indeed were the size of cannonballs. Today they have been carried away by curio hunters in such numbers that they are very rare.

The mouth of the Cannonball, which Evans said was 150 yards wide, marks the south end of a high, steep bluff that extends for four miles upriver along the west bank of the Missouri. It was here that William Clark "walked on Shore, in the evining with a view to See Some of those remarkable places mentioned by evens, none of which I could find."[22] Unfortunately, we cannot determine what those "remarkable places" might have been by looking at Evans's narrative; if it was consulted by Clark, it is no longer available for us today. Nor are there clues to their identity in Clark's subsequent notes, perhaps because he did not begin his search until he had passed the mouth of modern Badger Creek, thus being upstream from three locations on Evans's map that modern viewers find so intriguing. But the map that Evans made of his voyage contains several clues to those "remarkable places." The four-mile-long bluff above the Cannonball is called "the Humitt" (or "Hermitt") on his chart—a term that so far defies explanation. Two features that he names on the rim of Humitt Bluff demonstrate that here he was following the river uplands on foot, for the features he notes would have been invisible from the river channel two hundred feet below its rim.

One notation reads "Jupiters fort," with a hand-and-finger pointing to the north side of the Cannonball River atop the south end of Humitt Bluff. There is no doubt that this refers to a prehistoric Mandan village at that location overlooking the mouth of the Cannonball. Today, archaeologists call this village the North Cannonball site. Not only was it in a defensive setting, but the village also was fortified by a curving ditch that isolated a level upland spur from the adjoining upland. The village today is badly disturbed by plowing, but from the air one can clearly see the fortification ditch and the numerous bastions protruding from it. Little wonder that Evans referred to it as a fort, though his reference to Jupiter is not explainable.

On the north end of the Humitt is an undecipherable symbol labeled "Jupiter's house." The house would have been set atop one of the level benches overlooking the Missouri floodplain, but no archaeological remains are apparent in this locality that might suggest why Evans penned such a notation, and a close inspection of aerial photographs has revealed no other clues. Jupiter was the Roman version of the Greek god Zeus, and one can only speculate that Evans's "Jupiters fort" or "Jupiter's house" alludes in some way to Jupiter's Temple, built on Capitoline Hill in classical Rome.

Other remarkable Indian village sites are found north of this stretch of the river, including the Lower Fort Rice, Cadell Homestead, and Huff archaeological sites. Each of these large prehistoric Mandan villages has elaborate, bastioned fortifications that Evans would have had no difficulty seeing as he walked along the river terraces. Huff, the only one of these sites excavated by archaeologists, contained more than one hundred houses, and Cadell Homestead appears to have been far larger.[23] Since each of these sites was ignored by Evans, it appears that he was by then walking along the water's edge or that he was traveling by water when he passed these conspicuous fortified communities, each of them as large and elaborate as the North Cannonball village.

A "Butifull High Plain" is the next landmark on Evans's map, and above it is "sugar loaf," depicted by a triangular symbol that usually is reserved on his map for Indian villages. Today, Sugar Loaf Butte is an easily recognized landmark on the west side of Highway 1804 about halfway between the river

Fig. 14. An aerial view to the southwest toward the North Cannonball village site, or Evans's "Jupiters fort," prior to the inundation of the Missouri valley by the Oahe Reservoir. (W. R. Wood, 1955, courtesy of the State Historical Society of North Dakota)

bank and the river bluffs four miles northwest of the nearly deserted hamlet of Huff. This feature was noted by Lewis and Clark on October 19, 1804, and is shown on Prince Maximilian's copy of Clark's route map, aptly recorded as a "Conical Hill of about 90 feet high," a description that is equally descriptive today.[24] The hill has eroded very little since Lewis and Clark's time, despite being made of soft clays that are only sparingly mantled by grass.

Beinecke Library Map, Sheet 6

The Heart River marked the beginning of Mandan country for Evans (see fig. 26). He notes this stream at the base of sheet 6 as "R & I[sland] du Couer." This stream has been known by several different names, most of them being French for "Heart." The area near its mouth was considered the "heart" of the Mandan universe, a fact that may argue for Evans's hypothetical companion having been an Indian knowledgeable about Mandan cosmology. Another river a short distance downstream is also labeled "R & I[sland] du Couer." This legend was scratched out on sheet 5, probably by William Clark, for it identifies not the Heart River proper but the Little Heart River.

The first Mandan town noted on Evans's map is a large village just below the river's mouth, one that Clark labels "Village Chiss.chect." The triangular symbol that he used to denote this village marks the location of the village today known as "On-a-Slant." It undoubtedly was deserted when Evans discovered it, for Lewis and Clark were told by the Mandan chief Big White in 1806 that it had been abandoned for about forty years, or since about 1766.[25] The village today is one of the two major attractions of Fort Abraham Lincoln State Park; the other attraction is the cavalry fort from which Col. George Armstrong Custer led his men to near annihilation on the Little Big Horn Battlefield.

Above the Heart River, Evans passed two bluffs ("Yellow Ecore"). To the right of the symbol for the first of them, on the east bank of the Missouri, a legend says, "here are human bones of a Large Size." There are numerous early historic Mandan villages in this location, but the most conspicuous of them is a village that Clark notes on one of his route maps as an "Old Indian Village destroyed by the Soux." Today this village, known as the Double Ditch site, is a North Dakota state historic site.[26] Above the second "Yellow Ecore" symbol is a horseshoe bend of the Missouri River. Eight years later Lewis and Clark found that the river had cut through the neck of the bend and left it an island. The abandoned meander today is the Painted Woods Lake.

On the Missouri's south bank above the horseshoe bend, Evans passed five "Mandan Old Villages" that he records on his map with open triangles and a "Ricara Village" that he designates by a solid triangle. The old Mandan villages cannot be positively identified today because there are many old village sites in this locality, but the Arikara village is probably correctly identified as the Greenshield site. This village was often ascribed to the Pawnees by other travelers. The Pawnees and Arikaras were closely related and both spoke variants of the Caddoan language stock.[27]

Sheet 6 shows that the five villages occupied by the Mandans and Hidatsas at the mouth of the unlabeled Knife River are in precisely the same locations that they occupied when David Thompson visited the area in 1798, and they remained occupied in Lewis and Clark's time. The combined population of the five villages in Thompson's time was about 2,900 individuals. Curiously enough, whereas Evans mentions the Hidatsas only obliquely, the village locations he shows on sheet 6 are coded by tribe: solid ovals represent known Hidatsa towns, and open ovals are Mandan towns. Above the mouth of the Knife was Big Hidatsa and just below its mouth, the Amahami site. Between these two Hidatsa villages was the Sakakawea site, a nominally Hidatsa village, but one Evans shows as Mandan. However, in David Thompson's journals and on a map of the villages that he prepared in 1798, this village is identified as having been jointly occupied by thirty-seven Mandan and fifteen Hidatsa households, and Deapolis is said to have consisted of "mostly all" Mandans, the others presumably being Hidatsas.[28] The two open circles farther downriver represent, on the southern bank, the Big White site, or the village of Mitutanka; and on the northern bank, the Black Cat site, or the village of Ruhptare. Curiously enough, there is no clue on sheet 6 as to the location of the British fort he was to dislodge—a major goal of his voyage.

Evans's upriver voyage ended at the Mandan village on the south bank of the Missouri, at Mitutanka. Beaching his vessels at the rock ledge that lines the river's edge, he was cordially received there by its residents and by visiting Hidatsa Indians, who would quickly have flocked to the village on hearing of this new arrival. In 1804 the chief of Mitutanka was a prominent Mandan named Big White, or Sheheke, who was to play a major role in the years following Lewis and Clark's visit. Although Evans never mentions the name of any Mandan individual or chief, it is entirely possible that Big White was a chief as early as the time of his visit. Sadly, Mitutanka has been destroyed by gravel pit operations and by the construction of a power plant on what was then left of its remains.[29] It resembled in general plan, however, other Mandan villages for which we have artist's renderings.

Beinecke Library Map, Sheet 7

Extant documents provide no direct leads to the origin of what I have called sheet 7 (see fig. 27), but that chart contains data that could only have been obtained from his native hosts. Whether the informant was Mandan or Hidatsa is unknown, but since it depicts with great accuracy what now constitutes the entire state of Montana, I am inclined to believe the informant may have been Hidatsa. That tribe was well known for its raiding parties that ranged as far west as the Rocky Mountains, where they preyed on the Shoshones (the Snakes, or "Gens de Serpent"). It was from one of the Hidatsa villages on the Knife River, in fact, that a Hidatsa war party captured Sacagawea, later to be taken as a wife by Toussaint Charbonneau and who accompanied Lewis and Clark to the Pacific Ocean. In contrast, the map that Clark prepared of the area west of the mouth of the Knife River based on information from the Mandan chief, Big White, illustrates only the eastern part of modern Montana, specifically the course and tributaries of the Yellowstone River.[30]

Evans's map illustrates a geography of the upper Missouri River rather different from the conceptions held in St. Louis. There are four ranges of "Montagne de roche" shown, not the single range that even Lewis and Clark had been led to expect. The geography as it is shown from the Mandan and Hidatsa villages becomes increasing distorted from actuality as one approaches the Rockies. The unlabeled Little Missouri River enters the Missouri halfway between the Knife and the "River yellow rock" (Yellowstone), and the "River blanc" (Milk) enters approximately proportionate to geography. The "Shell River" (Musselshell) is depicted much too near the "the fall," or the Great Falls of the Missouri River.

The "Gens de Corbeau" (Crow) Indians are represented as living on the upper Yellowstone River, but the identity of the "Village de Boitife" on the middle reaches of the Yellowstone remains unknown as does that of the "Shevitoon," shown north of the mouth of the Yellowstone. The same term was applied to an Indian group shown on the 1791 Jarvis and Mackay map and on the 1795 Arrowsmith map downriver from the Mandans.[31] From its listing between the "Sious" and the "Corbeaus," surely it is the name of a nomadic group, the identity of which is speculative. Another symbol, apparently intended to depict a fort at the mouth of the Columbia River, probably denotes a Russian trading post.

By mid-September, summer had fled the northern plains. Along the river breaks, silvery patches of buffaloberry bushes, splotched with reddening clumps of berries, clung to the slopes of gullies mantled with yellowing grass. In the bottomlands as in the uplands, the yellowing leaves of giant cottonwoods rustled in the wind. Evans's party had only barely reached the Mandans before the onset of winter. The paths from the British post to the Mandan villages soon froze, becoming iron underfoot, and Evans was about to exercise his diplomacy in evicting the Nor'westers—as the North West Company employees often were known—from their fort and their trade along the Missouri. In the meantime, Mackay had returned from a summer bison hunt with the Omahas and had added yet another significant expedition to his roster of discoveries.

ACCOMPANYING AN
OMAHA INDIAN SUMMER BISON HUNT

It was June 1796 on the Great Plains. Winter had gone, although it could return unheralded. Late blizzards were common, and on the northern plains it is possible for the thermometer to drop to freezing any day of the year, even July 4. The spring weather led to a flurry of travel by the Spanish emissaries on the Missouri River. Evans left Fort Charles on June 8 for the Mandans and the Pacific Ocean, and sometime that same month Truteau left for St. Louis. Mackay remained at Fort Charles, and he and Chief Blackbird planned a spectacular gathering that was to take place in the early summer of 1796. The purposes of the gathering were to impress the Indians of the region who stood in the way of the navigation of the Missouri with the power and glory of imperial Spain and to wean those tribes away from the British councils along the Mississippi River. Zenon Trudeau described it as follows in a letter to Governor General Carondelet on April 2, 1796: "In the month of June the Mahas chief, the man, the most despotic, like *Glorieux* of the establishment of the French and [because] of the immense presents he has received, should assemble all the nations which might put an obstacle to the navigation of the Missouri in order to harangue them in our favor, which cannot fail to produce very good effects."[32] A meeting of this sort probably was impossible, given the intertribal rivalries and hostilities of the time, and its planning may have been still another excuse for Blackbird to fleece the Spanish out of yet more goods. Whatever the case, we hear nothing more of this grand gathering. Having failed in this endeavor, Mackay may have tried to obtain information on the fur potential of Omaha country by going on his tour of exploration west and south of Fort Charles.

Mackay's activities on that tour, while Evans was gone, can be traced only by roundabout means. Perhaps he went farther up the Missouri, for his "Table of Distances" provides landmarks as far upriver as the mouth of the White River. It is well to keep in mind, however, that Evans had penetrated to the White River in late 1796 before he was forced to retreat. The distances in Mackay's table, therefore, surely came from his subordinate's travels, for in his reports Mackay, as leader of the expedition, did not distinguish between what he had done and what Evans had accomplished. No other source confirms his statement, "I explored the Country as far as the Mandaine village about 5 or 6 hundred leagues above the Entrance of the Missoury," although Evans had done so.[33]

What we do know of his activities derive from cartographic sources that trace his explorations during the summer and perhaps early fall of 1796. Mackay left Fort Charles in the hands of a subordinate, perhaps Antonio Breda, for whom he had expressed admiration, and journeyed over much of northeastern Nebraska. It is certain that he did not do so alone or just with his employees, but rather he tagged along on a bison hunt with the Omahas, accompanying them deep into central Nebraska as far southwest as the North Loup River. The Omahas annually went on such a hunt after their corn crop was established and weeded, normally by late June or early July. They returned in early September for the green corn harvest, having been gone perhaps for ten weeks.[34] Indeed, some of the notations concerning Indian villages that appear on maps illustrating Mackay's travels are far beyond the route he took as traced on the maps, and only his Omaha hosts would have been able to provide that information.

If Mackay did indeed accompany an Omaha bison hunt, his route on that trip provides the only documented track of such an excursion and illustrates the mobility and awesome distances that plains village tribes would travel. On this occasion they encircled a substantial part of northeastern Nebraska over a distance of nearly six hundred air miles; on horseback, following the terrain, the distance would have been much greater. The need for water for both horses and people would have determined the specific track of the route they took, which certainly must have changed with circumstances from year to year. On his trip Mackay gives us the first description of that area, not in a narrative journal, unfortunately, but in a detailed trace with legends that are preserved on three early maps.

One of these maps is by François Marie Perrin du Lac dated 1802. A dotted line, labeled "Traces de Jaques Machay 1796," depicts Mackay's full route to and from Bad Village just north of Fort Charles. In his accompanying narra-

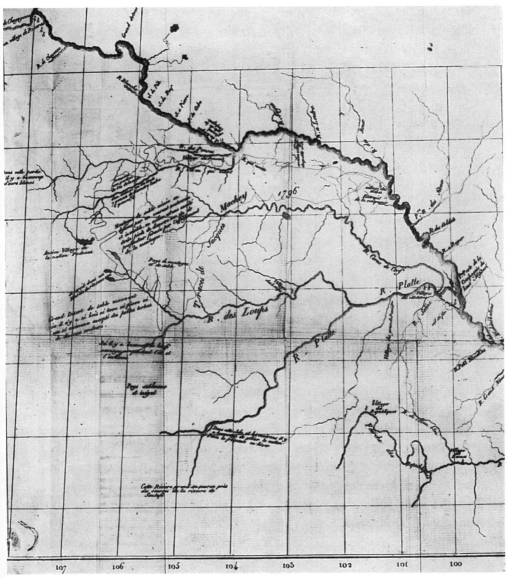

Fig. 15. Detail from François Marie Perrin du Lac's 1802 map showing James Mackay's route through northeastern Nebraska in the summer of 1796. (From Wood, *Atlas of Early Maps of the American Midwest*, plate 9; and Perrin du Lac, *Voyage*)

tive, Perrin du Lac claims that he had ascended the Missouri River in the spring of 1802 as far as the mouth of the White River. There is no reason to accept his claim. Rather, he probably obtained his information from Mackay or Evans. Perrin du Lac's published map duplicates (and also augments) a French-language manuscript chart in the papers of the French explorer Joseph N.

Nicollet in the Library of Congress.[35] The origin of this chart is unknown, although it is likely that Nicollet obtained it from the Chouteau family in St. Louis, an important source of other information for him. Like the Perrin du Lac map, the Library of Congress version provides a strikingly accurate depiction of the streams and other features in modern northeastern Nebraska and adjacent South Dakota as far north as the White River.

The French manuscript map shows only that part of Mackay's journey west of about present-day Norfolk, Nebraska, labeled "Route de Jacques Mackay en 1796." By combining information on both charts, we not only have an exact idea of the route that Mackay took, but also the first Euro-American commentary on Nebraska place names, geography, and paleontology, thanks to the expansive legends along his track. The legends on the Library of Congress manuscript are somewhat more complete than those of Perrin du Lac, suggesting that the latter is a derivative. What was the source for these two depictions of northeastern Nebraska? It surely was a chart prepared by Mackay himself.

Mackay's route, in modified form, also is depicted on a map made in 1806 by Nicholas King based on an original field map (now lost) made by William Clark. It was this former map that led Aubrey Diller, a professor of Greek at the University of Indiana, to trace and annotate Mackay's route through Nebraska.[36] Where Clark got the information to place "Mr J. Mackays Route" on this map is not certain, though it is likely that Mackay had given both him and Meriwether Lewis oral information on his whereabouts in 1795–97, together with the cartographic data he provided. Clark's map so closely mirrors the route shown on the Perrin du Lac and Library of Congress maps that he had to have had a chart that revealed Mackay's trace. Sadly, the excerpts we have of Mackay's journal make no mention of his trip through northeastern Nebraska with the Omahas, but the excursion is richly annotated by the Perrin du Lac and Library of Congress maps.

ON THE TRAIL

Mackay's trail led west, not from Fort Charles, but from the Omahas' Big Village. It is not difficult to envision a cavalcade of men and women, horses, and dogs trailing west from the village across the Missouri floodplain. In which direction did they go when they left the Missouri valley? There is no direct evidence on any of the maps, but they either went west toward the Niobrara River—as most previous summaries of this expedition assume—or they went west-southwest toward the Elkhorn River. In 1859 the Omahas took the latter route; the direction they took on other occasions is not known. Here we follow precedent in assuming they went west toward the Niobrara.[37]

This route would have led them west, up the broad, gently ascending valley of Fiddlers Creek to the rolling, loess-mantled hills that flank the west bank of the Missouri valley. The hills west of the valley are steep sided but become more gently undulating as one moves toward the Niobrara. The party moved parallel to the course of the Missouri River but well to its south. Their trail crossed several small, north-flowing tributaries of the Missouri, crossing the headwaters of Bow Creek and proceeding on to the "R. qui monte" (Climbing River, or modern Bazille Creek), a stream in a broad, deeply incised valley that flows north parallel to the lower reaches of the Niobrara. Moving north down that stream to a point just south of the modern town of Niobrara (set on a hill near the mouth of that stream), they then descended the bluffs to the Niobrara River valley, or the "R. qui court." They forded the Niobrara and moved west between that river and Ponca Creek, the "R. des Poncas." About a mile west of the mouth of Ponca Creek they either came near or visited the "Village de Poncas," a fortified village known today as Ponca Fort. The village was perched on a high hill overlooking Ponca Creek and the Missouri River bottomlands.[38] The Library of Congress map shows the group bypassing it a little to the south, but the Perrin du Lac map shows their route touching the village symbol.

The map then shows that they moved west in an irregular path between Ponca Creek and the Niobrara, but in actuality they must have followed the broad, flat floor of the Niobrara valley, for the land between the streams in this area is very rugged, which would have made travois travel difficult. West of the town of Spencer the uplands become very level to gently rolling, which would have made it possible for the party to easily cross this terrain, certainly prime bison-hunting country. Moving south, they crossed the valley of the Keya Paha and again approached the north bank of the Niobrara. The Keya Paha flows to the southeast out of present-day South Dakota through a land with low, mound-shaped erosional remnants, a fact that led to their Indian designation as *Keya Paha Wakpa*, or Turtle Hill River. Two buttes stand in the uplands north of the mouth of the Keya Paha that provide the only geographic features on the hunting expedition that a modern traveler would regard as a "landmark." An indeterminable distance to the west, on the headwaters of the stream in South Dakota, is the legend, in French, "In this country there are many white bears," or grizzlys.[39]

Between the Keya Paha and the Niobrara River is a legend that reads "Found here the middle part of the thigh-bone of an animal, the large end of

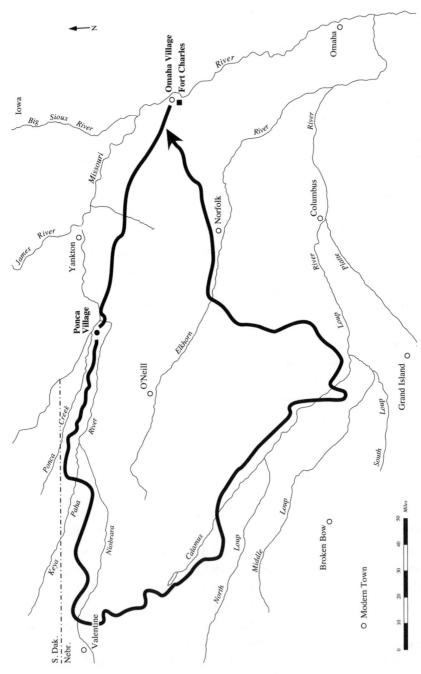

Fig. 16. James Mackay's route through northeastern Nebraska superimposed on a modern map. (W. R. Wood ©2001)

Fig. 17. Artist's restoration of a Middle Miocene *Gomphotherium* (formerly *Tyrilophodon*). Mackay may have discovered a fragmentary fossilized thigh bone of this animal in northeastern Nebraska. (From Osborn, *Proboscidea*, vol. 1, fig. 268)

which was 7 inches in diameter and the other 6 3/4 inches." Diller notes that there are large fossil deposits in Brown County, and the recently established Ashfall Fossil Beds State Historical Park in northern Antelope County, not far east of the town of O'Neill, bear evidence of the richness of the region's paleontological deposits. The identity of the beast that Mackay discovered cannot be established from his description alone, but the size of the bone is consistent with its identification as one of an ice-age mammoth (*Mammuthus*). The specimen usually is so identified, but it might well be from a four-tusked late Miocene mastodon (*Gomphotherium*), another relative of the elephant whose ten-to-thirteen-million-year-old fossils are common in the area.

The bones are not identified on the maps that depict Mackay's track, but it seems obvious that he talked about them on his return to St. Louis. There must have been discussions there that led to their identification as mammoths, and this information was placed on a few maps. The fossil discovery appears, for example, on a map made in New Orleans in 1803 by James Pitot, one that bears unmistakable evidence of having borrowed from the 1795 Soulard map. The words "ossements de Mammouth" appear here on the north side of the Niobrara River near where Mackay made his discovery. The words "Ossemens de Mamouth" also appear on a variant of this chart, and other legends nearby allude to Mackay's trek through the area. No one knows what happened to the bone, the first paleontological specimen described from Nebraska, assuming that Mackay indeed collected it. Its discovery, in any event, may well have been one of the elements that helped fuel the search for exotic animals by Lewis and Clark, for President Jefferson had asked them to make a special search for such creatures in their tour of the West. Before leaving St. Louis, Evans too had been asked by George Turner to make a special search for exotic animals, though Turner made no mention of seeking fossils.[40] The idea that the unexplored West contained living examples of animals known in the East only as fossils was to expire only after the return of Lewis and Clark.

The Keya Paha was unknown to Europeans before Mackay forded it and the stream found its way onto maps. It was first christened "Mackeys River" on William Clark's 1810 manuscript map of the trans-Mississippi West, but the name subsequently vanishes from later maps, even those prepared by Clark. Curiously enough, Robert Frazer, a member of the Lewis and Clark expedition, prepared a postexpeditionary manuscript map on which the Keya Paha is labeled as "Cold Spring" near its mouth, noting that there are "much White Bears" on its upper reaches. Private Frazer (or his cartographer) obviously had data from Mackay's expedition available to him. The first allusion to the stream by its modern name is on Joseph N. Nicollet's great map of 1843. On its lower reaches it carries the legend "Large Mammalia Fossil Bones have been found here," evidence that Mackay's discovery had not been forgotten in the intervening half-century.[41]

The party continued to move west over a gently rolling plain, lightly mantled by sand dunes along the north bank of the Niobrara, to the vicinity of the present-day town of Valentine in northeastern Cherry County. They descended the pine-mantled bluffs that line the walls of the Niobrara valley and forded the stream somewhere east of Valentine. In this locality the south wall of the valley slopes gently to the uplands, and they entered the Sand Hills region of Nebraska.

Mackay found himself on the west rim of what must have been an awe-inspiring sight for one accustomed to the landscapes of the humid East. The Sand Hills, where the monotonous rhythmical swells of the treeless, grass-mantled sand dunes creep away to the horizon, is unmatched anywhere else in North America. These ancient dunes may reach heights of four hundred feet and be twenty miles long, and they are interspersed with broad meadows, ponds, and lakes; streams, however, are rare, for rainwater quickly seeps into the sand and becomes groundwater. The nature of the country is illuminated by the Arabia Ranch, through or near which their trail now passed, the dune formations having inspired the ranches' name: the landscape is described here by the notation "Sandy rolling country" and in the legend "Great desert of drifting sand without trees, soil, rocks, water, or animals of any kind, excepting some little varicolored turtles, of which there are vast numbers." This reference to the ornate box turtle leads one to wonder why this small reptile was chosen for mention in the late summer or early fall, for they are most conspicuous during their mating season in June.[42] There is no note of herds of bison or of elk and pronghorns, nor any mention of the many local and migratory birds of the region.

The party zigzagged through the lake country along the border between Cherry and Brown Counties and on south to an unnamed stream that surely was the Calamus River. This stream heads in an area sprinkled with lakes southeast of Valentine, then flows through the eastern Sand Hills in a shallow, treeless valley. Near its headwaters Mackey's course passes to the east of a legend reading "Old village of the Padouca tribe," but no accompanying village symbol locates this Apache settlement. Mackay's Omaha traveling companions often had warred with the Apaches, and at one time the Omahas had even tracked the Apaches to a fortified village in the Nebraska Sand Hills.[43]

North of the head of the Calamus River is a note describing a "Hill of sand undermined by an underground stream of water, the middle of which has settled and formed a pit 100 paces wide and 150 feet deep." Such a feature in this landscape certainly was not formed by water, but it is readily identifiable to anyone familiar with the Sand Hills. It was a blowout, an erosional feature scooped into the soft sand by the ever present wind. Its diameter is no exaggeration, though its depth might be; most blowouts are of more modest dimensions, but giants of this width are not unusual.

South of Valentine the water table is very near the surface, and there are numerous meadows and small lakes scattered among the rolling dunes. The nature of this lake country is conveyed in the notation "In these marshes there is some wild rice or wild oats." Wild rice (*Zizania aquatica*) is indeed a major component in the marshes and along lakeshores in the Sand Hills and would have been particularly conspicuous in the fall, when it sometimes attains heights of six to eight feet. This is the same species of aquatic grass that provided such an important source of food for the American Indians in the Minnesota region.[44] Mackay's Omaha party continued down the Calamus, leaving the Sand Hills after traversing nearly a hundred miles of its trackless waste. They passed the junction of the Calamus and the North Loup Rivers and then crossed the Loup for what must have been a foray in search of bison, for here the land is a gently rolling prairie that would have been prime pasture for them.

Along the Loup River Mackay notes, "Here there are many wild oxen [bison] in summer and autumn." This would, indeed, be the kind of herds the Omahas coveted on their bison-hunting expeditions. They moved north some-where in the vicinity of the junction of the North and Middle Loup Rivers, perhaps up the valley of Beaver Creek to avoid the hilly uplands. It is equally likely that they took this track to avoid contact with the Pawnees, whose vil-lages were not far downstream. As they moved overland, the Omaha party crossed the high country between the Loup and Elkhorn Rivers, where they often had vistas of dozens of miles in every direction. They continued to move overland to the Elkhorn River, the "R. Corne de Cerf," where the Perrin du Lac map bears the notation "Sandy hilly country." The party descended into the broad valley of the Elkhorn and forded the river somewhere in the vicinity of the modern town of O'Neill. Here is located the last notation con-cerning Mackay's route on the Library of Congress map: "There are many beaver in this river." Following the level river valley for a time, the party then moved again into the loess-mantled hills of northeastern Nebraska for the final leg of their trip. The Perrin du Lac map shows us that Mackay returned directly to the Omaha village, not to Fort Charles, another clue that he had accompanied the Omahas.

A number of Indian villages are shown on the Perrin du Lac and the Library of Congress maps. Most of them are readily identifiable and known both histori-cally and as archaeological sites. The bison-hunting party visited or came within view of only one of them, Ponca Fort, which has already been dis-cussed. The others were far removed from their path. The first was a former Omaha village of the Little Bow (Ancien Village du Petit Arc) on the banks of the Missouri near the mouth of Bow Creek. Another site that Mackay's party did not visit was a Pawnee village (Village des Loups) on the Loup River well to the south of their track. This village cannot be correlated with any specific Pawnee archaeological site, for several of them exist in the general area shown on the map. Sometime in the 1790s the Omahas had fought the Skiri Pawnee in the grasslands between the Niobrara and the Platte Rivers in pre-cisely the area that Mackay and his Omaha hosts traversed. A village of the Grand Pawnee (Village des grands Panis) on the south bank of the Platte River and near the mouth of Skull Creek was probably the Linwood village, and the two symbols for an Oto Indian village (Villages des ottotatoes) on the Platte River just upstream from the "R. Saline," or Salt Creek, was undoubtedly the Yutan site. The twin symbols may derive from the fact that remnants of the Missouri Indians were living with the Otos there. Even more interesting is the depiction of a Republican Pawnee village (Village des Republiques) on the lower reaches of the Republican River in modern north-central Kansas. This Republican Pawnee village, known today as the Kansas Monument Site, was more than 120 miles south of Mackay's track. The precision of the village location shown make it obvious that Mackay was obtaining very accurate information from his informants.[45]

How long was Mackay absent from Fort Charles? There is no clue about how much time the expedition took for its circuitous over six-hundred-mile route through northeastern Nebraska. If it was indeed a bison-hunting expedition traveling with women and children and establishing tipi camps nightly, it probably consumed no less than twelve weeks. The only event with which it can be compared is the eleven-week period that it took a band of horse-mounted Crows to travel the five hundred miles from the Mandan and Hidatsa villages in west-central North Dakota to the present-day location of Billings, Montana. The trip was documented in the journal of François-Antoine Larocque in the spring and summer of 1805, when he accompanied a band of Crow Indians back to their home on the Yellowstone following a trading excursion to the Missouri River.[46]

Why did Mackay take this long furlough from his duties as commandant of Fort Charles? We can only speculate, for we do not have a clear notion as to what was expected of him as leader of the expedition. Exploring the country about the fort he had built would have been a reasonable course of action, and the notation on his map about the many beavers to be found in the Elkhorn River could be expected to be good news to the St. Louis merchants who were backing his venture. It is, however, probable that he had no idea of the length of time he would be absent from his post, and surely he was impatient to return to his duties. He must have felt great relief upon reentering its stockade after what had to be a long and exhausting journey.

As Mackay settled back into his routine and resumed command of Fort Charles, his second in command was confronting the Nor'westers at the Mandan villages after an arduous journey up the Missouri.

CHAPTER FIVE

Dénouement and Disillusion

"The Two Most Famous Travelers of the Northern Countries of This Continent"

Near the Mandan villages, the swiftly moving Missouri River cut its channel through bluffs of soft, layered beds of earth-toned sediments that confine it to a mile-wide trench. Autumn-colored foliage blotched the steep slopes as John Evans's party moved upriver. The Missouri's waters fell until its bed was exposed in long, bleached sandbars that in the spring would be stippled with seedling willows and cottonwoods. Evans came in view of the Knife River valley on September 23, 1796 (though his letter to Samuel Jones in Philadelphia in July 1797 says that he arrived in August).[1] He tells us nothing about the villages clustered about its mouth nor of his immediate destination, the trading post that René Jusseaume had built between the Mandan and Hidatsa villages two years earlier.

JUSSEAUME'S POST

We know little of Jusseaume's Post, the first trading establishment built in the area. Juan Fotman (or Jean Tremont) told the Spanish in St. Louis that it was constructed after Jusseaume's party arrived on the Missouri on November 27, 1794. In 1795, however, Robert Goodman, the master at the Hudson's Bay Company's Brandon House, reported that the fort had been built the preceding summer. Goodman's hearsay report is perhaps the more accurate statement, for the 1795 Soulard map bears the notation "The English fort located near the Mandan nation on the upper Missouri was built by the English Company of the North in July of 1794." There is a brief account of its construction by one of its builders, Juan Fotman, who had deserted the North West Company expedition that built it. In a declaration to Zenon Trudeau, Fotman said that he

Fig. 18. General area believed to be the location of Jusseaume's Post south and east of the mouth of the Knife River and between the Mandan and Hidatsa villages. The power plant on the right overlies the former site of the Mandan village, Mitutanka, or Deapolis. (W. R. Wood, ©2000)

and five other assistants had established "a small fort and a hut" for René Jusseaume between the Mandan and Hidatsa villages. The following April "Jussome took his skins and went back to the fort from which he had come [River La Souris], leaving the witness with three others to complete the work on the fort and house, on which they were to run up and did run up the English flag every Sunday."[2]

Where was it built? We do not know except in very general terms. A map, in French, based on Evans's travels, bears a rectangular symbol resembling others used on that chart to depict forts set below the mouth of the Knife River midway between two villages to the east and two villages to the west of the "wanutaris & wantuns & mandans."[3] The most plausible interpretation of the map is that the symbol represents Jusseaume's Post and that it was set between the Mandan and Hidatsa villages, an unassailably favorable position for a trading establishment to serve the two groups. Despite close scrutiny of aerial photographs and intensive foot reconnaissance of this area, however, no clues to its location have been detected. Railroad and highway construction along the riverbank in this locality may have destroyed any trace of it.

Fig. 19. Artist's reconstruction of Brandon House 1. During Evans's visit to the Mandans in 1797, this Hudson's Bay post was under the direction of factor James Sutherland. (Courtesy Historical Resources Branch, Manitoba Culture, Heritage, and Tourism Department)

We are equally ignorant of the post's size and appearance. Hearsay evidence recorded by Edwin James in his report of Maj. Stephen Long's expedition of 1819–20 speaks only of a "stockade trading post."[4] There is no reason to suspect that it was any more complex than those three words suggest: simply a stockaded log house.

RELATIONS "UNDER THE MASK OF FRIENDSHIP"

Evans's arrival at the Mandans must have come as a surprise to the Mandans and a shock to the Nor'westers. Surely the Mandans had told the British of earlier visitors from the south, for Jacques D'Eglise had been there in 1792, only four years before, and he had tried to return in 1793 with the goods he had promised the villagers on his visit. But Evans represented a threat to the Nor'westers' trade monopoly', and his first acts set in motion a series of events that nearly led to his murder. There surely was deep resentment among the British traders that a fellow countryman was attempting to evict them and usurp a profitable trade on behalf of a foreign power. It is unfortunate that most of the story of Evans's travails among the Mandans depends largely on his account alone, though it is augmented by a few terse letters written by his Canadian adversaries at their posts along the Assiniboine River.

The Welshman acted promptly: he confiscated Jusseaume's Post on September 28, 1796, renaming it "Fort Makay." The act was not precipitous, for he had been among the Mandans for nearly a week, obviously appraising the situation. His surviving records say nothing about whether or not the post was occupied at the time, but the lack of debate suggests it was not. It was a decisive action: "At that moment, John Evans stood at the very rim of European empire in the Americas. Had the Spaniards been able to equip him properly, he might well have made that classic crossing by land to the Pacific a decade before Lewis and Clark."[5] But the Spanish had not. Evans was to become discouraged and eventually leave what became an untenable situation, compounded by the profoundly and personally devastating revelation that the Welsh Indians of the Missouri River were an illusion.

For the moment, however, Evans hoisted the Spanish flag over Fort Makay, and after delivering a speech to the Indians, he began to distribute medals, flags, and other goods to his audience in the name of the King of Spain. He had a respite of almost two weeks before a detachment of North West Company traders from the River La Souris post, led by either Neil or Donald McKay, arrived on October 8. The Canadians were greeted enthusiastically by the Indians. James Sutherland, the factor at Brandon House, the Hudson's Bay post on the Assiniboine, tells us that "so fond were they of the English" that the Indians carried the sleds of the visiting traders into the villages. Evans may have been upset at the warm reception given the traders, but he nevertheless confronted them with a proclamation, written at Fort Charles by James Mackay the previous May 27, denying them the right to trade in Spanish territory:

> To all British Subjects Trading to the interior parts of N. America, and all other persons of whatever description who may frequent the said Country
>
> His Catholic Majesty having granted to his subjects (the Missurie Company) that part of his dominions siteuated on both sides of the Misssurie to its Westernmost source and from its source to the coast of

the Pacific Ocean, and North to the hight of land, that divides the waters that empties into the Missurie from those that falls into Hudsons Bay

I am therefor commanded to forbid and prevent all forigenrs whatever (especially all British subjects) who are or may be in the neighborhood of his Majestys dominions. To enter any part of the said chartered dominions on pain of confiscation of all such offenders propperty and such punishment as the law of the land may inflict on the conveyars of such propperty—

Given under my hand at Fort Charles this Twenty seventh day of May Anno Domini

One thousand Seven hundred and ninety six.[6]

There was consternation among the Canadians when Evans refused to allow them to trade their goods with the Indians, although he softened his action by purchasing their goods himself and paying for them with furs; one cannot but wonder where he had obtained furs in such quantity. Evans forced the traders to return to Canada with their goods, but McKay was told that he was not to return with further goods to trade. At this point matters were tense but still relatively cordial, for John Macdonell heard, or at least he alleged that he had heard, "that Mr Evans was a *bon garçon*." The traders hurried back to River La Souris with their disconcerting news and a copy of Mackay's proclamation—news that quickly reached Brandon House and other North West Company posts along the Assiniboine. René Jusseaume must have been especially upset: his wife and children were with the Mandans as were a large number of his pelts. On November 5 he wrote to Evans asking for the pelts and begged him to look after his family. There is no hint that Evans returned the goods to him.[7]

It would be interesting to know what Evans or Mackay might have felt had they known that Great Britain had gone to war with Spain in October. Certainly, they were not acting in the best interests of their homeland by expelling the British traders, but both of them had become naturalized Spanish citizens and were performing their duties accordingly, as they had sworn to do when taking their oath of allegiance to the Spanish crown.

The Canadians did not return until March 13, 1797. Jusseaume was with the party and was angry enough that he plotted to have the Indians murder Evans. The Welshman, however, had had six months to ingratiate himself with his native hosts, and they informed him of the plans on his life. Other Indians guarded his quarters from "some of the inferior class" that Jusseaume had bribed with gifts. Evans credits his unnamed interpreter with saving his life when Jusseaume himself entered Evans's quarters and tried to kill him.[8]

Saving Evans's life must have had an economic motive. How he was able to win the friendship of the Mandans who protected him is never made clear: the Mandans probably would have preferred the superior British goods, but Evans was the Mandans' guest and the British were not. Doubtless the Indians wanted as much competition among the Europeans as possible to keep down the price of their goods. If we read Evans's journal correctly, Jusseaume refused to engage in a duel offered by his nemesis, and the Frenchman and his disgruntled party returned to Canada a few days later, not to return until after Evans's departure.

Some correspondence between the Canadian posts and Fort Makay survives from the months after the confrontation. Letters from James Sutherland at Brandon House remained warm and cordial, but the Hudson's Bay Company had little economic interest in the Missouri trade. Employees of the North West Company, however, had a different attitude, for on February 25 two traders arrived at the River La Souris post from the Mandans with the story that Evans would not permit them to trade with the Indians but had forced them to trade with him at unfavorable terms. The next day John Macdonell angrily wrote a letter to Evans in which he rejected the Spanish claim to the region, charging, "there is most complicated vilainy carried on this year at the Missouri," alluding to the real or imagined desertion of North West Company employees (three men named La Grave, Garreau, and Chayé) to the Spanish. Macdonell told Evans he was sending Jusseaume and Jean Baptiste La France to the Missouri to confront Evans with charges he had made against them and to bring back Jusseaume's family.[9]

Unfortunately, the record of what happened next between the Canadians and Evans has not survived. The story does not resume until November 12, 1797, when we learn from the Brandon House journals that Macdonell had sent a Canadian to the Mandans with some Assiniboine Indians to "learn if the Spaniard is there," and if he was not, a party was ready to go to the Missouri. The same entry also tells us that surveyor and explorer David Thompson was expected to arrive at Brandon House very soon. He was to go to the Missouri River and determine the latitude and longitude of the Mandan villages and put to rest the matter of their proper jurisdiction. Thompson arrived a few days later, and he left River La Souris post on November 28.[10] By the time he reached the Mandans, however, Evans had been gone for seven months and, indeed, was back in St. Louis.

We know nothing of Evans's activities during the winter except that he obtained from his Indian hosts a map of the Missouri River west of the Mandans, a map that illustrates almost the entirety of the present-day State of Montana (see fig. 27). It is reasonable to assume that he traded with the villagers and may even have obtained a reasonable quantity of furs. However, for reasons that he never made clear, Evans abandoned the idea of reaching the Pacific and left Fort Makay the following spring. He and his party headed downriver on May 9, 1797, or perhaps a little earlier, having been at the Mandans for a little more than seven months. Before leaving, Evans had promised the Mandans (perhaps in good faith or perhaps tongue-in-cheek) to return and furnish them with guns and ammunition. But this was not to be. When Black Cat, the Mandan chief of Ruhptare, visited William Clark at Fort Mandan in 1804, he complained that Evans had "deceived" them since he had never returned.[11]

Of Evans's return trip we know only that he left the Mandans about May 9. He returned to St. Louis on or before July 15 after a journey of more than two months (sixty-eight days, he reported).[12] We have no appraisal from his own hand of the success or failure of his mission among the Mandans and the aborted trip to the Pacific Ocean. Yet it is not hard to surmise why he turned back where he did. The map of the western regions obtained from his hosts surely revealed that the Pacific was too distant even to contemplate the attempt. His supplies may also have been depleted during his winter among the Mandans. Given the hardships of the later Lewis and Clark expedition in crossing the Rocky Mountains, Evans clearly made the right decision; he would have perished.

In late December 1797, seven months after Evans's departure, David Thompson left Macdonell's House and arrived at the Knife River villages, having been guided there by a group consisting of Jusseaume, Hugh McCracken, and seven others. His purpose was not to trade but to determine the latitude and longitude of the Mandans and to try to induce them to establish a regular exchange with the North West Company. He spent nineteen days in the villages, meeting and conferring with several Canadian traders and with both tribes of Indians.[13] The party, especially Jusseaume, must have been delighted to see that the "Spaniard" was gone.

Curiously, Thompson says not one word in his journals about Evans's visit either directly or indirectly, despite his association with the Welshman's mortal enemy, Jusseaume, and the fact that Evans's presence had been the stimulus for his having gone to the Missouri in the first place. Nor does he or any other traveler in the area ever again allude to Jusseaume's Post: as far as the documents are concerned, it was utterly forgotten. Did Evans burn it down when he left? It would have been a reasonable course of action to deny the Canadians its use. The Welshman's brief but tempestuous visit among the Nor'westers was ignored if not forgotten. After all, Evans had been responsible for only a momentary interruption in the illegal Canadian trade into Spanish lands along the upper Missouri River. They continued their trade, and the Indians forgot the Spanish; after all, they had not returned with any goods, and British traders were there with merchandise. It was as though Evans had never been there. With the American purchase of Louisiana in 1803, the frequency of visitation by the North West traders began to diminish, and by 1818 their visits to the Missouri ended.[14]

What were Evans's emotions as he approached, then visited, and passed the now abandoned Fort Charles? He recorded nothing about the defunct post but hurried on to St. Louis. Evans must have worried about his reception by the Spanish officials.

By spring, having lost touch with Evans and assuming that his lieutenant was on his way to the Pacific, Mackay abandoned both his upriver hopes and Fort Charles after having spent a year and a half among the Omahas. In all likelihood he was ordered home: a man of his determination would scarcely have abandoned an enterprise, even one this disappointing, on his own initiative. By early May 1797 he was back in St. Louis. Fort Charles was left to molder, and no known effort was made to reclaim or reoccupy it. By July, Evans too was back in the city. Truteau had returned to St. Louis a year earlier, arriving about June 1796. It had been expected that Mackay and Evans would be gone a full six years in prosecuting their orders for the Missouri Company, but they were back in St. Louis in less than two years, far short of their anticipated return in 1801. The Spanish presence on the Missouri River promptly evaporated save for the few, usually nameless, *coureurs du bois* who continued to try their hand at the trade during the eight years prior to the arrival of Lewis and Clark. The dying embers of the Spanish Empire were extinguished along the upper Missouri River.

CARTOGRAPHIC RESULTS OF THE EXPEDITION

The Mackay and Evans expedition made the two men celebrities throughout Spanish Louisiana. More important, the geographical knowledge they obtained made available for future scholars what many of those involved in the fur-trading community of St. Louis had known, at least indirectly, for many years. This information was widely disseminated throughout Louisiana, from St. Louis to New Orleans. Copies of their maps and journals likewise found their way into the hands of American officials in Indiana Territory as well as in New Orleans and thence to Washington, D.C. Little wonder, for their charts were the most precise made before the Corps of Discovery traversed the area.

During the planning and execution of their journey up the Missouri, Lewis and Clark consulted the journals and maps generated by the Scot and Welsh leaders. The maps produced by these two men, indeed, laid out in detail the entire first year of the Lewis and Clark expedition. The captains carried copies of the Mackay and Evans charts with them and regularly inspected them during their voyage.

The Indian Office Map of 1797–98

Perhaps the most important single document resulting from the Mackay and Evans expedition is the Indian Office map, a large-scale chart that illustrates the Missouri River from St. Charles, Missouri, to the Mandan villages. It was first described by Annie H. Abel, a historian, after it was discovered in 1915 in the Bureau of Indian Affairs—hence its name.[15] It is the only detailed map of the Missouri River of the period, especially since the maps of the lower Missouri River made by William Clark have been lost. Although the Missouri Company made several copies of this chart, only one draft is now known to exist. Scholars agree that it is a version of one produced by James Mackay in St. Louis in 1797 following his expedition's return. Mackay assumed responsibility for its compilation based on his notes and those of Evans.

James Mackay returned to St. Louis from his upriver voyage a few days before May 13, 1797. Two men eagerly awaited his report on the expedition's activities and discoveries: the director of the Missouri Company, Jacques Clamorgan, and the Spanish lieutenant governor of Upper Louisiana, Zenon Trudeau. As one of his first tasks, Mackay produced a map illustrating the area his men explored. Before his departure, Spanish officials had directed Mackay to pay particular attention to this cartographic assignment, and "he had pledged himself to procure this map with careful attention for the government."[16]

A week or two after his return, Mackay prepared a map of the Missouri River from its mouth to that of the White River in present-day South Dakota. On May 26 Trudeau wrote baron de Carondelet, governor general of Louisiana, in New Orleans that Mackay had "made a very good map of the Missouri

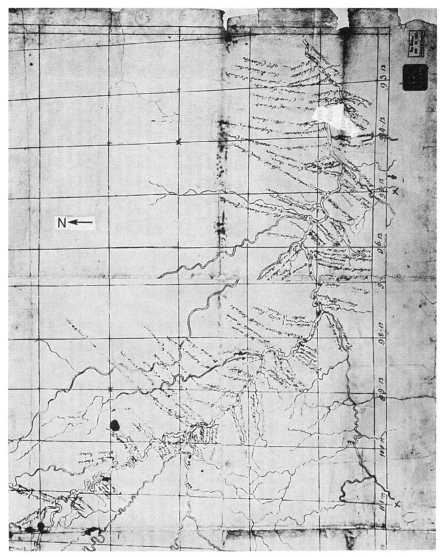

Fig. 20. The Indian Office map as prepared by James Mackay. (Courtesy National Archives and Records Service, Washington, D.C.)

from its mouth as far as the *riviere Blanche* [White River, South Dakota] which includes about three hundred and fifty leagues. You will receive this map as soon as it is *distinct*."[17] Any final map purporting to illustrate the expedition's full range of discoveries would have to await Evans's return, for Mackay himself is not known to have gone up the Missouri beyond Bad Village, though he had been along the lowermost reaches of the Niobrara River. Evans did not return to St. Louis until about July 15. During his excursion, he had made a map of his voyage to the Mandans, illustrating the river from Fort Charles to their villages. Without Evans's contribution, Mackay's product could not have shown the Missouri River above the White River. The Indian Office map is, therefore, a composite product of the two men.

At least two separate copies of the enlarged map appeared over the next few months. Clamorgan received the first of them. When Mackay reported to Clamorgan upon his return, the director dutifully passed this information on to higher Spanish authorities. On October 14, five months after Mackay's return to St. Louis, Clamorgan forwarded to Secretary Manuel Andrés Lopez de Armesto a copy of "the map of the Missouri well drawn up at the cost and expense of the company."[18] If this draft remains in the Spanish archives, it has yet to be discovered.

The second enlarged map was drawn up for Zenon Trudeau. Three months after Clamorgan sent his map to New Orleans, Trudeau sent Manuel Gayoso de Lemos (Carondelet's successor in New Orleans) a map of the Missouri River. This version, apparently now "distinct," included the course of the river "as far as the Mandan nation." Trudeau wrote: "I am enclosing to Your Excellency a *relacion* of a voyage which M. Mackay has made in the Upper Missouri, and the map of the said river, as far as the Mandan nation, made by the same person, which I believe to be the most exact of those which have been formed up to the present."[19]

One of the Chouteau brothers of St. Louis, on a periodic business visit to the capital in 1798, delivered the map to Gayoso de Lemos. A letter to the governor general by Trudeau documented this delivery and specified that Mackay was "the author of the map which Mr. Chouteau will deliver to you."[20] No trace of this map remains.

Mackay, in a letter to Gayoso de Lemos dated June 8, 1798, claimed to have made a map of the Missouri from its mouth to the "wanutaries [Hidatsa] nation."[21] His claim did not mention the contribution made by his assistant Evans. Mackay earlier, of course, had visited the Mandan and Hidatsa villages, but he did so by coming down from Canada in 1787, before he moved to St. Louis. Possibly, some of the details on this small upper portion of the map could reflect his own personal experiences during that previous visit.

Another copy of the map, also now lost, came into the possession of Daniel Clark Jr. of New Orleans. Clark, a native of Ireland, came to New Orleans in 1786, becoming a wealthy merchant and attorney. He served for a time as a clerk in the office of Governor Gayoso de Lemos. In this position many official documents of the period passed through his hands. Clark became an American citizen in 1798, and for a few months he acted as a temporary U.S. consul; Pres. Thomas Jefferson appointed him a regular consul at New Orleans on July 16, 1801. When Andrew Ellicott, the American commissioner in charge of setting the boundary between American and Spanish lands, visited the city in January and February 1803, just before the Louisiana Purchase, Clark served as an intermediary between him and Gayoso de Lemos.[22]

Clark obtained a copy of the Mackay map through his Spanish contacts. In 1803, in response to a request for information by President Jefferson, Clark wrote: "The Map of the Missouri taken at the expence of the Company of the same name I sent to be presented to [President John] Adams . . . in 1799.—this survey is certainly the best that was ever made in that Part of the world, & the map must now be in Mr. Adams possession."[23] The wording in this passage is ambiguous as to its cartographic author. But the identification of the map as having been made at the expense of the Missouri Company closely follows the wording of Clamorgan regarding Mackay's chart of the expedition: "the map of the Missouri well drawn up at the cost and expenses of the Company." Apparently, this copy also did not survive.

The only known extant copy of Mackay's map is the one that was carried on the Lewis and Clark expedition. On November 5, 1803, William Clark wrote a letter to William Henry Harrison, governor of Indiana Territory, asking him for a copy of the chart. Harrison responded a week later with a copy of the map and the comment, "The map mentioned in your letter of the 5th Instant had been taken from me by Mr. Jones who claimed it as the property of Mr. Hay of Cahokia but as it was still in the possesion of Mr. Jones I have had it copied & now send it to you by the Post rider." An inscription on the back of the map, in Harrison's hand, reads, "For Captn William Clark or Captn Meriwether Lewis on their voyage up the Mississippi"; the governor obviously was confused about their destination. Meriwether Lewis mentions having obtained this map of the Missouri River "from it's mouth to the Mandane nation" in a letter to President Jefferson the following month.[24]

The Indian Office map and the Beinecke Library map of the Missouri River from Fort Charles to the Mandans, contributed to the construction of many derivative maps in French, Spanish, and English.[25] Several of these charts, produced in St. Louis, circulated among local fur traders, their employers, and local mapmakers. Other copies were obtained by visiting explorers and scientists active along the Missouri River before and after Lewis and Clark, including François Marie Perrin du Lac, Antoine Soulard, and Joseph N. Nicollet.

Other mapmakers who drew on this source obtained their copies in New Orleans. One such map, drawn in France in 1803 by James Pitot, relied on sketches provided by Barthelemy Lafon. These charts also contributed to two other maps in Spanish. One is an anonymous map of about 1800; Jose Pichardo compiled the other one in 1811.[26] Pichardo was a Jesuit employed by Spain to determine the boundaries between its territory and that of the United States. He obtained a great number of contemporary papers and maps in conducting this task—at least one of them was obviously a Mackay and Evans product. Both trace their inspiration for the course of the Missouri River to a copy of the Mackay map sent to officials in New Orleans.

No less than five copies of the latter map were made. The best documented ones include the incomplete draft showing the Missouri as far as the White River, the two enlarged copies that Clamorgan and Trudeau sent to New Orleans, the copy obtained by John Rice Jones of Vincennes, the Indian Office map, and the copy Daniel Clark sent to President Adams. The many derivative maps that exist give reason to suspect that some may remain, unrecognized, in Spanish or American archives.

The Indian Office map and the Beinecke Library map clearly illustrate that Lewis and Clark were not trailblazing until they left Fort Mandan in 1805. As Charles Hoffhaus writes: "During the first half of the route," the French *voyageurs* on the expedition "were merely showing Lewis and Clark what had been their own backyard for over a century. . . . The idea that [the American expedition was] 'exploring' country they and their fathers and grandfathers had traversed annually for decades would surely have struck them as a good joke."[27]

The Beinecke Library Map

This map shows Evans's route up the Missouri River from Fort Charles to the Mandan and Hidatsa villages. This landmark map in Missouri River cartography illustrates in detail the major features of the Missouri River channel and shows all of its principal tributaries.

The Beinecke Library map was important to Lewis and Clark. William Clark on occasion referred to it and verified observations recorded there. The map by Evans (whose name Clark variously spelled "Evins," "Evens," and "Ivens") named all of the major tributaries of the Missouri in the area of his journey upriver. Indeed, it remained for Lewis and Clark to name only a few minor streams between the mouth of the Missouri and the Mandan and Hidatsa villages. Until the captains reached those villages, they made only "secondary and supplementary" maps of the Missouri River, so precise and detailed was their predecessors' work. Evans's chart was a major "road map" of the expedition for no less than seven hundred miles of its course.

The original map that Evans produced of his exploration from Fort Charles to the Mandan and Hidatsa villages has been lost, but a copy of it is now in the Beinecke Rare Book and Manuscript Library at Yale University. This copy first resurfaced in 1903, when it was discovered by Reuben Gold Thwaites in New York in the Clark-Voorhis Collection of Lewis and Clark documents. Thwaites reproduced it in his edition of the original journals of Lewis and Clark, believing that the map was a Clark original of the river beginning at St. Charles, Missouri. This error came about because he did not examine the maps carefully, for he misread "Fort Charles" as the lower Missouri River town of "St. Charles." This blunder, precipitated in part because Clark's own route maps from Camp Dubois to the Mandan and Hidatsa villages have been lost, had the effect of concealing the identity of the Evans map for forty years. Its correct identification was made in 1946 by Aubrey Diller, who first recognized its significance.[28]

Diller reported that this copy of the map had been "sent to Lewis by Jefferson 13 January 1804 and [is] cited by Evans' name in Lewis and Clark's journals." President Jefferson lost no time in dispatching the Evans map to Lewis: "I now enclose you a map of the Missouri as far as the Mandans, 12. or 1500. miles I presume above its mouth. It is said to be very accurate, having been done by a Mr. Evans by order of the Spanish government." Jefferson obtained this copy from Governor Harrison of Indiana Territory.[29] (The extant map clearly is not the original: not only did Harrison say it was a copy, but also the sheets are clean and show none of the wear that one would expect of a map that had been produced in the field.) Nine days later Jefferson dispatched another letter to Lewis in which he told him that Evans's journey had been to go in search of the Welsh Indians.

The Beinecke Library map comprises seven sheets. Six show the Missouri River from Fort Charles to the mouth of the Knife River. These may be overlaid, using the one-inch grid subdividing each sheet, to form one continuous map of the river. The scale is variable but ranges from about eight to ten miles to the inch. The map's precision indicates direct observation by an eyewitness. A seventh sheet is a chart of the Missouri River from the mouth of the Knife River to the Rocky Mountains. It is of necessity based on hearsay information that Evans obtained during his stay with the Mandans, although there is no clue as to who provided him with it. It is on a much smaller scale than the preceding sheets and carries no grid, but like the first six, it is labeled in either French or English written in the same hand. All notations on each of the sheets were made in ink.

Whoever composed the map spoke English, for all of the notes on major features along the river, plus all astronomical observations, are in English. Evans probably obtained the French names for some streams from his own *engagés*, and he may also have met French fur traders on the river, as the note on sheet 5 that refers to a man named "W Jacque" suggests. The precision with which the map was drawn demonstrates that its author was a person competent in the surveyor's craft. We know that Evans was a surveyor in Cape Girardeau, Missouri, for a time after his return from the expedition. Although it is unlikely that anyone other than Evans drew the original map above the White River, the surviving portion of his journal sheds no light on this issue. Regardless of authorship, the map provides the earliest place names for this area of the Missouri basin. Most of these names have continued in use to the present time, although some of them have been translated into English.[30]

Some of the inscriptions on the sheets are difficult to read. This occasionally led to errors by Clark, not to mention by others who were not familiar with the map and the history of the area it depicts. To choose the most notorious example, lack of clarity in writing the word "Ponca" led Clark to misread and record it as "Pania" (that is, as "Pawnee"). This error was accepted by many later students of western history, thereby producing what Diller describes as a "paper invasion by the Pawnees, and a paper colony of the Pawnees on the Missouri."[31]

In order to resolve these and other ambiguities, a new draft of the map was prepared to make it more useful and accessible to scholars, based on an inspection of the originals in the Beinecke Library at Yale University. All symbols of physical features are reproduced on the transcriptions exactly as they appear on the original. The positions of the grid, the directional symbols, and the identifying numbers of the sheets are retained, although some inscriptions have been rotated 90 or 180 degrees so they may be read without turning the map. A few inscriptions on the original map were scratched out, apparently by William Clark. Some of these inscriptions can still be read, in whole or in part, on the original. I have indicated in parentheses what I believe to be the wording in these instances. All wording on the map has been transcribed, including several marginal notations on sheets 1 and 2. Most of these notations consist of figures in Clark's hand, although the figures directly south of "R &

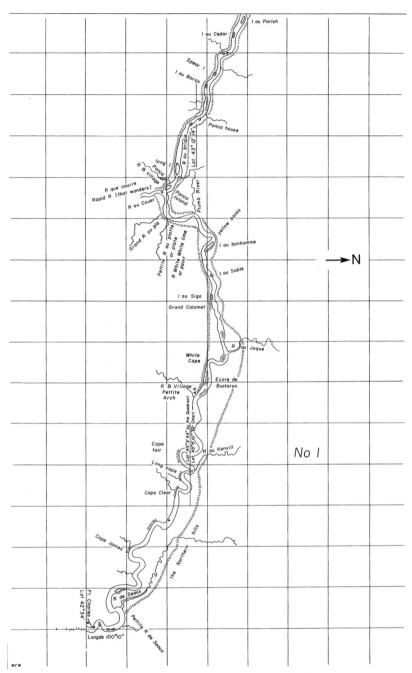

Fig. 21. Sheet 1 of the Beinecke Library map, from Fort Charles (near modern Sioux City, Iowa) to "I au Parish" (former Hamilton Island, South Dakota). (Courtesy *Great Plains Quarterly*, from vol. 1 no. 1[winter 1981])

village Pettite Arch" on sheet 1 are in a hand not identifiable as that of either Clark or the original copyist.

Although the map is essential for understanding the geographical knowledge of the northern plains in the years before Lewis and Clark, it must be used with caution. It contains not only the data recorded by Mackay and Evans in 1796 and 1797 but also additions made by William Clark during the expedition.

Inscriptions in Clark's hand appear on each sheet. On sheet 1 Clark wrote "Rapid R" and "R que courre" at the mouth of the Niobrara River. There are no anomalies on sheet 2, although there is reason to believe that Clark scratched out a legend that alluded to an "old volcano" in what is today northern Gregory County, South Dakota. But on sheet 3 a triangular symbol labeled "Teton" is shown on the bottomlands just above the mouth of the "Little Missurie" (now called Bad River). Clark added this notation because of the large Teton Indian encampment that the Corps of Discovery met at this location. An unidentified triangular symbol also appears on the west bank of the Missouri about halfway between the mouth of modern Chantier Creek and that of the Cheyenne River on what appears to be the bluff edge approximately opposite the later site of the second Fort Sully. Clark may have added this symbol to denote the Teton Indians he refers to in the journals at this location. Both Indian camps are marked on a copy of his field map. Another feature on this sheet that appears to be Clark's handwork is the sketch of the horse in the lower left-hand corner. This image resembles other sketches believed to have been made by Clark, although why he would have made it on this map is unknowable. Furthermore, it seems unlikely that a copyist would duplicate such a sketch, even if it had appeared on the original map.[32]

Other examples of Clark's additions appear on sheet 4 where "Marapa R," or modern Oak Creek, is placed above the Grand River. A nearby island he labels as "I au Brim" probably represents modern Ashley Island. Another inscription in Clark's hand reads "I Ricaras," probably in reference to the Arikara village that was located on this island above Oak Creek. Above this island Clark labels two streams that enter the Missouri from the northwest as "Kakawissassa or Light[ing] Crow" and "Parnorni." Two oval symbols set on either side of the latter creek denote the twin Arikara villages now known collectively as the Leavenworth site. "Kakawissassa" Creek was named by Clark after an Arikara chief.[33] Since the captain so carefully noted new information on this part of the map, perhaps he added the symbols for the Leavenworth village site. Clark also labels modern Spring Creek, shown on the

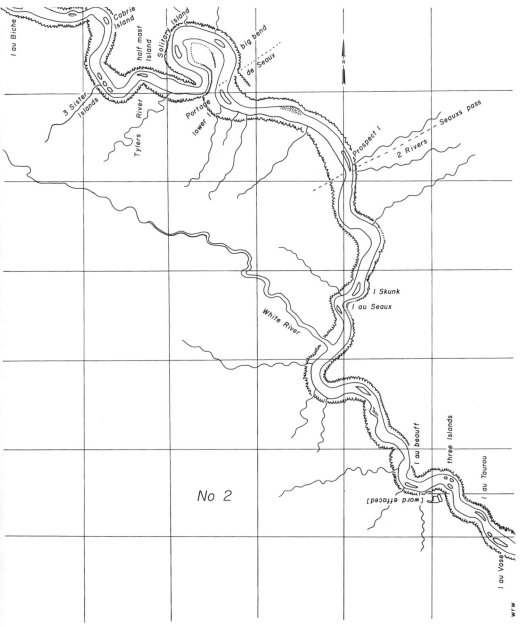

Fig. 22. Sheet 2 of the Beinecke Library map, from "I au Vase" (former Mud Island) to "I au Biche" (probably former Fort George Island), just east of Pierre, South Dakota. (Courtesy *Great Plains Quarterly*, from vol. 1, no. 1 [winter 1981])

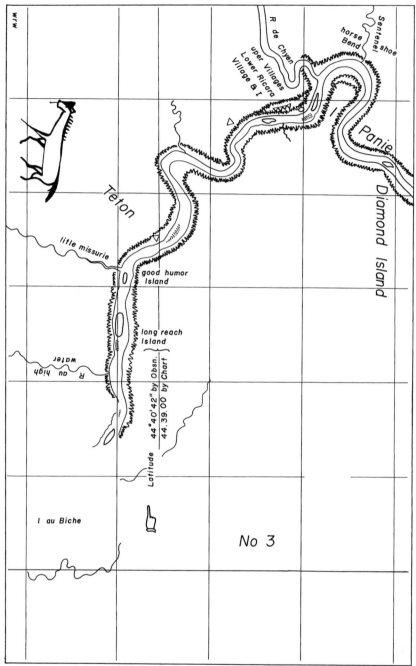

R de Chyen

uper Villages
Lower Ricara
Village & I

horse
Bend

Sentenel

Panie

Diamond Island

Teton

litle missurie

good humor
Island

long reach
Island

R au high
water

Latitude 44° 40′ 42″ by Obsn.
44. 39. 00 by Chart

I au Biche

No 3

Fig. 23. Sheet 3 of the Beinecke Library map, from "R au high water" (modern Antelope Creek) to "Diamond Island" (former Fishermans Island), South Dakota. (Courtesy *Great Plains Quarterly*, from vol. 1, no. 1 [winter 1981])

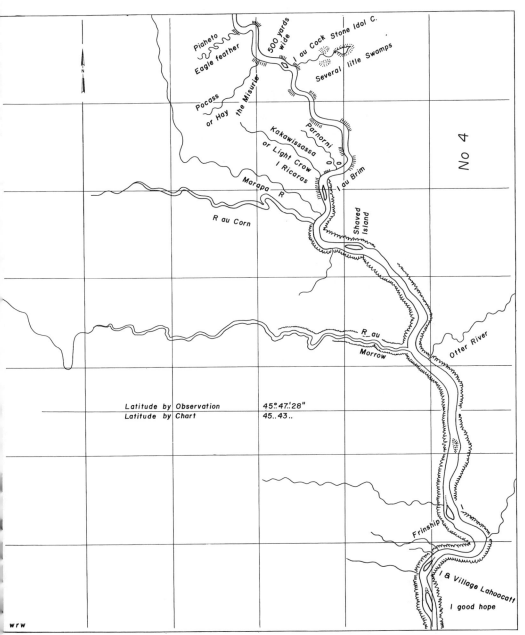

Piaheto
Eagle feather

500 yards wide

I au Cock Stone Idol C.

Several litle Swamps

Pocass
or Hay
the Misurie

Parnorni

Kakawissassa
or Light Crow
I Ricaras

I au Brim

Marapa R

R au Corn

Shaved
Island

R au
Morrow

Otter River

| Latitude by | Observation | 45°.47'.28" |
| Latitude by | Chart | 45..43.. |

Frinship

I & Village Lahoocatt

I good hope

wrw

Fig. 24. Sheet 4 of the Beinecke Library map, from "I good hope" (a former unnamed island) to "Piaheto/Eagle feather" Creek (modern John Grass Creek), South Dakota. (Courtesy *Great Plains Quarterly*, from vol. 1, no. 1 [winter 1981])

Evans map as heading in a lake a few miles east of the Missouri River, as "Stone Idol C."

Near the top of sheet 4, two streams are shown entering the Missouri from the northwest; both are labeled in Clark's hand. The lower one is "Pocass or Hay" and the upper one, "Piaheto or Eagle Feather." Both streams were named after Arikara chiefs and probably are modern Blackhawk Creek and John Grass Creek, respectively. Pocass, Kakawissassa, and Piaheto (as Clark spelled them) were the names of the chiefs of the three largest divisions of the Arikara Indians, as Pierre-Antoine Tabeau notes. Tabeau had wintered at the Arikara villages near the mouth of the Grand River in 1803 and was a valuable source of information for Lewis and Clark.[34]

On sheet 5 the term "Chiss.check" was applied by Clark to modern Little Heart River. An inscription on an unidentified creek to the south of it was scratched out, perhaps also by Clark.

Evans's sheet 6 depicts the area between the Heart and the Knife Rivers. The course of the Missouri in that area is shown much as it appears on later and more detailed maps except that the tight horseshoe bend near the center of the map had not yet been cut off to form modern Painted Woods Lake. The bend had been cut off to form an island by the time Lewis and Clark passed it on October 14, 1804. In his field notes Clark dates the cutoff as having taken place seven years earlier, that is, the date of Evans's visit.[35]

There are at least two notations on sheet 6 in Clark's hand: "Village Chiss.chect R" on the right bank of the Heart River and "Wah hoo toon—Wind" on the map margin. The meaning of the latter term is unknown. Another notation is in the hand of James Mackay, a judgment based on a 1797 sample of his handwriting reproduced by Nasatir.[36] This inscription appears north of the mouth of the Knife River and shows the "Track to Catepoi river." The spellings of "Catepoi river" (Q'Appelle River) and "Lake Ouinipique" (Lake Winnipeg) are also the same (except for one letter) as those used in Mackay's journal. Mackay probably added this notation sometime after he visited Lewis and Clark at Camp Dubois on January 10, 1804.[37] Since this visit occurred three days before Jefferson dispatched the Beinecke Library map from Washington, it is obvious that Mackay must have visited the explorers again at a later date and added the notation to the map at that time.

Bluffs along the Missouri are shown by hatch marks on sheet 6 and are twice designated by the term "Yellow Ecore," a corrupted spelling of the French word *accore*, "bluff" or "bank." The "R du Coer" on Evans's map is the present-day Heart River. Most of the Mandan and Hidatsa villages on sheet 6, marked

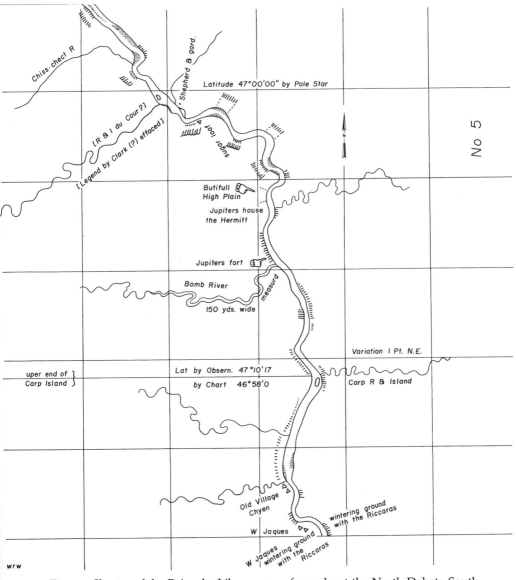

Fig. 25. Sheet 5 of the Beinecke Library map, from about the North Dakota-South Dakota boundary (around Porcupine Creek) to "Chiss.chect R" (the Little Heart River, North Dakota). (Courtesy *Great Plains Quarterly*, from vol. 1, no. 1 [winter 1981])

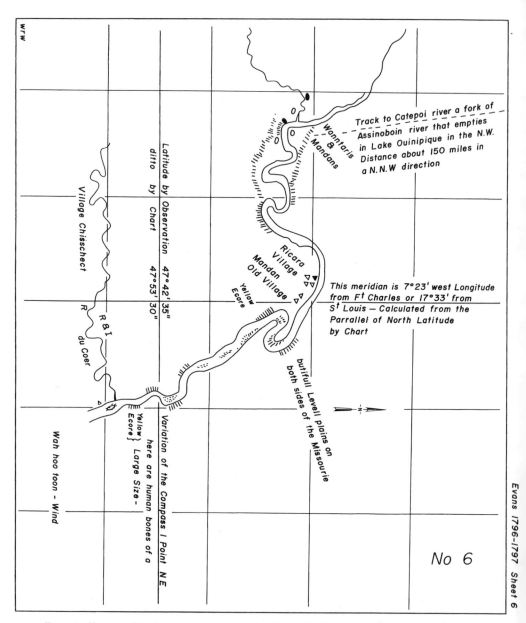

Track to Catepoi river a fork of
Assinoboin river that empties
in Lake Ouinipique in the N.W.
Distance about 150 miles in
a N.N.W direction

Wanntaris
&
Mandans

Village Chisschect

Latitude by Observation 47°42'35"

ditto by Chart 47°53'30"

R 8 I

R
du Coer

Ricara
Village

Mandan
Old Village

Yellow
Ecore

This meridian is 7°23' west Longitude
from F^t Charles or 17°33' from
St Louis — Calculated from the
Parrallel of North Latitude
by Chart

butifull Levell plains on
both sides of the Missourie

Variation of the Compass 1 Point N E

Yellow}
Ecore} Large Size —

here are human bones of a

Wah hoo toon - Wind

No 6

Fig. 26. Sheet 6 of the Beinecke Library map, from the "R du Coer" (the Heart River) to the Mandan and Hidatsa villages at the mouth of the (unlabeled) Knife River, North Dakota. (Courtesy *Great Plains Quarterly*, from vol. 1, no. 1 [winter 1981])

"Manutaris & Mandans," can be precisely identified with modern archaeological sites because they are described by later travelers and shown on more
detailed maps.

The Mandan and Hidatsa villages at the mouth of the Knife River are
depicted by two symbols: open circles and solid ones. Donald J. Lehmer
believed that the open circles were Mandan villages and the solid ones were
Hidatsa. The open circle farthest down the Missouri River is the Mandan
Deapolis site, and the one directly across the river to the northwest is the
Black Cat site. The solid symbol north of the Knife River is the Big Hidatsa site,
and the one on the Missouri below the mouth of the Knife is the Amahami
site. The open circle between the latter two sites is probably the Sakakawea
site. The dichotomy in symbols suggested by Lehmer is supported by information obtained by David Thompson when he visited the Mandan and Hidatsa
villages between December 1797 and January 1798, which is contained on his
1798 map and in his field notes. Thompson was in those villages during the
winter following Evans's departure in May 1797 and observed that the middle village consisted of thirty-seven Mandan and fifteen Hidatsa dwellings.
Under such circumstances it is reasonable that Evans would have plotted it
as a Mandan community.[38]

Sheet 7 contains information that Evans obtained from Mandan or Hidatsa
informants (or from resident Europeans). "Conjecturall" is written in Clark's
hand, upside down, across the Rocky Mountains along the upper reaches of
the Missouri River, reflecting his pessimism about the map's precision. A
symbol obviously intended to depict a fort on a stream flowing west from the
Rocky Mountains is shown. Perhaps, as John Allen suggests, this indicates
"a European establishment (possibly Russian since the Louisiana Spanish of
Evans's time knew of Russian posts in the Pacific Northwest)."[39]

Two other puzzling features appear on this sheet. One of them is the notation "Shevitoon" just north of the mouth of the Yellowstone River. This term
is also applied to an Indian group shown on the 1795 Arrowsmith map down
the Missouri River from the Mandans. A group called the "Shevitaun" is also
noted in Mackay's journal.[40] From its listing between the "Sious" and "Corbeaus" (Crows), one is led to suspect that the group was a nomadic one, but
its identity is unknown. The other puzzling feature is the "Village de Boitife"
(the spelling is not distinct} on the middle reaches of the Yellowstone River.
Its identity also is unknown.

Although Mackay had given Evans detailed instructions for crossing the
continent, there is no evidence that Evans ever went west of the Mandan and

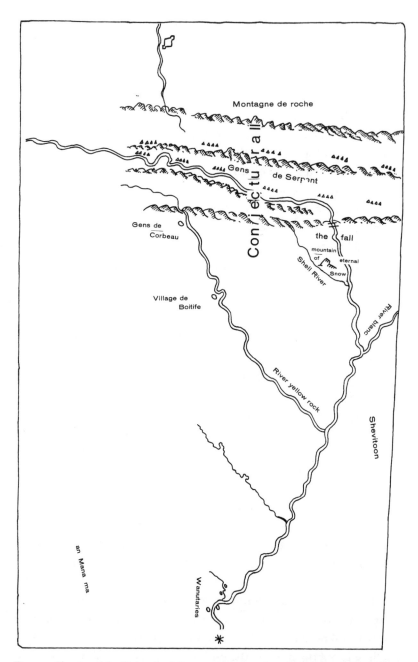

Fig. 27. Sheet 7 of the Beinecke Library map, showing the Missouri River from the Mandan and Hidatsa villages in North Dakota to the Rocky Mountains in Montana. (Courtesy *Great Plains Quarterly*, from vol. 1, no.1 [winter 1981])

Hidatsa villages. The information on sheet 7 about the area west of those villages could only have come from Indian sources or from Canadian traders Evans met at the mouth of the Knife River, who, in turn, could only have obtained it from native informants.

Evans's map of his explorations of the Missouri in what is now North and South Dakota in 1796–97 is the earliest known eyewitness map of the area. It is important to remember, however, that the copy of this chart carried by Lewis and Clark had been modified by a number of legends added by William Clark and by James Mackay. By deleting Clark's additions, we obtain a more precise notion of the original. Furthermore, Evans's map served as a basis for later English, Spanish, and French maps until the publication of Clark's own map of what was to become the western United States, first published in Nicholas Biddle's edition of the expedition in 1814. This chart rendered all earlier maps of the area obsolete and became the standard map of the West for another half-century.

MAN PROPOSES

What economic rewards did the Missouri Company reap from their investment of more than a quarter million pesos? Virtually none, and if profit-and-loss figures were available, they probably would have registered an overall deficit. The Spanish could not provide sufficient goods to attain and retain native respect and still maintain a reasonable margin of profit. Three years after the expedition's return, Spain sold Louisiana to France, but before any effective French control could even be contemplated, Napoleon resold the territory to the United States in May 1803. It was not until the following March that Spanish officials formally relinquished control of Upper Louisiana to the French, and the next day the United States took over the region. During the time these negotiations were taking place, the Missouri Company went bankrupt, although *coureurs du bois* continued their incursions into the Missouri valley. An "unregulated infusion of trade goods was destabilizing regional and tribal politics. Natives openly questioned whether the Spanish government's stepchildren, the French Canadians and French-Indians, were 'marking out the road in good understanding.'"[41]

Save for geographical information, there was no scientific advancement from the expedition: despite Turner's plea, no skins or horns of animals unknown to science, like those of the bighorn sheep, were returned. Mackay did find large fossils in his trek through northeastern Nebraska—those of a mammoth or mastodon—but neither these nor any minerals or ethnographic specimens are known to have been returned to St. Louis, nor were any plant specimens carried home. Naturalists apparently learned nothing from this venture, although the cartographic and narrative products the duo produced were valuable sources of information for everyone.

News of the expedition's discoveries could not be kept secret. The returning *engagés* would have spread information among their friends and neighbors, and a stream of independent traders continued to paddle their way upriver with cargos of trade goods. Lewis and Clark met a number of such entrepreneurs on their outbound passage, all of them operating out of St. Louis. The traffic the Americans met on the Missouri was, indeed, rather impressive; it included no less than twelve small vessels or rafts from the Grand Osages, Kansas, Pawnees, Omahas, Sioux, and Mandans operated by no less than eighteen men. Most of these men remain anonymous, but the captains met others who are named: Pierre Dorion, who had been living with the Sioux for twenty years (since about 1784); Joseph Gravelines, who had been on the river with the Arikaras for a like amount of time; Pierre Dorion Jr.; Pierre-Antoine Tabeau; and Régis Loisel.[42] They met still other traders on their return trip.

Mackay's Rewards

What compensation did Mackay and Evans reap from their two-year stint as employees of the Missouri Company? As the "principal explorer and director of the company's affairs in the Indian country," Mackay was to receive an honorarium of four hundred pesos a year. But we do not know the wages that Evans drew as co-leader of the expedition.[43] Their postexpeditionary fortunes, however, are illuminated in Spanish documents. Gov. Gen. Manuel Gayoso de Lemos, on November 22, 1798, wrote Don Francisco de Saavedra, secretary of state in New Orleans:

> Foreseeing the importance of this matter [of keeping the English out of the Missouri basin], I tried to keep to our cause the two most famous travelers of the northern countries of this continent; one Don Jayme Macay and the other Don Juan Evans, both natives of the Island of Great Britain, who, displeased with the Canadian companies, entered the services of our Missouri Company. But when this company failed due to its poor management and great losses, I knew that necessity would oblige these two valuable subjects to solicit employment among the

referred to Canadian Companies to our own very great loss. In order to avoid this inconvenience, after having had Macay at my side for some time, in order to assure myself of his principles, I have decided to locate him at San Andrés, a new establishment near the entrance of the Missouri, naming him commandant of that post, under the dependency of the Lieutenant-Governor of Illinois. Not having any position to give Evans, I have preferred to maintain him at my cost, keeping him in my own house, in order to prevent his returning to his own country, or for his own convenience, to embrace another cause.[44]

On May 1, 1798, Mackay was appointed a captain of militia and the commandant of San André del Misuri, which despite its Spanish name had been laid out by a man named John Henry. San André (or St. Andrew, also sometimes known as Bonnehomme) was a small community on the southern bank of the Missouri a few miles upriver from St. Charles between the present-day town of St. Albans and Bonne Homme Island (nearly opposite the north-bank town of Defiance, near which Daniel Boone later settled). Louis Houck tells us, without revealing his source, that a Frenchman, John Lafleur, had settled in this area in 1799. This man had been one of the *voyageurs* on Mackay's expedition, and he received a land grant through Mackay for his services on that journey.[45]

San André was short lived, for it was abandoned and in ruins by 1811, and because it had been built in the fickle bottomlands, in a matter of years its site fell into the shifting channel of the Missouri River.[46] The month following his appointment as its commandant, on June 8, Mackay petitioned the governor general for additional compensation, including an appointment in the Spanish army. The new commandant assumed his duties at San André on October 1. Although Gayoso de Lemos had contemplated employing both Mackay and Evans to assist a commission in setting the boundary lines between the United States and Great Britain, nothing came of this proposal.

Mackay, then, was richly rewarded, but not by his appointment as commandant of the settlement at San André, for his compensation in that regard was trifling. Rather, he also became the commandant of St. Charles, on the north bank of the river and downstream a few miles from San André, in 1801. More important, he was the recipient of several large land grants totaling more than 55,000 arpents (some 46,470 acres), or more than seventy-two square miles. One such grant included 400 arpents (about 300 acres) of land above the mouth of the Lamine River in present-day Howard County in central Missouri that included a salt lick, later called Mackay's Saline. Zenon Trudeau awarded him this land on May 31, 1797, and Mackay himself surveyed it and prepared a plat map dated December 2, 1804.

Perhaps because he was consumed by his duties as commandant and by other business interests, he neglected to meet the minimal requirements for land confirmation, and the Spanish government never confirmed this grant. The lick later passed into the hands of two of Daniel Boone's sons, Nathan and Daniel Morgan, and it attained fame not as Mackay's Saline but as Boone's Lick. Mackay also accumulated land north of St. Louis, one of his holdings consisting of 16,665 arpents (14,177 acres) along the banks of the Cuivre River in present Lincoln and St. Charles Counties, Missouri. The Cuivre River flows into the Mississippi near the town of Old Monroe upstream from St. Louis.[47]

Other land Mackay owned included the future site of White Haven, which for a time was the home of U.S. president Ulysses S. Grant. (The locale today, in the town of Affton, a suburb of modern St. Louis, is encompassed by the Ulysses S. Grant National Historic Site, a unit of the National Park Service.) On May 31, 1797, in St. Louis, Mackay wrote a letter to Zenon Trudeau asking for a concession of land on the Bonne Femme River (in present-day Boone County, Missouri) and on numerous other plots in and near St. Louis. Trudeau directed Antoine Soulard to plat the land, but this concession was not confirmed until 1833, eleven years after his death.[48]

On February 24, 1800, forty-year-old James Mackay took a bride, seventeen-year-old Isabella L. Long, a resident of San André but a native of Virginia and the daughter of John and Elisabeth Benit Long. The bride was Protestant, whereas James asserted he was Catholic. The wedding took place at St. Charles Borromeo Catholic Church in St. Charles. This vertical log building was the first religious institution in that town. No trace of the structure remains today. Nothing is said of James's original religious persuasion in the marriage record, but it is more than likely that a conversion to Catholicism was made when he became a Spanish citizen and an employee of the Crown. The couple had ten children: John Zeno(n), Eliza Lucie, Julia, Catherine May, Julia Jeanne, Georges Antoine, Amelia A., Isabella L., William (Guillaume) Robert (who died in childhood), and James Bennet. The many descendants of the couple today are widely scattered over the United States.[49]

During the next two decades, Mackay acted in a wide variety of capacities. He was a deputy surveyor for his friend Antoine Soulard, the former Spanish surveyor general; he was appointed by Gov. William Henry Harrison as one

Fig. 28. Mackay's Saline, known today as Boone's Lick, in Boone's Lick State Historic Site, Missouri. (Undated photo from a glass-plate negative, collections of the Missouri Geology and Land Survey, Missouri Department of Natural Resources, Division of State Parks, Jefferson City)

of the first judges of the Court of Common Pleas and Quarter Sessions; he served as justice of the peace; and he became a valued informant and map source for Lewis and Clark. Mackay and Antoine Soulard remained close friends and, indeed, were coexecutors of the estate of Zenon Trudeau in June 1816.

Of his private life we know almost nothing, but one of his descendants apparently was the source for the statement that he was "a fine musician, and brought with him from Scotland a violin and flute," the former having "been in use so long that a hole was worn through it by the friction of the chin." In 1819 Mackay built a handsome home on the south side of St. Louis worthy of his stature in the community; it is reputed to have been the first brick house built in the city.[50]

Despite his fame and reputation, Mackay's wealth was not secure, for titles to his extensive Spanish holdings never were clear, and a man named John Baptiste Charles Lucas became the bane of his life. Lucas attempted to disprove Mackay's Spanish land grants and then buy them for himself. Indeed, Mackay's vast holdings became a major temptation for him, so much so that he literally hounded Mackay beyond the grave in pressing claims for his land.[51] At varying times some of the Scot's holdings were noted in the *Missouri Gazette* as being delinquent in taxes, and he often placed notices in that newspaper warning people not to cut timber on his property and demanding that settlers vacate his land if they had no legal right to be there.

Mackay remained the commandant of St. Charles until the Louisiana Purchase. His prominence as a citizen did not lag after that sale, and in 1816 he was elected as a representative of St. Louis County in the legislature of the Missouri Territory.[52]

James Mackay died "after a painful illness of a few days" on March 16, 1822, at the age of sixty-three. He had explored by horseback, foot, canoe, and pirogue more of western North America than any other resident of what was soon to become the State of Missouri; in the United States, only William Clark could equal his breadth of geographical experience on the continent. A glowing obituary, appearing in the *St. Louis Enquirer* on Saturday, March 23, reflected the esteem in which he was held by his fellow citizens of St. Louis.[53]

At the time of his death, Mackay was living in the two-story brick home he had built two years earlier, just south of the city limits and near the Church Street Bridge, which spanned the creek that carried runoff from Chouteau's Mill Pond. (The location today is about ten city blocks southwest of the Jefferson Memorial Expansion Arch.)[54] He was buried in a small cemetery just south of his home, a cemetery that has now vanished and lies in part beneath modern

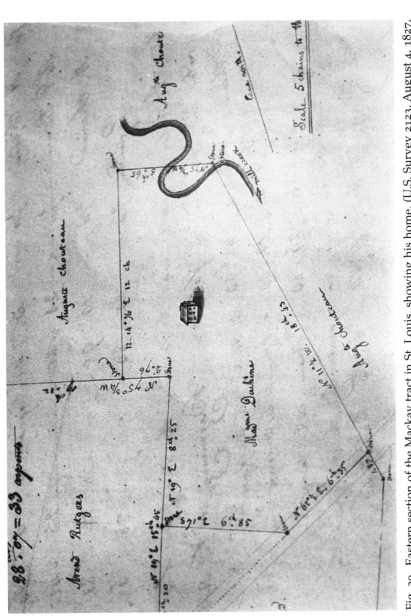

Fig. 29. Eastern section of the Mackay tract in St. Louis, showing his home. (U.S. Survey 2123, August 4, 1827, Recorder of Deeds, St. Louis. Mo.; courtesy Thomas C. Danisi)

Interstate 55. His gravesite too has disappeared. After his death his property was purchased by John Mullanphy, but his home later became the Convent of the Sacred Heart; the house is no longer standing. A man of his esteem and reputation in the community certainly must have had a portrait made, but none is now known. His name is memorialized in St. Louis today only by a two-block-long street that recently was renamed Mackay Place.

Coincidentally, Mackay's obituary in the *St. Louis Enquirer* appeared on the page immediately before one of the series of famous advertisements that William H. Ashley addressed "To Enterprising Young Men" to ascend the Missouri River to its source. (Ashley also had placed the same ads in the *Missouri Gazette* and the *Missouri Republican* in February and March.) Ashley had joined forces with his friend and neighbor Andrew Henry to sponsor an expedition into Blackfoot Indian country along the distant upper Missouri River.[55] The competition for the fur resources of that region and in adjoining Canada was heating up: even in Canada the bitter competition between the Hudson's Bay Company and the North West Company had led to their merger in 1821. In the years prior to his death, Mackay must have heard a great deal about the commercial excitement that was taking place in the region he had once explored, and surely he entertained many of its participants in his home in St. Louis.

John Evans's Fate

Whereas James Mackay attained an enviable level of prominence and affluence after his return, co-leader John Evans fared poorly. His dream of finding the lost Welsh Indians among the Mandans had been quashed. Only days after his return from the upper Missouri, he despondently wrote to Dr. Samuel Jones on July 15, 1797, "Thus having explored and charted the Missurie for 1800 miles and by my Communications with the Indians this side of the Pacific Ocean from 35 to 49 Degrees of Latitude, I am able to inform you that there is no such People as the Welsh Indians." Extracts concerning the fabled Welsh Indians from this and other reports by Evans appeared in publications throughout the United States and in at least one journal in Wales.[56]

Evans did not prosper as did Mackay. Zenon Trudeau was prepared to provide him a land grant, and he asked Evans to search for a plot of land that he would like. Evans chose a location on the upper reaches of Zenon River (present-day Hubbell Creek, a south-flowing stream south of present-day Jackson, Missouri) and petitioned Trudeau for ownership. He was becoming despondent (or philosophical) at this time, manifested in a statement that he made on the "shortness of life and the frowns of Delusive fortune." Historian Gwyn Williams tells us that Evans was busily employed at Cape Girardeau through the winter of 1797–98, helping Americans settle in the area just northwest of Cape Girardeau. Evans, however, soon became discouraged and left the area, and before July 18, 1798, he went to live in St. Louis, where he became a guest in the home of Jacques Clamorgan.[57]

Sometime in 1798 Mackay, perhaps accompanied by Evans, traveled to New Orleans to seek employment for his former lieutenant. Mackay praised Evans as "a virtuous young man of promising talents undaunted courage" and perseverance. The visit and recommendation must have impressed Gayoso de Lemos, who "placed him [Evans] in a Comfortable situation at New Orleans" and probably was seeking a position for him when Evans died in May 1799. Gayoso de Lemos, indeed, had taken the Welshman into his own home and was anxious to reward him.[58]

We do not know why the Spanish were so generous to Mackay and so niggardly toward Evans, but certainly his poor health was a factor. Those who knew Evans in New Orleans were concerned about him, and one of them, Daniel Clark (a clerk in the office of Gayoso de Lemos), spoke of him as "being for some time deprived of his reason. Chagrin and disappointment in his Views contributed, I fear, to hasten his end." We have some information on his last days in a letter that Gayoso de Lemos wrote Mackay from New Orleans on May 20, 1799: "Poor Evans is very ill; between us, I have perceived that he deranged himself when out of my sight, but I have perceived it too late; the strength of liquor has deranged his head; he has been out of his senses for several days, but, with care, he is doing better; and I hope he will get well enough to send him to his country."[59]

John Thomas Evans died later that month at the age of only twenty-nine, just two years after his return from the Mandans, during an outbreak of malaria in New Orleans. Illness and, if one is romantically inclined, a broken heart, brought Evans to his end. The location of Evans's grave is unknown, and since he died during an epidemic, he may well have been interred in an unmarked mass grave. There was good reason for Daniel Clark to speak of him as "being for some time deprived of his reason," for the effects of chronic malaria are severe. Evans's illness on his way to St. Louis in 1793 surely was an attack of malaria, which can recur repeatedly and even kill its victim. But when Gayoso de Lemos spoke of liquor having "deranged his head; he has been out of his senses for several days," he was misreading symptoms of the disease. A severe case of malaria can mimic mental illness and drunkenness; the more plausible explanation for Evans's demise is chronic malaria, not alcoholism.[60]

Some romantic revisionist historians, clinging to the old myth that the Welsh Indians were real, have suggested that Evans himself, on the demand of the Spanish, refuted evidence that the Mandans were Welsh. Why would he lie? It would of course be in the Spanish interest that reports of British (that is, Welsh) Indians in their territory were denied once and for all. And the testimony of a Welshman who had journeyed to the very frontiers of the New World would be a priceless testament. Gwyn Williams suggests that Evans's letter home may have been censored, for Evans was of course still firmly in Spanish hands. Such perjury, Richard Deacon asserts, would have been ample reason for the Spanish to offer him land and employment as a surveyor.[61] The fact there were no Welsh Indians to find makes such attacks on Evans's integrity little more than character assassination.

Evans's discovery and reports hardly stifled the legend. Stories of Welsh Indians continued to circulate widely in the following years. It was still fresh in many minds in 1832 when western traveler and renowned artist George Catlin again tried to prove a Welsh presence among the Mandans. It was still taken so seriously later that century that Jacob V. Brower attempted to suppress the myth in his monograph, *Mandan*. Brower had begun collecting Mandan artifacts from their village sites in North Dakota in 1896 "to be used in ascertaining whether there was or is any foundation for the statements made by Mr. Catlin that the Mandan people were descendants of a Welsh ancestry. . . . Industrious archaeologic explorations and study covering a period of nearly ten years . . . have absolutely failed to secure one single fact to sustain Mr. Catlin's contention." Nor has any archaeological confirmation of their presence ever been detected in the century following Brower's investigations. But even his statement did nothing to stifle the Welsh legend. That the Welsh Indians were said to have "white skins, blue eyes, blond and even red hair [was] a surprising ethnological change for Madoc's colonists, being Welsh, must mostly have been swarthy and black-haired."[62] Myths are immortal, however ludicrous and anachronistic.

Today, even some Indians of Mandan descent on the Fort Berthold Reservation have accepted the Madoc myth, and the fraud is being kept alive by some Welsh and other romantics. (It is also reinforced on television, as in the 1997 British Broadcasting Company "documentary" *Before Columbus*, produced by Sunstone Films.) Myths are indeed immortal, while the accomplishments of once-historical figures like James Mackay and John Evans are all but for-gotten. These shadowy figures nevertheless live on, their deeds memorialized not in statues but in the minutiae of local histories.

FATE DISPOSES

Both men certainly earned the respect and admiration of Spanish officials. Gayoso de Lemos's allusion to "these two valuable subjects" as "the two most famous travelers of the northern countries of this continent," however, was a short-lived accolade.[63] The turn of the nineteenth century was a time of breathtaking change: Spanish Upper Louisiana and St. Louis were acquired first by the French, then by the Americans. Lewis and Clark were dispatched to the Pacific; their explorations became national news, and they were trans-formed into national heroes. The accomplishments of Mackay and Evans were nearly forgotten as the fame of the American explorers gripped the new nation. Even the images of the two men have been lost, if they were ever made, for there are no known contemporary portraits of either of them.

The Mackay and Evans expedition was the single most important probe into the North American Great Plains prior to Lewis and Clark. The geogra-phical information they gathered remained the best available for the region until 1805, when William Clark sent a map of what was to become the western United States to Washington from Fort Mandan.[64] The much earlier explora-tions of Pierre Gaultier de Varennes, the Sieur de La Vérendrye, and his sons in the northern plains (1738–43) and those of Francisco Vásquez de Coronado in the southern plains (1540–41) also were important French and Spanish entradas into the West. The La Vérendryes had visited the Mandans and Arikaras in present North and South Dakota, and Coronado had visited the village Indians of central Kansas.[65] But these travels had little effect on later history, and more to the point, their discoveries remained essentially unknown in American circles until the twentieth century; Jefferson and his expeditionary team had no knowledge of what these men had seen and recorded.

Lewis and Clark will remain giants in the history of the exploration of western North America, but that luster should not be permitted to diminish the accomplishments of their predecessors, the two now-shadowy expatriates from Great Britain. Truly, James Mackay and John Thomas Evans had marched "with long strides upon unknown soil" and paved the way for the first half of the transcontinental journey of the Corps of Discovery. They were, after all, the first English-speaking explorers known to have penetrated the wilderness that Lewis and Clark would bring to the attention of the world, yet their well-deserved monuments exist only in the dusty footnotes of historians of the American West. No memorial exists for them in either the United States or in Wales, although in all probability the accomplishments of the duo are more celebrated today in Wales than in the land where their deeds came very near to becoming legendary.

Selected Documents, 1796–1822

The following primary documents written by participants represent the bulk of those that provide a contemporary record of the Mackay and Evans expedition. Most of the documents may be found in A. P. Nasatir's monumental *Before Lewis and Clark*, but these have been augmented by texts from rare or hard-to-obtain published sources and from the archives of the Hudson's Bay Company, Manitoba Provincial Archives, in Winnipeg, Canada. Other documents not reproduced here provide only marginal supplementary data on the expedition. These sources are cited in the body of the text.

DOCUMENT 1: MACKAY TO CLAMORGAN, PLATTE RIVER MOUTH, OCTOBER 24–27, 1795

By means and individuals that go unmentioned, Mackay dispatched a letter written at the mouth of the Platte River to Jacques Clamorgan in St. Louis. In this extract, which contains the first of his calendar of events along the river, he advised the Missouri Company officials— fruitlessly as it turned out—of his views on how the trade in this region could profit by changes in trading policy. He was ignored. Reprinted from Nasatir, *Before Lewis and Clark*, 1:351–54.

To Messrs. Clamorgan and Reyhle, directors at St. Louis.

I arrived here the fourteenth of this month after a forty-four days' march. The bad weather and one of the pirogues of my convoy, which has continually filled with water, delayed me, and will delay me in reaching the Mahas.

I must recommend to you never to load your barges or *voitures* too much and always to have at the head some leaders of ability. I ought not to [have to] tell you, nor to forewarn you, of the indispensable necessity of having a person possessed of a great talent with the Indians remain at the post of the Mahas at the head of your operations. You know that this is a place of importance for the new commerce and for communication with the Mandans.

I am informed at this time by the Othos that the pirogue which left in the month of April last, in order to go to the Mandans, consigned to Truteau and conducted by Léquiyé [Lécuyer] is at the Poncas where the merchandise has been pillaged. The one named Breda whom you dispatched after him must have arrived too late to give aid and take possession of it.

If the Company is to continue its commerce in this distant country, it is absolutely indispensable to have the village of the Othos in your power. Otherwise, your pirogues will be more or less pillaged each year. I have promised them that you will have a fort built among them next year, in order to protect them against their enemies; and that they would have many guns for their hunt; for they complained of not having a fourth of that which they have need. In these two types of promises, I hope that you will not make me out a liar, seeing that the first, under the guise of favoring them, will serve to hold them in check, and that the second is absolutely inseparable from our interests. I have contracted this obligation with them, on condition that they behave well towards the agents that you will send them and toward the boats which might ascend to the Mandans. They have decided on the spot where they wish the fort to be built—at the entrance of the Platte River, where they intend to place their village. This situation will be advantageous. The agent that I have placed there for the trade with them will apprise you of their conduct, and of means of subjecting them to our interests. If it should occur that the Othos do not keep their word and behave themselves badly, deprive them of all help the next year. We will gain much from this by showing them that their need depends absolutely on the good will of the Company, and that, in default of us, they must no longer count on the aid of other traders, each accustomed to lie to them in pursuance of his own interests. But if their conduct is honest remember well to carry out my promise. You can not conceive the difficulties one has in passing through this nation, in spite of the presents we must give them. The chiefs have no command, and this nation is so rough that one has trouble to move them, even in their own interest. They complain that Motardi, Quenell, and the other traders who have come among them for several years, have spoken so much deceit, have cheated so much, and have made them so many promises of which not one has ever been fulfilled, that they wish to believe nothing now without seeing. To tell you the truth, they are in a kind of anarchy which will lead them to become dangerous enemies of all the commerce of the Upper Missouri. [This danger will increase] if this post continues to be open as usual each year to all types of traders who are only interested in the present, and do not worry about the future.

I am satisfied enough with the equipment of my whole convoy, but I wish that you had given me better interpreters for the Maha. Many of those people at St. Louis who think they understand the Indians and who on that basis, wish to be sent out to the [Indians], when they arrive here, are only children. We need some good, shrewd interpreters.

If the government, as well as the merchants, do not take combined measures for the continuation of the commerce in the Missouri, by prohibiting the entrance of those who are capable of breaking away or eluding them, this country is lost for all time, both to His Majesty and to his subjects. The commerce of foreigners on the one hand and the bad behavior of our traders on the other are enough to throw all the nations into insurrection and anarchy at once. Only one year is necessary for that; but how many would be necessary to restore them to order and submission?

The Othos desire that the same agent whom I left them for the trade be continued. He appears to be well-liked there; consequently will be more than any other capable of leading them to our purpose, for [which is] the passage to the Upper Missouri of the boats, which could not escape them, due to the continual stationing of various strong parties, hunting all along the banks of the river, where they will establish themselves more than ever, in order to intercept our communications—whenever they are tempted to do so by their usual inclination to do evil—now that they know of our new enterprise. If the government does not grant the Othos to you as the key to our distant interests, it is absolutely necessary to purchase [that trade] from those men who might be [its] proprietors, if, however, you think that we might be able to sustain the increase of expense. Otherwise, we must retire [withdraw] as well as we can from the career of discoveries, and renounce now, rather than later, our ruinous [enterprise].

In case the favors of the government are distributed far enough in advance to us, so that we may have them, and arrange at our pleasure the absolute needs of all these nations, through whom we must pass, do not fail to give at least two swivel guns to the agent of the Othos, in order to have the fort that you will have built there respected.

This will especially please that nation, since it will consider them a protection against an attack by their enemies.

27th of October, eight leagues above the Platte River.

This morning six men belonging to the Company and coming from the Poncas arrived at my camp. They belonged to Lecuyer's expedition or that which Antoine Breda was leading which you had sent after him, but which arrived too late to help him. This autumn the Poncas killed a Ris who was coming as a messenger [*en parole*]. I am much afraid that I will experience great difficulties in passing through this nation next spring to reach my destination. The thing which has just happened to our merchandise has entirely destroyed our stock, and I do not know how to replace it.

Tabeau, one of the *engagés* of Lecuyer's expedition, not only should be deprived of his wages, but also severely punished, in order to serve as an example to the future. He is an infamous rascal. Lecuyer, the leader, who has not had less than two wives since his arrival among the Poncas, has wasted a great deal of the Company's goods, even as you will see by the account which I have received, and am sending to you.

I have a difficult task to fill, but I do not lose courage. Next spring I will inform you of all that I will have done.

DOCUMENT 2: MACKAY'S JOURNAL, OCTOBER 14, 1795–JANUARY 18, 1796

The following narrative is the first of two first-person narratives of James Mackay's expeditionary experiences on the upper Missouri River. Unfortunately, it begins only after the party reached the mouth of the Platte River a month and a half after leaving St. Louis, and it includes nothing of his trek through northeastern Nebraska the following fall or his return to St. Louis. We gain from this fragment all that we know of the construction of Fort Charles, details of the interaction between Mackay and the local tribes that took place there that winter and the following spring, and his attitudes toward British traders in the area. This narrative is reprinted from Nasatir, *Before Lewis and Clark*, 1:356–64.

October 14, 1795

On this day I reached a place one league below the mouth of the Chato River [Platte]. I camped in that place in order to visit the Othochita [Otoes] and take fresh provisions there. On the following day I reached a place one-half league above the said river, in order to construct a house for the wintering of the traders whom I left there on the 20th day [of the same month] following. The principal men of said tribe arrived to the number of sixty. On the following day I assembled the chiefs in council, in order to chide them, and point out to them with vigor, their evil conduct with the whites whom their Spanish Father had sent to them for the purpose of furnishing them the goods that they needed. Convinced of the truth, they gave me weak excuses. I made them perceive the consequences that might result, if they did not change their conduct immediately. Their reply reduced itself to saying in effect that they would change their conduct toward the whites, if I kept the word which I gave them; in respect to the fact that they had never, until the present, had any but traders who deceived them by telling them all sorts of lies, in order to get hold of their furs, only giving them [in return] great promises which never were fulfilled. I told them that their Father, in his desire to render them happy, had formed a Company to supply them with all the things that they needed; that this Company, of which I am here as its agent, would never deceive them in its promises, if they behaved well toward us. In that case the Company will have a fort built for them next autumn, in order to protect them from their enemies; in which there will always be merchandise, without them having to go to the English, who desire to deceive them more than do the traders. After this speech which I made to them through my interpreter, I perceived that it had not failed to produce an effect, because, although they were accustomed to pillaging the boats destined for the most distant posts, they absolutely did not touch a thing, except what I wished to present to them of my own accord, and they did not even dare to enter into any of the pirogues laden with goods for the Mandans and other tribes of the Upper Missouri.

I remained eleven days with the Othoctatas in order to make them some suggestions and attract them by means of mildness to our side. I imagine that my harangues will not fail of success. If such be the case, will Your Excellency remember to fulfill the promises which I have made to them. In case of the contrary, I beg Your Excellency, for the future prosperity of the Company, to deprive them entirely of everything they need. In that regard Your Excellency may interest yourself with the Government, in order that no one may be permitted, for the general welfare of the country, to penetrate to this tribe, whether for trade or hunting. Without doubt Your Excellency will find the necessary aids for preventing those who go to the Panis and the Lobos [i.e., Loups, or Wolves] and Abenaquies from giving them any aid secretly, by passing through any other road than the abovementioned Chato River, on whose banks are located the Othocatatas who would doubtless pillage them. In case that their conduct with the Company permits the sending of goods next year, I must inform Your Excellency that at least one hundred guns are needed for this tribe, without which, as has happened, the returns will be very doubtful, since three-fourths of the tribe are idle all winter, so that the trader suffers a considerable loss in furs.

On November 3, the son of Pájaro Negro [Blackbird] who was in St. Louis the past summer, came to meet me with a band of young men, as soon as he heard of my speedy arrival among his tribe. His father sent him to protect me from the obstacles that I might meet on my way. They accompanied me overland for the two day's march to their village. The cold and the snow have been so great that my voyage has been retarded considerably.

On November 11, I reached a place below the village of the Mahas with the great chief Pájaro Negro who came to meet me a day's journey distant. He showed great affection and friendship to me, as did the other smaller chiefs who accompanied him. As soon as we reached the village, he placed a guard in my boats to watch all night, and to see that his people did not take anything.

On the 12th and 13th, the weather was so bad that I was unable to unload my boats. Consequently, during these two days, I held long conferences with the Great Chief on various important matters, both for the Government and the Company. I found him in those conferences, to be a man full of experience, intelligence, and capacity.

The rigor of the weather having moderated on the fourteenth, I unloaded my berchas and pirogues and placed them in security.

On the 15th I assembled the Great Chief and the principal men of the tribe in Council, and represented forcibly to them the bad conduct that they had observed toward the traders who went to their tribe. I told them that their Spanish Father sent me, in order to ascertain whether they had any intention of changing their conduct; that, if they acted well, a Company, formed for the Missouri, would never allow them to want for anything, and they would not need to have recourse to the goods which the English bring annually; that then they would have whites with them all the year whom the Company would leave for their needs; and that, if they did the contrary, they would be deprived of everything.

They answered me that the traders who had been sent to them hitherto were very bad, and the last of all the men whom they had seen among the nation [were the worst?]; but that now they were satisfied at seeing in their village a white chief whom they could call their Father, on whose word they could count; and that they would behave better if they had many guns with which to hunt, in order to support their families. Now Your Excellency may see how important it is for the Company to supply them with arms and ammunition, although it may be necessary to make a present of it to them; for when a savage has many furs, trade is easy with him; but when he has few, quite the contrary happens.

This village contains seven hundred warriors, and I have promised them two hundred muskets for next year, even though this number is too few for the number of men there. If this is not possible, Your Excellency must expect a general discontent on their part, and the sure loss of the trade that might be carried on with them. They care for only the English guns and not the French ones which burst in their hands, and good powder, for bad powder is regularly sent to them, which is of the greatest consequence for the hunt. Today I began to trade with them, which I stopped at the setting of the sun. That has surprised them greatly, since they are accustomed to trade at all times, and when they please, without considering the convenience of the trader. I announced to them that the first one who dared to violate my intentions would repent it, and that threat has had all the effect that I desired.

The Mahá Chief, their sovereign, is the soul of the village and many others. He appears to be my sincere friend since my arrival. He is more despotic than any European prince, and, in addition, is most courteous and of great talent. His present conduct toward us must not be forgotten, since he is the one to decide whether our communication remains open and free.

November 21, the Indians, contented and satisfied, went to hunt and it was necessary for me to send part of my men with them, as there were no provisions in the village, for maize was totally lacking, and there was not one-half minot of this grain which has not cost me a blanket [*demande*]. This scarcity of food retards a trifle the construction of the fort which I am building, but will not prevent me from finishing it soon. I saw a Ponca chief who left on the next day for his village. Through him I have sent severe reprimands to his tribe. I showed him my *bercha*, and, in order to mortify him, I told him that it was charged with goods for the purpose of going to his tribe; but that since his whole village was incapable of anything else than doing evil, I would punish it by never sending any more, and depriving their women and children of whatever they needed; that now they would get no guns or powder with which to get their living; that they would die of hunger; and that the Great Maha Chief would unite with me, in order to avenge me. After hearing my long and severe speech, he could do naught but shed tears over the conduct of all his tribe.

After that, I declared a plan to the Maha prince in regard to my voyage to the head of the Missouri, presenting to him the famous medal and *patentes* which pleased him greatly, especially as they were accompanied by the present given him by the Company. However he was surprised at not finding in it a large flag, telling me that the English always gave one with the medal, and that though they had frequently invited him to accept both, he had never made use of either of them, abandoning them to his children, in order to make it clearly understood by the English that he had no intention of abandoning the friendship of his Spanish Father. However he believed that the latter did not appreciate the affection which he professed for him, and besides, it would be shameful for him not to receive a large banner and a present proportional to his importance, since the English, his neighbors, constrained him to receive their friendship and their presents which they send him annually, in order to attract him with this tribe to the San Pedro River, in order to trade his furs with them. Thus they insinuated to him and his tribe the scant heed that their Spanish Father gives them, who did not love them, while, on the contrary, their English Father was so affectionate to them, and showed such great generosity to the red men that they would not lack anything, if the latter would give him their hand. In proof of this they annually receive presents in his name, both for the support of their families and to clothe them; and, notwithstanding, without heeding so many promises on the part of the English, and without trusting to the deceits of the traders of the Missouri, he only desired to conserve the friendship of his Spanish Father, for his heart was happy because the latter had sent a chief to visit him, and truly make him recognize his word, which so many other traders had hitherto falsified, deceiving him. On that account he would endeavor to assist me in all my plans, especially in opening a road of communication with the Upper Missouri, and reuniting the various tribes, who could oppose the conservation of the peace and tranquillity. He himself in person with his tribe would go to convoy my boats to the Ricaras, if there were the least sign of danger or opposition. He would reduce the Poncas to their duty, avenging the wrong and injury which they had committed against our boat, conducted by Lecuyer. He ended his speech with testimonies of regret over the past, protesting that his heart had never been happy until this day, and that he saw in me his true friend whom his Father had sent him, and that he was speaking the truth.

Seeing that I was constructing a fort in which large guns, that is to say canons, were to be placed, in order to protect their tribe from all those who refused to enter into relations of peace with them, I told him that, reckoning on his good actions in favor of the Government and of the Company, he could be absolutely sure of their friendship and protection against all those who attempted anything against his tribe or who disturbed the good harmony and concord in which his Father, the Spaniard, desired to have them live. Consequently, he would send them two great guns next summer, in order that they might be placed in the fort, and they would remain there continuously, both to protect them from their enemies, and to open the road from [to] the Upper Missouri; in regard to which, I hoped that he would keep his promise. He answered me that the Master of Life was witness of his promise and of mine, and that the universe would see which of us two failed. On that score we, respectively, reiterated our promises, and took as witness of our oaths the sun which lighted us. Afterward he asked me for my patents or despatches from his Great Father, the Spaniard, who lived on the other shore of the Great Lake, that is, in Europe, in order that he might see whether, as I told him, I was the bearer of his word among the tribes of this continent, in order to direct, assist, or compel to peace the evil tribes, whether by mildness or by force, clothing me with his authority in order that I might clear the road of the Upper Missouri, and remove all the obstacles placed there by the tribes through whom one must cross, in order to reach the proposed end; that, without it, he would not dare to undertake a task which could grieve his Father, the Spaniard, who would be angry with him and with me, if he did it without his permission. I replied to him that in such a question he demanded from me prudence to convince him that the word which I gave him had already been announced to him three months before by our Spanish Father, Don Zenon Trudeau, by means of his [i.e., the chief's] son when the latter presented himself in St. Louis in the month of July last; that the desire of our Great Father was to make all the red men happy; and that our Father, Don Zenon Trudeau, was entrusted with this commission, in consequence of which he had sent a member of the Company to announce to him his word. I told him that our Great Father, being informed that for many years the tribes of the Missouri were showing evil inclinations against the whites and his trader, had made him take the precaution of sending a chief to him, who, showing him his friendship and good intentions, should be supported by his power through the likeness which he has with him in authority, judgment, and sentiments, to bring the tribes of the Upper Missouri to reason, who might oppose themselves to the good-fortune and tranquillity of those who desire to live in good fellowship with the whites, who can at any moment deprive them or procure for them whatever they need when they judge it suitable. He answered me that his Father, the Spaniard, as well as myself, has always charged him to be good; that such have always been his intentions; but that he did not have sufficient ascendency among the other tribes to cause himself to be perfectly respected, without making presents to their chiefs, in order to show them his superiority by means of his power and generous conduct, which he had with the common chiefs of each tribe, whenever they assembled to form a pact of friendship and alliance among these same tribes and the whites, who came sent by his Father, the Spaniard; that, in such case, the presents would make them adopt my advice and my counsels, receiving the calumet of peace and the Spanish flag, notwithstanding how ordinary it might be; for the Sioux, as well as other tribes of the northern district, who, receiving only silk flags from the English, would cause them to despise ours. Notwithstanding, he is about to send to seek out all the tribes, but he tells me that this cannot be done without great presents of cloth, blankets, kettles, tobacco, guns, and ammunition; [and] that he was not asking for these articles for himself, but rather for me, and to make it known that his Father, the Spaniard, loved and showed his affection to the Indians who behaved well. He told me that he would send [*correos*] posts this winter with a calumet to all the tribes, especially to the Sioux, who frequenting the Missouri between the Poncas and Ricaras, might be induced to come to see me next spring, with the object of adopting measures and means of peace with them, and opening forever a free communication with the Upper Missouri; [Thus] allowing my boats to pass without committing any outrage; but that, when they came, presents would be necessary, and he had nothing to give; consequently, it would be necessary for me to stand the expense; [also] that a large flag was absolutely necessary for him, in order to distinguish him from the other chiefs, and to lend importance to his mission.

A few days after my arrival here, I received information that a Ponca had killed a Ricara, who had come to his village with a message last summer. This occurrence, together with the previous outrages committed upon the Sioux, placed great obstacles in my passage. I hope, nevertheless, with the aid of the Maha prince and with a number of presents suitably placed, to find a means of opening the road, although these two casualties will occasion reiterated expenses, and will retard our march.

November 24. Not having had any information of the Ricaras, and not being able to send by water, I had a well-accompanied detachment set out overland with the order to go to said tribe, and inform me of what is happening there. But, unfortunately, they had to return, because they discovered a considerable band of Sioux who were hunting buffalo, at sight of whom, believing that their lives were not safe, they came here on the sixth of January, on which occasion the great Maha Chief renewed his promise to me that he would assist me to succeed in my enterprise.

On the 29th, the Prince came to visit the fort which was being built in a plain located between the very village of the Mahas and the Missouri River, on the shore of a small river which flows into the latter, and is fairly navigable. This plain is very extensive, the land excellent, and never inundated by the waters. The location of the fort seems to have been prepared by nature. It is in a commanding district, which rises for a circumference of about one thousand feet. It looks on the shore of this river, as if to command the rest of the area. I have established my settlement and my fort there, although at a distance from the woods; however, the horses of the Prince are at my service.

On December 18, the Missouri had ice, and on the 19th of December, was completely frozen.

January 18, 1796

Two Mahas arrived from the hunt.

[The clerk or official who copied or translated the original journal here merely synopsizes]. Note: *Monsieur* Mackay goes into great details here on the pillage of the Poncas, which it is useless [for me] to mention, since I had already given information of what happened among this tribe, because of the bad conduct of the conductor [of the boats], Lecuyer.

He [Mackay] continues after to say: The autumn having passed, I ordered Antonio Breda, our commissioner, to hide the rest of the goods, which the Poncas took, and which remained in their village, announcing to them that I was sending for them in order to give them to the Mahas. Antonio Breda executed my orders faithfully. That mortified the Poncas greatly who counted on taking possession of the rest, which is very little, at whatever price they wished. I hope that in the future, it will not be so, if my friend, the Great Chief, the Maha Prince keeps his word with me. He expressed himself as greatly irritated against the Poncas. Some time ago he sent them a message, and he himself, accompanied by the chiefs of their village, is going thither to make them deliver the few furs that they have obtained in their hunt, on account of what they have stolen. I believe that his journey will not be without success, and, although he will not bring back more than a little from a hunt to which no necessity incited them, the consequence will always be advantageous for the interests of the Company, since it will serve as an example to the other tribes in the future. And then, Your Excellency, do not doubt that my friend the Maha Prince has a right to a generous recompense [and this will] increase our losses and expenses. But it is important to sustain the authority of this intrepid man by the ostentation and particular distinction of elevating him above every other chief, especially for his personal interest. This man deserves consideration, and must not be abandoned, for I consider him one of the chief instruments of our projects. A present worthy of him and one of consideration ought to be given him annually. It is necessary to give this on account of his character, and does not Your Excellency believe that that is a small thing; it is better to fatten one who rules as a despot over various tribes, than to feed many at less expense. However, the Government must come to our aid, for he is one of the chief supports for our navigation. The intrigue of the English, in order to attract the tribes of the Missouri, has planted such deep roots among these peoples, that it is necessary to apply a prompt remedy, unless we desire to see ourselves exposed to abandon this magnificent country which must some day be a great resource to the prosperity and glory of the state.

The presents which the English send annually to the various tribes, where they can penetrate, give much weight to their intrigues. The English of the river of San Pedro had concluded among this tribe last autumn the construction of a fort for them on the shore of the Missouri, which they were resolved to maintain against all resistance. My arrival here changed all their projects, while the presents which I have given to the tribe and to my friend, the Prince, have turned them in such manner to his favor, that they have made disappear and have destroyed the measures agreed upon with the English.

The latter have at present thirty pirogues of goods on the San Pedro River within four days' journey from these places. They sell the blanket for two furs, and the rest in proportion. It is probable that they will come this spring to visit the Missouri. The jealousy that has always existed among the merchants of Canada, has not only ruined trade with the Indians in their territory, but also with the vassals of His Catholic Majesty on the western part of the Mississippi to which they daily penetrate.

The traders of the River of Monigona [Des Moines] have sent twelve horses, laden with goods, to trade with the Panis and the Loups [Lobos, or Wolves] on the Chato River. The caravan crossed the Missouri in the month of last December. I would be glad to be able to deal them a blow on their return.

Since my arrival here, I have sent many messages to various tribes, which has occasioned me great expense, although that is inseparable from our interests, if we wish to open up communication for our explorations and to reach the Pacific Sea, we must expect to see them increase daily, until our project sees complete fulfillment. We need the aid of the Government to resist and destroy the ambition of foreigners. Otherwise, the ruin of the Company in its infancy is inevitable.

Through my fear of arriving late next summer at the Mandans, I am going to send out a detachment within a few days under the charge of *Monsieur* Even [Evans], until he meets Trudeau [Jean Baptiste Truteau who was in command of the first expedition of the Company], who must have already constructed his fort among the above-mentioned Mandans, if he has experienced no opposition on the part of the English, who have had the audacity to unfurl their banner there. *Monsieur* Even is to leave there with picked men, who occasion us great expense, in order to visit the head-water of the Missouri and *La Cadena de Rocas* [Chain of Rocks, or Rocky Mountains], and follow to the Pacific Sea, according to the enclosed instructions of which he carries a copy.

DOCUMENT 3: MACKAY TO EVANS, FORT CHARLES, JANUARY 28, 1796

From the beginning of their first expedition, the goal of the Missouri Company was to reach the Pacific coast and open trade there for the Spanish. Mackay's instructions to John Evans for the conduct of his excursion from Fort Charles to the Mandans and then to the Pacific Ocean were both long and, ultimately, impossible. His guidelines on how Evans was to travel and comport himself with the American Indians he encountered must have been based on his prior experiences in the Canadian West. Reprinted from Nasatir, *Before Lewis and Clark,* 2:410–14.

Instructions, given to Jean Evans for crossing the continent in order to discover a passage from the sources of the Missouri to the Pacific Ocean, following the orders of the Director of the company, Don St. Yago Clamorgan under the protection of His Excellency, Mgr. le Baron de Carondelet, Governor-General of the Province of Louisiana, and Mr. Zenon Trudeau, Lieutenant-Governor of the Province of Illinois.

During the time of your absence from this place and during your journey to reach the Pacific or any other place, you will observe the following instructions:

Art. 1. From the time of your departure from this fort until your return to the place where I will be living on the Missouri, you will keep a journal of each day and month of the year to avoid any error in the observations of the important journey which you are undertaking. In your journal you will place all that will be remarkable in the country that you will traverse; likewise the route, distance, latitude and longitude, when you can observe it, also the winds and weather. You will also keep another journal in which you will make note of all the minerals; vegetables; timber; rocks; flint-stone; territory; production;

animals; game; reptiles; lakes; rivers; mountains; portages, with their extent and location; and the different fish and shellfish which the waters may contain. You will insert in the same journal all that may be remarkable and interesting, particularly the different nations; their numbers, manners, customs, government, sentiments, language, religion, and all other circumstances relative to their manner of living.

Art. 2. You will take care to mark down your route and distance each day, whether by land or water; in case you will be short of ink, use the powder, and for want of powder, in the summer you will surely find some fruit whose juice can replace both.

Art. 3. In your route from here to the home of the Poncas, trace out as exactly as possible a general route and distance from the Missouri as well as the rivers which fall into it; and although you cannot take the direction of each turn and current of the Missouri, since you go by land, you can mark the general course of the mountains which will be parallel to each bank. You will observe the same thing for every other river [landmark] which you may see during your journey, whether river, lake, ocean, or chain of mountains which may effect your observations.

Art. 4. Be very accurate in your observations concerning the nations, their size, their dwellings, their land, and their productions.

Art. 5. Mr. Truteau, our private agent, whom you will find among the Ricara or Mandanes, will give you what you are bound to need. You will consult with him on the most practical route and he will give you guides that he will obtain from the nations where he will be.

Art. 6. You will take for provisions on your route some well-skinned dried meat, which is very nourishing and a very little quantity of which satisfies your appetite as well as your fancy. Always lay up some provisions and keep them for a last resource.

Art. 7. You will take heed not to fall in with some parties of savages, where there are neither women nor children, as they are almost always on the warpath. It would not be prudent to appear at any nation if you can avoid it, unless it be in their villages; and in spite of this be well on your guard. You will never fire any guns except in case of necessity; you will never cut wood except with a knife unless it should be strictly necessary; you will never build a fire without a true need, and you will avoid having the smoke seen from afar, camping if it is possible in the valleys. You will not camp too early and will always leave before daybreak; you will always be on guard against ambushes and will always have your arms in good condition, changing the tinder evening and morning, and you will never separate them from you or place them in the hands of the savages. When you will see some nations, raise your flag a long way off as a sign of peace, and never approach without speaking to them from a distance. When you will enter a village, stop and ground arms at a small distance until they come to receive and conduct you. Appear always on guard and never be fearful or timid, for the savages are not generally bold, but will act in a manner to make you afraid of them. If, however, they see that you are courageous and venturesome they will soon yield to your wishes. You will recollect that the pipe is the symbol of peace and that when they have smoked with you there is no longer any danger; nevertheless you must beware of treason.

On all occasions be reserved with your detachment as well as with the savages; always give to your conduct the air of importance and show good will toward everyone white or red.

You will carry with you some merchandise, consisting of various small articles suitable for new nations, in order to make presents to the savages which you will discover; but you must be careful of your generosity in this even as in all other things which you carry and bring with you, seeing that the time of your return is uncertain.

Say to the savages whom you will meet on your route that the white people, who come to meet them, speaking of our Company, still have many other kinds of merchandise for them. If they wish to trap some beaver and otter in order to give the skins in exchange for whatever they need, then it is necessary to show them the process of stretching and cleaning them in the same way as all other kinds of peltry are treated.

If you discover some animals which are unknown to us, you will see that you procure some of this kind, alive if possible. There is, they say, on the long chain of the Rockies which you will cross to go to the Pacific Ocean, an animal which has only one horn on its forehead. Be very particular in the description which you will make of it if you will be unable to procure one of this kind.

When you will have crossed the sources of the Missouri and will have gone beyond the Rockies, you will keep as far as possible within the bounds of the 40th degree of north latitude until you will find yourself nearly within the 111th to 112th degree of longitude west meridian of London. Then you will take a northerly direction to the 42nd degree of latitude always keeping the same longitude in order to avoid the waters which probably are destined to fall in California. This might induce you to take a route away from the Pacific Ocean. After all, you cannot travel over so great an expanse of land without finding some nations which can inform you about rivers which go toward the setting sun. Then you will build some canoes to descend these rivers, and will watch carefully since there may be some water falls on them which can carry you away, since the distance in longitude from the Rockies to the Pacific Ocean ought not to be above 290 leagues, perhaps less, which condition makes it necessary for the rivers to be very rapid or else to have great falls, in comparison with the distance which exists between the sources of the Missouri which runs over a space of about 1000 leagues to come to the sea by entering the Mississippi whose waters are very violent. This is so if it is true that this chain of mountains serves to divide the waters of the west from those of the east.

Mark your route in all places where there will be a portage to pass from one river to another or from one water-fall to another by cutting or notching some trees or by some piles of stones engraved and cut; and take care to place in large letters Charles IV King of Spain and below [that] Company of the Missouri, the day, the month, and the year when you do this in order to serve as unquestionable proof of the journey that you are going to make.

There is on the coast of the Pacific Ocean a Russian Settlement that they say is to the north of California, but there is reason to believe that it is not the only one and that the nations of the interior of the continent ought to have knowledge of it. Then, when you will have discovered the places that they inhabit, you will cease to make any sign of taking possession, for fear of having spring up with these foreigners any jealousy which would be prejudicial to the success of your journey. You will not neglect any interesting observations on the sea-shore and, although there may be some things which do not appear to merit the least attention, nevertheless, in a journey of this nature, everything is sometimes of great importance. Do not fail to measure the rise of the sea in its ebb and flow.

As soon as you will have visited the sea-shore sufficiently, you will return from it immediately, with as much vigilance as you can to this place, or to the spot where I may be at the time, either among the Mandanes or elsewhere. You will take steps to return by a different route from that which you have taken on your way out if you believe it practical; but mind that if you find the route by which you will have passed rather straight and easy for traveling by water in canoe or other craft, it will be wiser to return by the same route, and, in case there are portages to make from one river to another or from one rapids to another, see whether the place permits the forming of a settlement.

If, however, you are obliged to search for a new passage to return here from the sea-shore, you will return from any latitude where you may be when you will take your point of departure to forty-five degrees north latitude; and on your entire route you will examine the most penetrable and practical places for foreigners to the north country in order to give an account of the means of forming a settlement and fort there to prevent their communication [coming into this territory].

On your journey you will not forget to tell every nation that you discover, that their great father, Spain, who is protector of all the white and red men, has sent you to tell them that he has heard of them and their needs and that, desiring to make them happy, he wishes to open a communication to them in order to secure [provide] for them their necessities; that for this purpose, it is necessary that all the redskins be peaceful in order that the whites can come to see them; and that, instead of making war, it is better that they should slaughter game with which to feed their women and children.

In your orders be strict with your detachment and take care that no offense is committed against the nations through which you pass, especially by the connection that they may seek to have with the women, a thing which is ordinarily the origin of dissatisfaction and discord with the savages.

Whereas the journey is of very great importance not only to His Catholic Majesty, his subjects and the Company especially, but even [also] to the universe since it ought to open a communication of intercourse through this continent, it requires the clearest evidence to prove the truth of everything and to leave no doubt about the boldness of this discovery.

Take care, above all, to bring with you a collection of the products of the sea-shore: animals, vegetables, minerals, and other curious things that you can find, especially some skins of sea-otters and other sea animals and shell-fish which cannot be found in any fresh water. A portion of each will be an unquestionable proof of your journey to the sea-shore; but, if you can find there any civilized people who wish to give you an affidavit of your journey in whatever language they speak, this will be an additional proof of the validity of your journey.

If on your return, God has disposed of me or I have left the place of my residence on the Missouri, you will not deliver or show to anyone anything relative to your discoveries, but you will go immediately to St. Louis to deliver all your papers, plans, charts, and journals to *Monsieur* Clamorgan, Director of the Company. In case he is dead or absent, you will deliver them to whoever will represent him at the time, but in the presence of *Monsieur* Zenon Trudeau, Lieutenant-Governor or any other who should represent him, keeping in your possession a copy of each thing to be delivered and sent to the said *Monsieur*

Zenon Trudeau by a safe means; this always in case Messieurs Zenon and Clamorgan should be dead or absent.

(Signed) Mackay.
Fort Charles, January 28, 1796

DOCUMENT 4: EXTRACTS OF MR. EVANS'S JOURNAL

Evans's own account of his upriver venture is the only detailed report of his journey and stay among the Mandans. Reprinted from Nasatir, *Before Lewis and Clark*, 2:495–99.

8th June 1796. After having received from Mr. James McKay Agent of the Missouri Company the necessary Instructions, as well as men, Provisions and Merchandizes, I sat off from the Missouri Company's Establishment at the Maha Village, to ascend the Missouri as far as the Pacific Ocean—After a long and fatiguing voyage I arrived the 8th of August following at the Village of the *Rik,ka,ras* on the South Side of the Missouri, 250 leagues above the Mahas, I here met with some difficulties to get along, the *Rik,karas* would not permit me to pass their Village and carry my Goods to those nations that reside above them, they said, they were themselves in want of Goods &c. Finding then that all my Efforts were in vain, to get on, I was obliged to stay among them. Some Weeks after my arrival, several Indians of different nations particularly the *Caneenawees and Shayenns* habitants of the Rocky Mountains, came to the village to see me. Their Chief in a very long and prolix discourse expressed to me the joy they felt to see the Whites, they assured me of their Love and Attach-ment for their Great father the Spaniard and for all his children who Came in their Country. Judging it necessary for the better insuring the success of my enterprise to take Possession of the fort built at the Mandaine Village by the English Traders of Canada, I succeeded in persuading the *Rikaras* to let me go so far as there with a few Goods. The 23 Sept. I arrived at the Mandaine Village which is situated about 10 leagues above the *Rikara* on the Same Side (south) of the Missouri, there I was visited by the *Munitarees* and *Wattassoons* whose villages are only a league above those of the Mandaines, those nations as well as the Mandaines received me very cordially. I gave their Chiefs in the name of their Great Father the Spaniard, who inhabits the other Side of the great lake and in the name of the Great Chief who inhabits this Side of the great Lake and also in the name of the Chief who resides at the Entrance of the Missouri, the Flags and Medals that were given me for that purpose by Mr. McKay. Besides those medals & flags I made some small presents, which were received with the greatest of Satisfaction, and testified their acknowledgment in the most expressive manner, promising to observe the most sincere attachment to their great father the Spaniard and his Chiefs, who have Sent to them from so far, their children the Whites with such great marks of their Esteem and of their Charity for the Red People; they added that they would hear what I had to say and had sent to all their Brothers, and hereafter they would follow my Counsels on all occasions—The 28th September in Conformity to the orders I had, I took possession of the English forts belonging to the Canada Traders, and I instantly hoisted the Spanish flag which seemed very much to please the Indians—

The 8.th of October arrived Several men at the Mandaine Village belonging to the Canada Traders that I have above mentioned, they had brought some Goods with them, not having a Sufficiency of men I did not strive to oppose their arrival, nor of their goods: I nevertheless found a means to hinder their Trade and some days after absolutely forced them to leave the Mandane Territory, I sent by them in the North the Declaration that I had received of Mr. McKay: forbidding all strangers whatever to enter on any part of his Catholic Majesty's Dominions in this Quarter under any pretext whatever—The 13th March 1797 Arrived at the Mandaine Village from the North, a man named *Jusson* accompanied by several Engagees he was sent by the English traders, with Merchandizes as presents for the Mandaines and neighboring nations, so as to be able to break off the Attachment & fidelity they had promised to his Majesty and his Subjects, the said *Jussom* and those who Accompanied him advised the Indians to enter into my house under the Mask of Friendship, then to kill me and my men and pillage my property; several of the Good Chiefs who were my friends & to whom *Jussom* had offered presents; refused them with indignation and shuddered at the thought of such a horrid Design and came and informed me of the Whole. Nevertheless the presents that *Jussom* had made to the Indians had tempted some of the inferior class, who joined him to execute his abominable Design, happily for me his presents had not the same Effect with some of the Principal chiefs, to undertake Such an enormous crime, therefore many of those chiefs Came to my house to guard me and were resolved to die in the attack if any should be made; this Resolution disconcerted entirely my enemies and totally put an End to their infamous Design. Some days after *Jussom* came to my house with a number of his Men, and seising the moment that my Back was turned to him, tried to discharge

a Pistol at my head loaded with Deer Shot but my Interpreter having perceived his design hindered the Execution—The Indians immediately dragged
him out of my house and would have killed him, had not I prevented them—
this man having refused me Satisfaction for all the Insults he had given me,
Moreover disgusted on the ill success of the Execution of his Black Designs,
left the Mandanes with his men some days after and returned to his people
in the north and bring them the News of his Ill success—I found out by all I
could learn that the Intentions of the British Traders were Not to spare trouble
or Expence to maintain a fort at the Mandaine village Not that they see the
least appearance of a Benefit with the Mandanes but carry their views further,
they wish to open a trade by the Missouri with Nations who inhabit the Rocky
Mountains, a Trade, that at this Moment is Supposed to be the best on the Continent of America.—The general Course of the Missouri from the Maha Nation
to the Mandaines is near about North West, it runs for the greatest part of this
space, on a Rocky Bottom & Gravel, it is Shut up like in Each side by a chain
of Rocky Mountains and of Sand, which in some places coming so near to one
another reduces the Breadth of the River to about 500 toises. The Land on both
sides of the River is at one time Mountainous & barren and at other times even
& fertile, but in the Back part a tree can hardly be found. The best Quality of
Land is found in the Mandaine Country, this quality of Land Extends itself
on the West as far as the East chain of the Rocky Mountains which are about
170 league to the West of the Mandaines, it is at these Mountains where the great
Meadows and Prairies terminate the Country then begins to be Absolutely
Covered with trees, even upon the Rocky Mountains and it is probable these
trees extend to the Pacific Ocean.—The Country from the Mandaines to the
Rocky Mountains is well watered by different Rivers that empty themselves
in the Missouri, particularly from the South West, many of these Rivers are
navigable for Boats of one or two tons burthen. The largest of these Rivers is
the Rivière Blanche (White River) Whose mouth is About 80 leagues above the
Mahas the River *Shayenn* 70 leagues higher—The River LaBombe about 65
leagues higher and the Yellow Stone River, (Rivière des Roches Jaunes) about
120 leagues further and about 80 leagues above the Mandaines, all these Rivers
Come from S. W. of Missouri and there is also a River that comes from the N.
W. and which joins the Missouri near the mouth of the Yellow Stone River, they
call it Rivière dufoin (hay river) they say it is a large and fine River in which
there is More Beaver and Otters than in any other part of the Continent.

 Mr. Evans measured the Missouri near the Village of the Mandaines And
he found it 500 toises large, which confirms me in my Opinion that the Sources

of the Missouri is much further off than what it is imagined, although the Indians who inhabit at the foot of the Rocky Mountains have but a Confused Idea of the upper parts of the Missouri; Nevertheless after all the Information I could collect, it appears that the Missouri takes it source in abt. the 40th deg. North latitude from Whence it Runs to the North (between the chains of the Rocky Mountains) as far as the 49th deg. Latitude that thence running East, it falls over the East chain of the mountains in the great plains across which it runs to the East till it reaches the Maindaines—There is no other fall, in the whole Course of the Missouri, but where it falls over the Rocky Mountains, in the plains, as I have said before. This fall it is Said, is of an astonishing height, from the Situation of the Country and the Meanders of the River I suppose this fall to be 200 leagues West of the Mandaines. Among the innumerable Numbers of different animals found on the Rocky Mountains, there is one that is really an Object of curiosity, it is near about the height of an Elk, its hair is like to that of a fallow Deer or Buck, it carries its horn like those of a Ram, but turned in a spiral form like a trumpet and of an immense size, some have been found of 8 inches Diameter in their thickest part. This Animal lives but about 10 or 12 years, by reason of their horns, that advance foremost, as to hinder the Animal from eating Grass, which is its only food, so that he becomes obliged to die for hunger; The Indians make spoons, cups &c of the horns, some of the latter are so large as to contain a Sufficiency to satisfy the Appetite of 4 men at a meal—There are also found on the Rocky Mountains, Ermines, and a kind of Wild Cat, whose skin is of a great Beauty, it is spotted as that of a Leopard; it is probable there are in those unknown Regions many other kinds of Animals which are not found in the other different parts of America. As to the manners and Customs of the Indians I found they differ but little one from the other. In the different parts of the Continent across which I voyaged, all that I could remark was, that the nations who had but an imperfect knowledge of the Whites (being yet in a State of Nature) were of a softer and better Character. Whilst those who have frequent Communications with the Whites appeared to have contracted their vices Without having taken any of their virtues.

DOCUMENT 5: GRANT TO EVANS, RIVER TREMBLANTE, OCTOBER 8, 1796

In this letter Cuthbert Grant, factor at the North West Company's Fort Tremblante on the Assiniboine River, is responding to Mackay's declaration of May 27, 1796, forbidding British trade in Spanish territory. He

asks for the return of property belonging to his employee, René Jusseaume, and assures Evans that he has no further plans to trade
along the Missouri. Reprinted from Nasatir, *Before Lewis and Clark,*
2:460–61.

Mr. Evans
  Sir

As I find by Mr. James Mackay's letter that the Missisourie is Chartered
by a Company I wish to withdraw what little property the N. W. Co. has their,
indeed it has been my wish for some time past as we have lost a good deal
of money by Mr. Gousseaume [Jusseaume] whome we have employed in that
business. I therefore beg you will be kind enough to deliver the bearer all the
property of whatever kind belonging to the said Gousseaume that may be in
your possession, he has wrote you himself to that effect he is to pass some
time here himself to settle his affairs but means to return to the Missisourie in
[the] course of next month. I am very much obliged to you for your kindness
in lending a man to Mr. Mackay as this is the last time any of our people will
go that way I hope you will be kind enough to give your assistance in getting
away the men who has deserted from us in that quarter and should any of
your people ever come this way you may depend upon it they shall be delivered up to you I hope you will be so good as send me an acct. of everything
you will deliver the men belonging to Gousseaume and you will oblige.
  Sir
  Your most obedient
  Humble servant
  Cuthbert Grant

DOCUMENT 6: SELECTIONS FROM
BRANDON HOUSE JOURNALS, BY JAMES SUTHERLAND,
OCTOBER 25, 1796–NOVEMBER 12, 1797

The journals kept by the factor at Brandon House, a Hudson's Bay
Company post along the Assiniboine River, preserve some of the cor-
respondence that John Evans had with the British traders in Canada.
The originals, in the Hudson's Bay Company Archives, Manitoba
Provincial Archives, are reproduced with permission. Reprinted from
Thomas D. Thiessen, "Excerpts from the Brandon House Post Journals

Relating to Trade with the Mandan and Hidatsa Indians, 1793–1830," 33–49. Entries between October 25, 1796, and November 12, 1797, are by James Sutherland; the entry for November 12, 1797, was penned after his death by his successor, John Mckay.

The first letter contains the text of Mackay's prohibition by the Missouri Company of British trade along the Missouri River; the remaining correspondence concerns the British response to this edict and their continuing desire to carry on that trade. On October 23, Sutherland tells Evans that his prohibition on British trade will not affect the Hudson's Bay traders, but he presumes there would be no objection to those traders obtaining horses and other materials not associated with the fur trade with the Missouri Indians.

B.22/a/4, fo. 14
October 25, 1796

Mr. Demurier and more Canadians arrived from above, as did also Mr. Neel McKay from the Mandals, one of his men deserted from him; Recd. the following declaration from Mr. McDonnell, Just come from the Mandals

To all British Subjects Trading to the interior parts of N. America, and all other persons of whatever description who may frequent the said Country

His Catholic Majesty having granted to his subjects (the Missurie Company) that part of his dominions siteuated on both sides of the Misssurie to its Westernmost source and from its source to the coast of the Pacific Ocean, and North to the hight of land, that divides the waters that empties into the Missurie from those that falls into Hudsons Bay

I am therefor commanded to forbid and prevent all forigenrs whatever (especially all British subjects) who are or may be in the neighborhood of his Majestys dominions to enter any part of the said Chartered dominions on pain of confiscation of all such offenders propperty and such punishment as the law of the land may inflict on the conveyars of such propperty—

Given under my hand at Fort Charles this Twenty seventh day of May Anno Domini

One thousand Seven hundred and ninety six.

Signed

J. Makay

To all who it may concern

B.22/a/4, fo. 16d
October 26, 1796

Wednesday. Snowy weather. The men variously, Stept over to the other House [River La Souris] to hear more news from the Mandals Mr. McKay says the above Mr. J. Mackay has not yet arrived at the Missurie, only a party under a Mr. Evans a Welsh Gentleman, who has come to explore the source of the River as far as the stoney mountains if not to the Pacific ocean in search of mines, some of which is already found, Mr. Evans permitted him to return for this time without confiscation of his property, but on promise of not returning again with any more goods.

B.22/a/4, fo. 20–20d
November 23, 1796

As Canadians are going from the other House to the Mandals I sent the following Letter to Mr. Evans, barly out of couriositey

Dear Sir

Your written declaration dated Fort Charles 27th of May last has come to our hands, forbiding all British Subjects from Trading at the Missurie, this may effect the Traders from Canada, but very little those from Hudsons Bay—I should be glad however to know if we may be permitted on any future ocasion to visit the Mandals and Trade Horses, Indian corn and Buffalo robes which articles we suppose to be unconected with the Fur Trade and consiquently expect you will have no objections to, with wishing to hear of your health and Success I Remain

Dear Sir
Your Obedient Humble Servant
        J. Sutherland

B.22/a/4, fo. 28–28d
January 16, 1797

Canadians arrived from the Mandals. Recd the following letter from Mr. Evans in answer to mine of the 23d of Novbr last

Fort Makay Decbr. 20th 1796

Dear Sir

Yours of the 23d of Novbr. came to hand, and I thank you. The Trade from the N. to this place being prohibited I believe cannot effect neither the Hudsons Bay nor the N W Company as they never met with anything but loss from this quarter

As to your requist concerning admission to Trade Horses, Indian Corn and Buffalo Robes it is not in my power to answer you on that head. But I have reason to believe the latter will not be permitted as it is the staple Trade of this Countrie, but however you will be propperly inform'd after the arrival of the Agent General and Lieutt. Mooroch at this Post, having no entertaining news of any kind to transfer to you,

I remain
Dear Sir
Your Obt Servt.
J. T. Evans

B.22/a/4, fo. 29
February 25, 1797

Saturday. Cloudy, cold weather, the men hauld home the Cattle kild yesterday, About 3 P.M. Slettar and Yorston arrived from the Mandals with 4 Sleds well loaded with Furs, Mr Evans was as cival to them as his wretched sitewation would admit, but would not permit them to Trade with the natives, he Traded all the goods they had and gave them furs for it, but would have bought it much cheaper had they dealt with the natives who was highly displeased with Evans on that account and some thinks will endanger his sitewation. On their arrival there they were met by above 300 Indians who carried their Sleds on their Shoulders into the vilage, so fond were they of the English. Mr. Evans hoisted his Spanish flagg

B.22/a/4, fo. 35–35d
April 14, 1797

Friday (Good Friday) snow all day Watson and Easter making a bed place for the Master upstairs, 2 making a door for the flesh house, the door of which has been stolen either by the Indians or Canadians. News from the Mandals, Mr. Evans and the Canadians was almost at fisticuffs in atempting to prevent them from Trading with the natives, and not having goods himself set all the Indians out against him, he was obliged to set off with himself and all his men down the River for Fort Charles, the Indians threatning to kill them if they refused being greatly exasperated against them for preventing the Subjects of G. Britain from comming to Trade with them. The Indians has plenty of Furs still among them particularly the Grovanders (or bigg bellys) and are determined to visit this place nixt fall or at least to meet Traders halfway, what a pity there is not men and goods to encourage this Trade—

B.22/a/5, fo. 18
November 12, 1797

Slater, Louttit, and Christian making ready to set off for the Mandles some time this night. I understand McDonell has sent one Cadian to the Mandles in company with a number of Assiniboils to learn if the Spaniard is there. I do not hear of any more Canadians being off, nor do I believe any will go until he returns. No one is sure whether that part of the Misoures where the Mandles are, belongs to the Spaniards. Mr. Evans last year acknowledged that the little Souris River was out of the line of the Spaniards, the head of which is but one days Journey from the Big Bellies. There my men will deposite the goods they have until they see how affairs stands in the villages. There is a Mr Thompson in the Canadian Service who is expected here every day to go to the Mandles and take the Latitude and Longitude of the place. I hope James Slaters reckoning will run to 300 at least. Thompson must stand at go.

DOCUMENT 7: SUTHERLAND TO EVANS, BRANDON HOUSE, JANUARY 21, 1797

This complimentary letter from James Sutherland to Evans at "Fort Makay" asks the Welshman when he expects his superior to join him at the Mandan villages, and, like John Macdonnell, Sutherland sends him small gifts of flour, sugar, and chocolate. He also asks what plans Evans may have about further exploration to the west and if his "agent general" is the same James Mackay that formerly traded on the Assiniboine (or Red) River. The Canadians' lost horses had been stolen by Arikaras. Reprinted from Nasatir, "John Evans," pt. 3, 587–88.

Brandon House, 21st Jany 1797
Dear Sir

By the arrival of Mr. De Murier [Desmarais] and men the 16th Inst from your place, I was favoured with yours of the 20th of Dec.br last, and although personally unknown to me, as a Country man I was pleased to hear of your wellfare.

It is not my business to enquire into the causes of your exposing yourself to such dangers and difficulties which from hearsay attends your situation [?], it is sufficient for me to suppose that your future views doubtless are adequate to your present hardships.

The Canadians, having lost their Horses the first or 2d night from the Missourie obliged them to leave their property behind, which they now return for, two of my men out of curiosity accompanys them to see the Mandan Villages and to try if they can purchase a Slave girl, they bring no goods with them of any consequence—I send by them 6# of Flour, two cakes of chocolate, and a little sugar as a small present, supposing you to be none [run?] out of such articles I am only sorry I have not any thing more worthy of your acceptance as my stock is near out, but hope you will take the will for the deed—all the news from this quarter you can hear from our men, a little from you would be very acceptable such as when you expect the gentlemen from below to your post, what your future Intentions are with regards to exploring further up the River &, if your agent general be the same Mr James Makay who was formerly a Trader here in Red River. These perhaps you will say are tedious enquiries, but I suppose a gentleman of your abilitys can have no objection to any communication which does not immediately concern the Companys affairs in so remote a country. I remain with Respect

Dear Sir
Your obedient Hble Servant
James Sutherland

DOCUMENT 8: MACDONNELL TO EVANS, RIVER LA SOURIS, FEBRUARY 26, 1797

Macdonnell's missive to Evans begins politely enough in response to the latter's "very acceptable favor" sent to him, but as he writes he warms to his dislike of the Welshman's mission. Asserting that "British subjects are not to be tried by Spanish laws," he doubts the legitimacy of Evans's trade prohibitions and scolds him for his use of Canadian deserters. Reprinted from Nasatir, *Before Lewis and Clark*, 2:502–3.

Dear Sir

I recd. your very acceptable favor by the two English Lads yesterday, & note the contents—As you mention that the men inform'd you of the cause of my not writing you I shall be silent on that head—I'm soray to find that the Horses are fallen in the hands of the Panees—they could not have gone to a worse place—as for ye Books be so kind as to deliver them to Jussoume.

As you speak much of La France in your letter I have ventured to send him with Jussome, he could not be in better company, as you seem to be as invete-rated against the one as the other; they have an opportunity of vindicating themselves from your aspersions in your own presence—Let their conduct be what it will you would expose yourself in acting agreeable to your letter—British subjects are not to be tried by Spanish laws, nor do I look upon you as an officer commissioned to apprehend oth[er] people's servants, if you serve a chartered Comy. why not show the Spanish Governors Orders, decla-rations, denounciations or manifestos, prohibiting others from frequenting that country—Then shall we leave you in peace—Be at bottom of it who will most certain I am [of the belief] that there is most complicated vilainy carried on this year at the Missouri in many respects witness the debauching of Chay last fall, and the offering 200 dollars to the English men arrived yesterday—If we were nearer neighbours than we are we could easily come to an explanation.

It must give any sensible person no grand idea of your Missouri Company making use of such *Canaille* [scoundrels] as I have reason to think many of your *Engagees* are by judging of the remainder by La Grave Garreau Chayé &c Such as are not run aways from here are Deserters from La prairie du Chien & other places in the Mississippi La France goes with Jussaume to help the latter in bringing his family [I am]—D[ea]r Sir Your very Humble Servt

John Mcdonnell

DOCUMENT 9: JOHN EVANS TO SAMUEL JONES, ST. LOUIS, JULY 15, 1797

On his return to St. Louis, John Evans wrote to Samuel Jones in Philadel-phia to report the details of his journey to St. Louis and up the Missouri

River and the failure of his mission to find the Welsh Indians. This letter is in Papers of Dr. Samuel Jones, Pennepek Baptist Church, Lower Dublin Township, Mrs. Irving H. McKesson Collection, Historical Society of Pennsylvania, Philadelphia; reprinted from Williams, "John Evans's Mission," 600–601.

Dear Sir,

It is such a long time Since I have departed from your part of the world that I am ready to supose every body of my friends in that Part of the world has given me up for dead. However after inumerable escapes from red and white people and [having] undergone some of the severest hardships I supose was ever experienced, I am, by kind providence, preserved to have the pleasure of informing you as well as my other Friends of some particulars of my Travells.

After I left your house I proceeded to Fort Pitt where I was kindly treated by a certain gentleman of the name of Dr. C. Wheeler for a month to wait for the high waters. From thence we was transported in a few days to Limestone in Kentucky. From there I travelled by land to Bourbon and from there through the wilderness to Cincinata. Here I was kindly received by General Wilkinson. Stayed here a few days. Then departed for Louisville and from thence for New Madrid in Louisiana. Here I was kindly received by Mr. and Mrs. Rees my countrypeople, but was obliged to take the Oath of Allegiance before I could be permitted to debark.

Now begins my life of misery and hardships. In 10 days after my arrival was taken by a Violent and Intermiting fever succeeded by a delirium. Thank God for friends, for I was paid the greatest attention to in my Sickness by my kind land lady and all the Great People of the place, otherwise I should have died in the greatest poverty, having undertaken the Voyage of discovery up the Missouri upon the Strength of my own Pockett which consisted of a dollar and three quarters when I left your house.

In 2 months my fever abated a little, my resolution and anxiety for proceeding on my voyage being hightened to such a pitch that I was determined to risk my life, feeble as I was, and start for the Illinois in Company with one man only. Neither of us knew the road, if it could be called a road, for it was so overgrown with grass that in several places not the least trace was left. However, such as it was, we had the bad fortune to lose it altogether in the Evening of the first day. Now lost in the infinite wilderness of America. Oh unsufferable Thirst and hunger is an amusement in Comparison to this. The parent sun who is so much courted in the northern nations has in this distressing moment turned my Enemy and threatens to beak my brains like a cake and withdraw from me my Pressuous Eye Sight. 3rd day, here my fever returned and my Eye Sight recovering. Came to a country overflowed with water. Travelled several miles in water from the hip to the Arm Pitt amongst a numerous crowd of the bigest water reptiles I ever saw. The 7th day arived at Virgen a Spanish Post in the Illinois. The night before, we slepd within 5 miles of this village, but on account of my weakness which kept me unable of Travelling above a hundred yards without rest, it took us all day nearly to get to the Village. In a miserable situation, I arived bear foot, bear legged and bear headed. Here stayed a day to rest myself. Next day went to Kaskaskia on the American side of the Mississippi where I was kindly received and treated by John Rice Jones, Esq, another Countryman. Here my fever turned nervous and I have been several days neither asleep nor awake.

I arived the same year as I left Philadelphia in the later end of July. Stayed here 2 years to wait for a passage up the Missurie, but that Country being under Spanish government and Engrossed by a Sett of Indian traders, I had no prospect till Christmass 1794, when I was informed of a gent. at St. Louis who was engaged to go up the aforesaid River for three years. Now or never, as I thought, it was my time to make aplication, so I went over the Mississippi. I thought within myself that it was rather a ridiculous busyness as it was a Critical time on Spanish side on account of the report of Clark's armie and I not able to speak one word with any body, they speaking French. However, I went and was taken for a Spy, Imprisoned, loaded with iron and put in the Stoks besides, in the dead of winter. Here I suffered very much for several days till my friends from the American side came and proved to the Contrary and I was released.

In August 1795 I started from St. Louis in Company with James Mackay Esq, Comandant of the Missurie. Wintered with him the same year at the nation Mahas on the Missurie. Here I started with the Indians to the hunting ground, with whom I stayed 25 days and returned to the said Port Maha where I stayed 2 months. In February 1796 started on my voyage to the West but at the distance of 300 miles from the Mahas was discovered by the Enemy the Sioux and obliged to retreat and returned to the Mahas. In June following undertook the same voyage and arived in August safe at the Mandans and Bigg Belly nation 300 leagues from the Mahas and 600 from the confluence of the Missurie with the Mississippi.

Description of the Country. 2600 [sic] leagues from St. Louis is a woody country. Where the Missurie runs through is a bottom from 12 to 18 miles wide. The Missurie in its turns touches some times the hills on the north side. The general run is under the south hills. For 400 leagues, it is full of Islands and receives several Considerable Rivers from R. Platte 190 leagues from St. Louis. Up to the Mahas the Missurie glides along in as curious turns as any River in the known world through a fine meadow as levell as a table 18 miles wide from one hill to the other. A traveller often imagines in going up that he descends the country on account of the curious meanders. From the Panias [Pawnees] to the Mandans 190 leagues, the Missurie by furious and revengefull Power in some far antient time has bursted its way through the mountains and miny hills.

Thus having explored and charted the Missurie for 1800 miles and by my Communications with the Indians this side of the Pacific Ocean from 35 to 49 Degrees of Latitude, I am able to inform you that there is no such People as the Welsh Indians, and you will be so kind as to satisfie my friends as to that doubtfull Question.

In July 1797 I arived at St. Louis after the long voyage of 2 years up the Missurie, Was well received by the Officers of this Please, but I suspect that I shall be obliged to undertake other voyages as dangerous as the former as there has allready Solicitations been made to me by government to undertake a voyage accross the Continent, which voyage I supose will keep me from having the pleasure of Seeing you as I think but very little of a trip to Philadelphia at present, having been so far up the Missurie that it took 68 days to come down with the furious Current of the Missurie.

Dear Sir, present my best respect and friendship to Mrs. Jones and Miss Sally, but I supose I may call her by some other name by this time.

I am, Dear Sir, with due respect, your very humble servant, J. Thomas Evans.

Do not fail writing by the first opportunity. Direct to be left at William Arundel, Esq., Cahokias, Illinois.

DOCUMENT 10: EVANS AND RHEES IN THE
GREAL NEU EURGFRAWN (CARNARVON, WALES) 1800

Morgan John Rhees extracted the substance of Evans's postexpeditionary letter and other reports for several American newspapers, including the

New York Daily Gazette and the *(Pennsylvania) Aurora*. Together with a letter from Rhees, the information also appeared in the *Monthly Magazine* for March 1798. It also appeared in the *Greal neu Eurgfrawn*, a Welsh magazine published in Carnarvon, Wales, in 1800. Again, Evans's sad conclusion was that "there are no such people [Welsh-descended Indians] in existence" anywhere on the continent.

This notice is reprinted from Thomas Stephens, *Madoc*, 107–8. The introductory paragraph below was translated by Dr. Geraint Evans of the University of Wales at Aberystwyth. The remainder of the text follows Stephens's translation, which omitted that paragraph, except for the use of "Seaux" (Sioux) and "Puncas" (Poncas) as spelled in the original Welsh version.

History of John Evans's Journey in America

Concerning the six years (or more), that have passed, it was announced publicly that a tribe of Welsh Indians had settled on the banks of the Missouri river; and that a young man of the name John Evans (who was born at Bettws Garmon, near Caernarfon) had taken in hand the task of locating the said tribe.

After overcoming various obstacles, he started on his journey from St. Louis, in August 1795, in the company of Mr. James Mackay, superintendent of the trade upon the Missouri river; and towards the end of the year he landed among a tribe of Indians called Mahas, about 900 miles up the Missouri, and wintered there. In February 1796 he recommenced his journey to the West, and advanced about 300 miles farther; but, finding that the Seaux Indians had assumed a warlike attitude, he returned to his previous station. In the following June he started again on the same route, and in August he landed among the Mandans and "the populous nations," 900 miles from the Mahas.

"The Missouri," says he, "for 780 miles from St. Louis, meanders and assumes a beautiful fern-like form; it runs through delightful dales, and sometimes runs on each side of the hills as smooth as a board; but its general inclination is southward to the plains for about 1,200 miles. It is full of small islands, and receives various streams, from the Mandas, and the Puncas, which flows for 600 miles. The river (Missouri) has its own way, and rushes impetuously through mountains and hills full of mines."

After surveying and delineating the river for 1,800 miles, he returned with the stream, in sixty-eight days, and reached St. Louis in July 1797, after an absence of nearly two years.

With reference to the Welsh Indians, he says that he was unable to meet with any such people; and he has come to the fixed conclusion, which he has founded upon his acquaintance with various tribes, *that there are no such people in existence.*

DOCUMENT 11: JAMES MACKAY'S OBITUARY, *ST. LOUIS ENQUIRER,* MARCH 23, 1822

James Mackay's death in St. Louis came as the fur trade of the Upper Missouri was being opened up to ever increasing commercial exploitation in the decades following the Lewis and Clark expedition. His obituary, reprinted here from the St. Louis Enquirer (page 3), reveals the esteem with which he was held by the Americans who came to displace the Spanish and French governments of Upper Louisiana.

DIED—On the 16th inst. at his residence near the town of St. Louis, after a painful illness of a few days, JAMES MACKEY, Esq.

We trust that in offering a small tribute to the memory of this worthy citizen, we shall escape the charge of being impertinent or rediculous—imputations that have well attached on divers "obituary notices" of late years. Mr. Mackey's life was one of considerable enterprise—about forty years ago he emigrated from Scotland, the country of his birth, to Canada; he there became engaged in the Indian fur trade, and had occasion to explore the region of the upper lakes and the country as far west as the Rockey Mountains—after some years past in the perilous occupation, he transferred his domicile to upper Louisiana and availed himself of the protection which the Spanish government extended to foreign settlers. By that government he was employed to explore the country watered by the Missouri and its tr[i]butary rivers, a region almost without a civilized man. On his return from that expedition he made a report to the Spanish government, which met its fullest approbation. In remunerations of his services he received a grant of a large tract of Land on the waters of the Missouri, when this grant was made the land was scarcely worth the expense of surveying, and from that moment to the present, the concession, in consequence of the delay of confirmation, has not only been unproductive but has been a positive annual loss to Mr. Mackey. It is to be hoped that the justice which has been so long withheld from the father will not be denied to the mother and the orphan. The Spanish government testified its sense of Mr. Mackey's merits, not only by this grant, but by investing him with different offices of importance, in all of which he was distinguished for his activity, intelligence, and disinterestedness. As military commandant of one of the subdivisions of Upper Louisiana, the duty devolved on him of providing for the settlement of a multitude of American emigrants, who were induced by the advantages which the government and country presented to establish themselves in Louisiana. There are many of them yet alive to bear witness to the kind and honorable manner in which Mr. Mackey conducted himself towards them. On the cession of Louisiana to the United States, he continued to co-operate with the constituted authorities until the second grade of government was organized and Upper Louisiana divided into districts—since that time he has served in the various capacities of Major of Militia, Judge of a District Court, and Representative in the legislature, with credit to himself and advantage to his fellow citizens. It is a consolatory fact that the last moments of his life were worthy of its whole blameless tenor. The perfect calmness with which he viewed his approaching dissolution was the best comment on the character of the man. Neither the illusions of superstition, nor the abstractions of philosophy, could create the bright serenity which marked his latter end—this could only have been the result of a quiet conscience—the best proof of his innocence in this world and his title to happiness hereafter.

Concordance of Physical Features on the Beinecke Library and the Indian Office Maps

W ords <u>underscored</u> on the Beinecke Library and Indian Office maps are in the hand of William Clark. Words in *italics* on the Beinecke Library map are in the hand of James Mackay. The side of the river is given as viewed downriver: (L) is the left bank, (R) is the right bank. Modern island names are taken from U.S. Army Corps of Engineers maps of the Missouri River predating the construction of the mainstem dams in North and South Dakota.

Beinecke Library Map	Indian Office Map		Modern Name
	Name on Map	Translation on Map	
St. Charles (L)	St. Charles		St. Charles
L'habitation (L)	The Habitation		site of two houses on the riverbank
I. au bonhomme	Good man's Island		Bonhomme Island
Taverne (R)	a Cave		Tavern Cave
I. Labadie	Labadie's Island		Labadie Bottoms
R.Dubois (R)	Dubois's River		Dubois Creek
R. au Charotte (L)	Charotte's River		Charrette Creek
R. St. John (R)	River St. John		St. Johns Creek
Island boef	Beef Island		Bouef Island
R. Berger (R)	Shepherd River		Big Berger Creek
R.a la outre (L)	Otter River		Loutre River
Channaill á laponsee (L)	Laponsee's Channel		unknown

River Gasconade (R)	Gasconade River	Gasconade River
Caverne á montbran (L)	Montbran's Cave	Montbrun's Cave
Riv. a Vase (L)	Muddy River	Auxvasse Creek
petite Cedre (L)	little Cedar River	Middle River
Osage River (R)	Osage River	Osage River
Riv. du Cedre (L)	Cedar River	Cedar Creek
R. petit manitou (R)	Little Conjurers River	Little Monitreau Creek
R. au la roche percée (L)	Split Rock River	Perche Creek
Saline (R)	Saline	Petite Saline Creek
R. au la bonne femme (L)	Good Woman's River	Bonne Femme Creek
Riv. a la mine (R)	Mine River	Lamine River
La 1ᵐᵉ prairie (R)	the 1st prairie	unnamed
Les deux R. Charletons (L)	the two rivers of Charleton	Chariton and Little Chariton Rivers
flait(?) Stones (R)	pierre a fleche	Arrow Rock vicinity
La Grande Riviere (L)	[not translated]	Grand River
wacanton ou Endroit des serpents (L)	[not translated]	Wakenda Creek
antient villages des petite Os (R)	antient village of the little Osages	Little Osage village site
antient vill des Missouri (R)	antient vill of the Missouri	Utz village site
vieux fort (L)	[not translated]	Fort Orleans
marais apaquis (R)	Flag Pond	Lake Hicklin
Prairie des Sakias (L)	Sakias Prairie	Sauk Prairie
Prairie du (R)	Prairie	Fire Prairie
L'Eau bleu (R)	blue water River	Little Blue River
Riviere des Kances (R)	Kanses River	Kansas River
petite Riv. platte (L)	Little Shoal River	Platte River, Mo.
Isles des Parques	Two Islands	opposite Leavenworth, Kans.
premier village ant. des Kance (R)	First old village of the Kances	first Kansas Indian village site
2nd vieux village Kances (R)	2d old village of the Kances	second Kansas Indian village site
Prairie de St. Michel (L)	St. Michael's Prairie	vicinity of St. Joseph, Mo.
Riv. Nadawa (R)	Nadouan(?) River	Nodaway River
R. des Loups (R)	Wolf River	Wolf Creek

	R. grand nimaha (R)	Big Nimaha River	Big Nemaha River
	R. Taquio (L)	Taquio River	Tarkio River
	Isle St. Joseph	St. Joseph's Island	near St. Joseph, Mo.
	R. & Chanaille de baton (L)	Cane River & Channel	Nishnabotna River
	petite R. nimaha (R)	little Rivr of the nimaha	Little Nemaha River
	Isle Chauvin	Chavin's Island	no modern analog
	R. Eau qui pleure (R)	Weeping Water	Weeping Water Creek
	I. du tabac	Tobacco Island	Tobacco Island
	du fer (R)	Iron Isld.	no modern analog
	I. des 5 Barrils	five Barrels Island	Nottleman Island(?)
	Premiere Poste de la Compagnie du Missouri (L)	the first post of the Missouri Company	Post of the Otos
	Riv. Platte (R)	Shoal River	Platte River (Nebr.)
	R. de Papillon (R)	Butterfly River	Big Papillion Creek
	Ecore de Aioas (R)	Aiouah Bluffs	unnamed
	R. á Boyer (L)	Boyer's River	Boyer River
	R. des Soldats (L)	Soldier's River	Old Soldier River
	Riv. de Sious (L)	Sious River	Little Sioux River
	Ecore des Cedre rouge (R)	Red Cedar Bluff	west bank of river
	[symbol not labeled (L)]		Fort Charles

Sheet 1

Fort Charles (R)			Fort Charles
	Maha village (R)	Maha village	Omaha Indian village site
Pettit R de Seaux	petite Riv. des Sious (L)	Little Sioux River	Floyd River
R de Seaux	River de Seaux (L)	Sioux River	Big Sioux River
Cape James (R)			unnamed
[unnamed bluffs (R)]			hills at Ponca State Park
Cape clear (R)			Boy Scout Hill
Long cape (R)			Rattlesnake Hill
Cape fair (R)			unnamed
R. au Kenville	Riv. á Renville (L)	Renville River	Vermillion River
R & village Pettite Arch	Riv. & village des petits Os (R)	River & village of the Little Osages [sic]	Bow Creek and Little Bow Creek Omaha village site
white Cape	Cap blanc (R)	White Cape	Campbell's Point
Ecore de Bustaron (L)			unknown
R au Jaque	R. a Jacques (L)	James River	James River

Grand Calumet (R)			Calumet Bluff, Gavins Point
I au Sigo	I. á Sego	Sego's Island	unknown
I au Sable	I. au Sable	Sand Island	unknown
I au bonhomme	I. au bonhomme	good man's Island	unknown
Plumb River (L)			Emanuel Creek
Pettite R au platte au plate	R. White White lime or Paint (R)		Lost Creek
Grand R au pla (R)			Bazille Creek
R que courre / Rapid R (that wanders) (R)	Riv. qui courre (R)	Rapid River	Niobrara River
	village des panis (R)	Panis Village	Ponca Fort
Ponca Island	I. au Panis	Panis Island	Ponca Island
Ponca R & Village (R)	R. des Panis	Panis River	Ponca Creek; Ponca Fort village
long I	Isle longua	Long View Island	unknown
R au brique (L)			
	I. au Basques (L)	Basque Island	Chouteau Creek
Ponca house (L)	Maison de Mr. Trudeau (L)	Mr. Trudeau's House	Ponca House
I au barqu [Boat Island]			Chicot or Big Cedar Island
Spear I			Martha's Island or Pease Island
[unnamed stream (L)]			Campbell Creek
[unnamed stream (R)]			Whetstone Creek
I au cedar	I. au Cedres	Cedar Island	Little Cedar Island
I au Parish	I. de periche	Peter's Island	Hamilton Island
Sheet 2			
I au Vase	I. au vase	Muddy Island	unknown
I au Taurou [Bull Island]	I. Bon	good Island	Pocahontas Island
three islands	Quatre Isle	the 4 Islands	La Roches Island
I au beauff	Isle au boeuf	Buffalo Island	Durex Island
	I. petite	little Island	unknown
[words scratched out] by Clark? (R)]	Vieu Volcano (R)	old volcano	no volcano existed
White River (R)	R. blanche (R)	White River	White River
I au Seaux	Isle des Sious	Sioux Island	unnamed island
I Skunk	I. bete puante	Pole Cat Island	American Island
unnamed stream (R)			American Creek
2 Rivers	I. des deux Rivieres (L)	Island of the two Rivers	Elm Creek and Crow Creek

	Portage des Sious	The Sioux carrying place	unknown
Prospect I			Cadotte Island
lower I	I au bas de grande	Island below the big bend	no modern analog
big bend			Grand Detour
Solitary Island	I. solitaire	Solitary Island	Johns Island
	I. demi-lune	half-moon Island	unknown
Tylers River	R. du vieux Langlois (R)	Old Englishmans River	Medicine Creek
half mast island			no modern analog
[unnamed stream (R)]			Cedar Creek
3 Sisters Island	I. de 3 Souers	Island of the 3 sisters	Dorian Island Nos. 1& 2
Cabrie Island	I. au Cabris	Goat Island	no modern analog
	Mr Louisells House in the Winter 1803 & 4		Loisel's Post
I au Biche	I. au Biche	Elk Island	Fort George Island
Sheet 3			
I au Biche	I. au Biche	Elk Island	Fort George Island
R au high water (R)			Antelope Creek
long reach island			no modern analog
good humor Island			no modern analog
Litle Misssurie (R)	R. petit Missouri (R)	Little Missouri River	Bad River
[symbol labeled "Teton"] (R)			where Lewis and Clark met the Teton Sioux
Lower Ricara Villages & I (R)	village des Panis (R)	Panis villages	Black Widow Ridge Arikara villages
uper [Arikara] Villages (R)			Cheyenne River Arikara village
I Panie			Cheyenne Island
	I de longue vue	long view Island	Mission Island
R de Chyen (R)	R. du Chien (R)	Dog River	Cheyenne River
horse shoe Bend			unnamed bend
Sentenel (R)			Fox Creek, or Charlie Creek
Diamond Island			Fishermans Island
Sheet 4			
I good hope			Pascal Island
I & Village Lahoocatt			Dolphees Island and Lahoocat Arikara village site

Frinship I			no modern analog
Otter River (L)	R. a la outre (L)	Otter River	Swan Creek
R au Morrow (R)			Moreau River
Shaved Island			Blue Blanket Island
R au Corn (R)			Grand River
Marapa R	R. Marapa (R)		Oak Creek
I au Brim			Ashley Island
I Ricaras			Arikara village site on Ashley Island
Kakawissassa or Light Crow (R)			unnamed creek
Parnorni (R)			unnamed creek dividing the Leaven-worth Arikara site
Stone Idol C (L)			Spring Creek
Several litl Swamps (L)			headwaters of Spring Creek
I. au Cock	I au Coc	Cock Island	no modern analog
Pocass or Hay (R)			Blackhawk Creek
Piaheto / Eagle feather (R)			John Grass Creek
W Jaques wintering ground with the Riccaras (R)			location near Fireheart Butte
W Jaques (R)			man's identity unknown
Old Village Chyen (R)	vieux village des Chians (L)	Old village of the Dog Indians	Cheyenne village site
Sheet 5			
[unlabeled stream (R)]			Porcupine Creek
Carp R & Island (L)	I. & R. ou Carp	Island & River of the Sucker Fish	Long Lake or Badger Creek
Bomb Riv (R)	R. a la Bombe (R)	Lebeaume's River	Cannonball River
Jupiters fort (R)			North Cannonball site
the Humitt (R)			unknown
Jupiters house (R)			unidentifiable
sugar loaf (R)			Sugar Loaf Butte
Shepherd & gard. (L)			mouth of Apple Creek
R & I du Couer [scratched out by Clark?] (R)			Little Heart River
Chiss.chect R (R)	R. du Cuivre (R)	Copper River	Heart River

Sheet 6

<u>Wah hoo toon—</u>			unknown
Wind			
Village Chiss.chect (R)			On-a-Slant village
R & I du Coer	R. du Cuivre (R)	Copper River	Heart River
Yellow Ecore: here are human bones of a Large Size (L)			near Double Ditch site
Yellow Ecore (R)			near Cross Ranch
butiful Levell plains			near Washburn, N.Dak.
on both sides of the Missourie (L)			
Mandan Old Village	Village vieux des Mandans (R)	old village of the Mandan	unidentifiable, near Bagnell site
Ricara Village (R)			Greenshield site
Manutaries & Mandans (R & L)			site of the five Man- dan and Hidatsa villages
Track to the Catepoi, etc. (L)			track of trader's route to the Assini- boine River

Sheet 7

Manutaries / Mandans (R)	Hidatsas and Mandans
Shevitoon (L)	unknown
River Yellow rock (R)	Yellowstone River
Village de Boitife (R)	unknown
Gens de Corbeau (R)	Crow Indians
River blanc (L)	Milk River
Shell River (R)	Musselshell River
mountain of eternal snow (R)	Little Belt Mountains?
The fall	Great Falls of the Missouri
Gens de Serpent	Snake or Shoshone Indians
Montagne de roche	Rocky Mountains
<u>Conjecturall</u>	Clark's assessment of details of Rocky Mountains

NOTES

1. BEFORE MACKAY AND EVANS

1. Mackenzie, *Voyages from Montreal*; Thompson, *David Thompson's Narrative*.

2. Jackson, *Jefferson and the Stony Mountains*, 94–96, 121–24.

3. See the documents relating to these expeditions reproduced in Jackson, *Letters of the Lewis and Clark Expedition*, appendix 1. These efforts to reach the Pacific have been recounted many times, but a convenient summary may be found in Jackson, *Jefferson and the Stony Mountains*, 42–62, 84.

4. Jackson, "Some Books Carried by Lewis and Clark," 3–13.

5. Moulton, *Journals of the Lewis and Clark Expedition*, 2:154; Lewis to Jefferson, Dec. 28, 1803, in Jackson, *Letters of the Lewis and Clark Expedition*, 1:155. The first, second, and fourth of these documents are reproduced in "Selected Documents, 1795–1822," docs. 1, 2, 4. Both journals were in French despite the fact they were prepared for the use of Spanish officials. But the Spanish presence in Louisiana was recent and ephemeral, and much of the region's official business was conducted in French because of the lack of literate Spanish clerks. Evans did not know French, although Mackay wrote and spoke both French and Spanish. But since the originals have not been discovered, we do not know whether Hay was transcribing the original Evans journal or a copy in French.

6. The Indian Office map was first described in Abel, "New Lewis and Clark Map." See also Jackson, *Letters of the Lewis and Clark Expedition*, 1:136 n. 3; and Wood, "Nicolas de Finiels." The Evans map is described in detail in Wood, "The John Evans 1796–97 Map." See also William Henry Harrison to Jefferson, Nov. 26, 1803; and Jefferson to Lewis, Jan. 13, 1804, in Jackson, *Letters of the Lewis and Clark Expedition*, 1:140–41, 163.

7. DeVoto, *Course of Empire*, 69.

8. The geographical contributions of Mackay and Evans have been richly treated in Allen, *Passage through the Garden*, esp. 140–77.

9. Jackson, *Jefferson and the Stony Mountains*, 139. For a claim that Jefferson "copied" Mackay's instructions for Lewis and Clark, see Williams, *Madoc*, 14. The president had never seen Mackay's instructions to Evans, nor were they among the documents that Meriwether Lewis obtained in St. Louis.

10. Flint, *Recollections*, 120.

11. Jackson, *Voyages*, 7.

12. The spelling here is from Jacques Marquette's 1673 autograph map. Tucker, *Atlas*, plate 5.

13. Delanglez, "Cartography of the Mississippi," 257–84; Wood, "Ethnohistory and Historical Method," fig. 3; Tucker, *Atlas*, plate 5.

14. Garraghan, *Chapters in Frontier History*, 57; Henning, "Oneota Tradition," 387–89.

15. For general references to these early journeys, see Nasatir, *Before Lewis and Clark*, 1:5.

16. Syrett, *Papers of Alexander Hamilton*, 11:24–25. According to Syrett, "Medad Mitchell (who was sometimes called Thomas Mitchell) was a surveyor and adventurer. He subsequently became a free-lance agent on the Spanish-American frontier." The editor also provides a brief biography of Mitchell.

17. Garraghan, *Chapters in Frontier History*, 61–62. See also the archival and published documentation that Garraghan provides.

18. Villiers du Terrage, *La Découverte du Missouri*, 32–40. See also Nasatir, *Before Lewis and Clark*, 1:9–10.

19. Villiers du Terrage, *La Découverte du Missouri*, 62–63.

20. Bray, "Utz Site," 9.

21. The most readily accessible copy of the map of the fort may be found in Norall, *Bourgmont*, 22–23.

22. The Padoucas Bourgmont encountered were not the Comanches, as early writers suggested, but the Apaches, as George Bird Grinnell first suggested. Later scholars, including specialists on the Jicarilla Apache, have confirmed that identification. See Grinnell, "Who Were the Padoucas?"; Gunnerson, *Jicarilla Apaches*; and Hyde, *Indians of the High Plains*, 28–35.

23. Norall, *Bourgmont*, 89.

24. Tucker, *Atlas*, plate 15.

25. Piazza, "Kaskaskia Manuscripts"; Nasatir, *Before Lewis and Clark*, 1:36, 41; Hoffhaus, *Chez les Canses*, 59.

26. Nasatir, *Before Lewis and Clark*, 1:36–37.

27. The history of this elusive post, whose location remains a mystery to this day, is told in Hoffhaus, *Chez les Canses*, 53–88.

28. Henning, "Guillaume Delisle," plate 1; Norall, *Bourgmont*, 27, 110.

29. Cox, *Journeys of Rene Robert Cavalier, Sieur de La Salle*, 1:160.

30. Finiels, *Account of Upper Louisiana*, 69.

31. Ibid., 56.

32. Nasatir, *Before Lewis and Clark*, 1:162, 229–30.

33. Ibid., 1:5.

34. Sayer, *Les Sauvages Americains*, 154.

35. Gates, *Five Fur Traders*, 38–39, 111.

36. General references to these villages and their characteristics may be found in Moulton, *Journals of the Lewis and Clark Expedition*, 3:401–4; Ronda, *Lewis and Clark*

among the Indians, 67–71; and Meyer, *Village Indians of the Upper Missouri.* See also Wood and Thiessen, *Early Fur Trade,* 3–8.

37. Rich, *Fur Trade and the Northwest,* 188.

38. Wood and Thiessen, *Early Fur Trade,* 12–15.

39. Jablow, *Cheyenne in Plains Indian Trade Relations;* Ewers, "Indian Trade of the Upper Missouri." See also Wood, "Plains Trade in Prehistoric and Protohistoric Intertribal Relations."

40. Ewers, "Indian Trade of the Upper Missouri," 430–31.

41. Jablow, *Cheyenne in Plains Indian Trade Relations,* 45–50.

42. Matthews, *Ethnography and Philology of the Hidatsa Indians,* 27.

43. Bruner, "Differential Change in the Culture of the Mandan," 201.

44. Catlin, *Letters and Notes,* 1:186; Clark, *Indian Sign Language,* 1–16, 334–39; Driver and Massey, *Comparative Studies of North American Indians,* 379.

45. Ewers, "Indian Trade of the Upper Missouri," 435.

46. Ray and Freeman, *"Give Us Good Measure."*

47. Finiels, *Account of Upper Louisiana,* 86 n. 151.

48. Nasatir, *Before Lewis and Clark,* 1:134–35.

49. Ibid., 1:208–9.

50. Finiels, *Account of Upper Louisiana,* 85.

51. Ibid., 113.

52. Nasatir, *Before Lewis and Clark,* 1:181, 161.

53. Ibid., 1:80.

54. Ibid., 2:388 n. 15.

55. Joseph Garreau, sometimes called the first white settler in South Dakota, later interacted with Lewis and Clark at the Arikara villages. Pierre and Antoine, his two sons by an Arikara wife, became traders and translators in the upper Missouri River fur trade. Moulton, *Journals of the Lewis and Clark Expedition,* 3:313–16.

56. Ibid., 1:234. The identity of the Tayanne is unclear. From their mention together with the Mandans, the term may allude to the Hidatsas, but an equally plausible identity would be the Cheyennes.

57. Nasatir, "Jacques D'Eglise," 2:133–34.

58. Nasatir, *Before Lewis and Clark,* 1:289.

59. Nasatir, *Before Lewis and Clark,* 1:266. Ponca Fort is described in Wood, *Ná{ⁿza}.*

60. Nasatir, *Before Lewis and Clark,* 1:266, 279–80, 287–93, 285.

61. Ibid., 1:87–91, 280–85.

62. Ibid., 1:285.

63. Ibid., 1:338, 91–92, 98.

2. THE THIRD SPANISH EXPEDITION TAKES FORM

1. Nasatir, "James Mackay," 4:200.

2. Morse, *Fur Trade Canoe Routes of Canada.*

3. Henry, *Journal,* 1:43. The Jarvis and Mackay map is reproduced in Wood, *Atlas of Early Maps of the American Midwest, Part II,* plate 11.

4. John C. Jackson, letter to author, 1998; Orser, "Explorer as Ethnographer," 20.

5. For an extended account of Donald Mackay, see Duckworth, "The Madness of Donald Mackay." Donald Mackay's relations with James Mackay are detailed in pages 26–29. See also John C. Jackson, "Inland from the Bay," 41. For a reproduction of the 1795 Soulard map and a discussion of its history, consult the latter part of this chapter.

6. Nasatir, *Before Lewis and Clark*, 2:492; Smith, *Explorations of the La Vérendryes*, 54.

7. Smith, *Explorations of the La Vérendryes*, 100.

8. Nasatir, *Before Lewis and Clark*, 2:492–93; Wood and Thiessen, *Early Fur Trade*, 118–19; Wood, *Atlas of Early Maps of the American Midwest*, plate 7.

9. Little, "Ulysses S. Grant's White Haven," 14–15 n. 40 (citing Danisi, "Honor without Title").

10. Nasatir, *Before Lewis and Clark*, 1:130–31.

11. Orser, "Explorer as Ethnographer," 19.

12. DeVoto, *Course of Empire*, 373.

13. Nasatir, *Before Lewis and Clark*, 1:181; Danisi, "James Mackay," 511; Nasatir, *Before Lewis and Clark*, 1:355–56.

14. Nasatir, *Before Lewis and Clark*, 2:586; Nasatir, "James Mackay," 188.

15. Nasatir, *Before Lewis and Clark*, 2:493.

16. Williams, "John Evans's Mission," 570. For more particulars on these bizarre events, see two books by Gwyn A. Williams, *Madoc* and *Search for Beulah Land*.

17. For biographical details on Evans, consult Nasatir, "John Evans," pts. 1–3. See also Nasatir, "John Thomas Evans," 99–101; and Williams, "John Evans' Strange Journey."

18. Houck, *Spanish Régime in Missouri*, 1:334.

19. Williams, "John Evans' Strange Journey," 600–601.

20. Ibid., 601. War did indeed erupt between Britain and Spain in October 1796.

21. Nasatir, *Before Lewis and Clark*, 1:316–17.

22. "Selected Documents, 1795–1822," doc. 10; Orser, "Explorer as Ethnographer," 19.

23. Nasatir, *Before Lewis and Clark*, 1:331, 95, 330–35.

24. Ekberg, *Colonial Ste. Genevieve*, 80–81.

25. Collot, *Journey in North America*.

26. Diller, "James MacKay's Journey in Nebraska," 179.

27. Ibid., 175.

28. Carter, *Territorial Papers of the United States*, 9:523; Ekberg, *Colonial Ste. Genevieve*, 435; Soulard to Gayoso, Dec. 15, 1797 (PC 213), Audencia de Ste. Domingo, legajos pertaining to Upper Louisiana, Papeles Procedentes de Cuba, legajos pertaining to Upper Louisiana, Archivo General de Indias, Seville; Nasatir, *Before Lewis and Clark*, 1:370.

29. Smith, *Explorations of the La Vérendryes*, 112.

30. Wheat, *Mapping the Transmississippi West*, 1:157; Nasatir, *Before Lewis and Clark*, 2:760 n. 1.

31. Nasatir, *Before Lewis and Clark*, 1:160, 330.

32. Ibid., 1:245, 275.

33. Ibid., 1:84–91.

34. Ibid., 1:119; Wheat, *Mapping the Transmississippi West*, 1:156–57; Tucker, *Atlas*, plate 15; Hamilton, "Early Cartography," 655.

35. Nasatir, *Before Lewis and Clark*, 1:253.

36. Diller, "Maps of the Missouri River," 507; Diller, "James MacKay's Journey in Nebraska," 178.

37. Nasatir, *Before Lewis and Clark*, 1:253; Wheat, *Mapping the Transmississippi West*, 1:157 n. 3.

38. Including the present author. See Wood, "Mapping the Missouri River through the Great Plains," 35.

39. Nasatir, *Before Lewis and Clark*, 1:346.

40. Ibid., 2:389 n. 20, 395, 406.

41. Consult the reproduction of this map in Nasatir, *Before Lewis and Clark*, 2:406 n. 55. A copy is also provided in Wood, *Atlas of Early Maps of the American Midwest, Part II*, fig. 5.

42. Arader, "Most Important Eighteenth Century Map."

43. Wheat, *Mapping the Transmississippi West*, 1:158, 244, map 235a.

44. Ibid., 244.

45. Diller, "New Map of the Missouri River." The map is illustrated in Temple, *Indian Villages*, plate 75.

46. Diller, "New Map of the Missouri River," 175.

47. Thwaites, *Original Journals of the Lewis and Clark Expedition*, vol. 1, p. li, vol. 8, map 2; Moulton, *Journals of the Lewis and Clark Expedition*, vol. 1, map 4; Wood, *Atlas of Early Maps of the American Midwest*, plate 2. See also Jackson, *Letters of the Lewis and Clark Expedition*, 1:156 n. 6.

48. Moulton, *Journals of the Lewis and Clark Expedition*, 1:5, 178 n. 34.

49. Wheat, *Mapping the Transmississippi West*, 1:158 n. 4.

50. Allen, *Passage through the Garden*, 148–50, 172; Moulton, *Journals of the Lewis and Clark Expedition*, 3:108–9. This river is not to be confused with another stream of the same name that enters the Missouri River above the Mandan and Hidatsa villages.

51. Nasatir, *Before Lewis and Clark*, 1:360; Wood, "Fort Charles," 2–7; Nasatir, *Before Lewis and Clark*, 1:87–90, 280, 294–96, 388–89.

52. Diller, "Maps of the Missouri River," 508–9; Wagner, *Peter Pond*, map 2; Innis, *Peter Pond*, map on inside back cover.

53. Carver, *Travels through the Interior*; Diller, "New Map of the Missouri River," 178; Van der Zee, "Fur Trade Operations," 361.

54. Tucker, *Atlas*, plate 15; Wedel, *Introduction to Kansas Archeology*, 60, 606. This village today is contained in Pawnee Indian Village State Historic Site near the town of Republic.

3. FROM ST. LOUIS TO FORT CHARLES

1. "Selected Documents, 1795–1822," docs. 1, 2. See also Nasatir, *Before Lewis and Clark*, 1:351 n. 2.

2. Houck, *History of Missouri*, 2:72–73 n. 147; Nasatir, *Before Lewis and Clark*, 2:416.

3. Thorne, *Many Hands*, 72–73; "Roster of St. Louis Militia Companies in 1780," in Houck, *Spanish Régime in Missouri*, 1:181–89.

4. Nasatir, *Before Lewis and Clark*, 1:340.

5. Finiels, *Account of Upper Louisiana*, 85.

6. Dunbar, *Life, Letters, and Papers*, 237–38; Baldwin, *Keelboat Age*; Chapman, *Architectura Navalis Mercatoria*; Haites, Mac, and Watson, *Western River Transportation*. See also the discussion of river vessels in Ekberg, *French Roots in the Illinois Country*, 273–82.

7. McDermott, *Glossary of Mississippi Valley French*, 6, 113.

8. Nasatir, *Before Lewis and Clark*, 1:340. The artifacts in figure 9 were selected from those illustrated in Wood, *Ná^{n}za*, figs. 9–11, 13. Truteau's inventory was taken individually from his narrative in Nasatir, *Before Lewis and Clark*, 1:260–311.

9. Brackenridge, *Journal*, 32.

10. Ibid., 33–34; Tabeau, *Narrative of Loisel's Expedition*, 65.

11. Maximilian, *Travels*, 22:237–38; Brackenridge, *Journal*, 33; Perrin du Lac, *Travels*, 166.

12. Finiels, *Account of Upper Louisiana*, 73.

13. Emmons, "Founding of St. Charles"; Houck, *History of Missouri*, 2:91–92.

14. "Selected Documents, 1795–1822," doc. 1; Nasatir, *Before Lewis and Clark*, 1:351.

15. Tabeau, *Narrative of Loisel's Expedition*, 63.

16. Moulton, *Journals of the Lewis and Clark Expedition*, 2:251.

17. Jackson, "Journey to the Mandans," 184.

18. Brackenridge, *Journal*, 77.

19. Moulton, *Journals of the Lewis and Clark Expedition*, 1:440–41; Nasatir, *Before Lewis and Clark*, 1:125–26. See also Blaine, *Ioway Indians*.

20. "Selected Documents, 1795–1822," doc. 2; Nasatir, *Before Lewis and Clark*, 2:489.

21. Abel, "New Lewis and Clark Map," 343; Wood, *Atlas of Early Maps of the American Midwest*, plate 4d.

22. Moulton, *Journals of the Lewis and Clark Expedition*, vol. 1, map 14, vol. 2, p. 445.

23. "Selected Documents, 1795–1822," doc. 1; Nasatir, *Before Lewis and Clark*, 1:354.

24. O'Shea and Ludwickson, *Archaeology and Ethnohistory of the Omaha*; Tucker, *Atlas*, plate 15; Dorsey, "Omaha Sociology," 211–13.

25. O'Shea and Ludwickson, *Archaeology and Ethnohistory of the Omaha*, 1–15.

26. For a summary of Blackbird's life, see ibid., 23–30. See also Ludwickson, "Blackbird and Son," for a more extensive statement and a resolution of the confusion between the elder Blackbird and his son.

27. Kinnaird, "Spain in the Mississippi Valley," 2:228; O'Shea and Ludwickson, *Archaeology and Ethnohistory of the Omaha*, 26.

28. Bray, "Utz Site," 129; Henning, "Oneota Tradition," 392.

29. Nasatir, *Before Lewis and Clark*, 2:494; Will and Spinden, *The Mandans*, 215.

30. Moulton, *Journals of the Lewis and Clark Expedition*, 2:435, 437 n. 3, 3:399, 9:78–79.

31. Gilmore, *Uses of Plants by the Indians*, 7, 68–77, 84.

32. Nasatir, *Before Lewis and Clark*, 1:126.

33. Ibid., 1:81–82, 88, 206.

34. Jablow, *Ethnohistory of the Ponca*, 81; Houck, *Spanish Régime in Missouri*, 2:168.

35. Wood, *Atlas of Early Maps of the American Midwest*, plates 3a, 4a; Moulton, *Journals of the Lewis and Clark Expedition*, vol. 1, map 19; Lt. Gouverneur Kemble Warren, manuscript map of the Missouri River, 1856, Q579, sheet 14, Record Group 77, National Archives and Records Service, Washington, D.C.

36. Nasatir, *Before Lewis and Clark*, 1:293, 2:378.

37. Chardon, "Linear League in North America."

38. Nasatir, *Before Lewis and Clark*, 1:90–91, 91 n. 44, 2:441–42.

39. Ibid., 1:374.

40. Perrin du Lac, *Voyage*; Wood, *Atlas of Early Maps of the American Midwest*, plate 9; Diller, "Maps of the Missouri River," 513, 519.

41. Nasatir, *Before Lewis and Clark*, 2:490.

42. Ibid., 2:710.

43. Ibid., 1:89.

44. "Selected Documents, 1796–1822," doc. 2; Nasatir, *Before Lewis and Clark*, 1:362.

45. Moulton, *Journals of the Lewis and Clark Expedition*, vol. 1, maps 7, 16; Wood, *Atlas of Early Maps of the American Midwest*, plate 4d.

46. Moulton, *Journals of the Lewis and Clark Expedition*, 2:467–68.

47. Carlson, "Nebraska State Historical Society Fort Charles Survey Project." For an example of how the channel has moved in this general area, consult the map of its changes between 1804 and 1894 in Monona County, Iowa, in Chittenden, *American Fur Trade*, 1:77 (opposite).

48. "Selected Documents, 1795–1822," doc. 2.

49. Ibid.

50. Nasatir, *Before Lewis and Clark*, 1:243–44, 280.

51. "Selected Documents," 1795–1822, doc. 2.

52. Ibid.

53. Nasatir, *Before Lewis and Clark*, 2:418. Derouin may have built another post for the Oto trade, perhaps south of the mouth of the Platte River. If he did, it may account for the conflicting locations that Mackay cited for the position of the Post of the Otos, for in his journal the Scot is clear that the post was above the mouth of the Platte. That site also was noted in 1795; the locations south of the Platte date from his 1797 "Table of Distances" and from the Indian Office map, by which time Derouin had been among the Otos.

54. Nasatir, *Before Lewis and Clark*, 1:109, 2:516–17; Prucha, *Indian Peace Medals*, 14, plate 5.

55. Nasatir, *Before Lewis and Clark*, 2:416.

56. Ibid., 1:269, 2:382.

57. Ibid., 1:363.

58. Ibid., 1:283.

59. Ibid., 1:354.

60. Wedel, "Le Sueur and the Dakota Sioux."

61. Tucker, *Atlas*, plates 13, 15.

62. Parker, *Journals of Jonathan Carver*; Wagner, *Peter Pond*.

63. Van der Zee, "Fur Trade Operations," 361.

64. Alan R. Woolworth, communication with author, Mar. 2000.

65. Nasatir, *Before Lewis and Clark*, 1:204.

66. Ibid., 1:80–81; Nasatir, "Anglo-Spanish Frontier," 304–5.

67. Nasatir, *Before Lewis and Clark*, 1:125, 126, 365; "Selected Documents, 1795–1822," doc. 2.

68. Nasatir, *Before Lewis and Clark*, 1:284, 322 n. 2.

69. Anderson, "Personal Narrative," 151–52.

70. Thwaites, *Original Journals of the Lewis and Clark Expedition*, 7:373; Jackson, *Letters of the Lewis and Clark Expedition*, 2:702.

71. Moulton, *Journals of the Lewis and Clark Expedition*, 3:356, 357.

72. Hurt, *Report of the Investigation of the Swan Creek Site*, 30.

73. Jantz and Owsley, "White Traders in the Upper Missouri."

4. THE MISSOURI RIVER BASIN EXPLORED

1. Burpee, *Journals and Letters of Pierre Gaultier de Varennes de la Vérendrye and His Sons*; Smith, *Explorations of the La Vérendryes*.

2. Jackson, "Inland from the Bay," 41–42; Ray, *Indians in the Fur Trade*, 105, fig. 35; Ramenofsky, *Vectors of Death*, 130; Moulton, *Journals of the Lewis and Clark Expedition*, vol. 1, map 28.

3. Shimkin, "Eastern Shoshone," 309.

4. Burpee, *Search for the Western Sea*, 307–64; Moulton, *Journals of the Lewis and Clark Expedition*, 3:435–36.

5. Wood and Thiessen, *Early Fur Trade*, 3–48.

6. Newman, "The Blond Mandan."

7. The map has been called the Evans 1796–97 map, but the hand of James Mackay is so evident in it that here we resort to using the repository name for it. The Mackay and Evans maps currently are undergoing an extensive revision. Thomas C. Danisi and W. Raymond Wood, "James Mackay's Charts of the Missouri River: Lewis and Clark's Route Maps" (manuscript in preparation).

8. Williams, *Madoc*, 14.

9. "Selected Documents, 1795–1822," doc. 3; Nasatir, *Before Lewis and Clark*, 2:410–14.

10. Cotter, *History of Nautical Astronomy*, 87–91, 189–92.

11. Hamilton Island, among other features in the Missouri River channel and floodplain, was flooded by the impoundment of the river by the Fort Randall, Big Bend, and Oahe Dams created by the U.S. Army Corps of Engineers in the years following World War II.

12. Moulton, *Journals of the Lewis and Clark Expedition*, vol. 1, map 22; McDermott, "Clark's Struggle with Place Names," 150; Tabeau, *Narrative of Loisel's Expedition*, 22–23, 26–27 n. 66; Smith, *Big Bend Historic Sites*, 47–50.

13. Smith, *Explorations of the La Vérendryes*, 112.

14. Ibid., 112, 99–101.

15. Moulton, *Journals of the Lewis and Clark Expedition*, 3:71; Porter, "Notes on Four Lithic Types," 267–68.

16. Lehmer, *Middle Missouri Archeology*, fig. 82.

17. Tabeau, *Narrative of Loisel's Expedition*, 138 n. 109.

18. Moulton, *Journals of the Lewis and Clark Expedition*, 3:168. The name does not appear on Prince Maximilian's copy of Clark's map. Ibid., vol. 1, map 26.

19. McLaughlin, *My Friend the Indian*, 9–10. Photographs of the monument appear in the appendix, 11–12. The tradition is recounted in Federal Writers' Project of the Works Project Administration for the State of North Dakota, comp., *North Dakota: A Guide to the Northern Prairie State*, 2d ed. (New York: Oxford University Press, 1950), 299–300.

20. Will, "Archaeology of the Missouri Valley," 299–300; Farrell, "Standing Rock," 1.

21. Moulton, *Journals of the Lewis and Clark Expedition*, 3:174–75, 9:85; Grinnell, *Cheyenne Indians*, 1:23–24, 27. See also Wood, *Biesterfeldt*, 64.

22. Moulton, *Journals of the Lewis and Clark Expedition*, 3:183.

23. Will and Hecker, "Upper Missouri River Aboriginal Culture," 93–95; Wood, *Interpretation of Mandan Culture History*.

24. Moulton, *Journals of the Lewis and Clark Expedition*, vol. 1, map 28; vol. 3, p. 184.

25. Ibid., 8:308.

26. Ibid., vol. 1, map 28; Will and Spinden, *The Mandans*.

27. Wood, "Cultural Chronology," 21–22. For examples of Pawnee attributions, see David Thompson's narrative in Wood and Thiessen, *Early Fur Trade*, 117; and Thompson's 1798 map in Wood, *Atlas of Early Maps of the American Midwest*, plate 7.

28. Wood, "David Thompson at the Mandan-Hidatsa Villages," 339, 337–41; Wood and Thiessen, *Early Fur Trade*, 117, 119, fig. 7.

29. Thompson, "Final Story," 143–53.

30. Moulton, *Journals of the Lewis and Clark Expedition*, vol. 1, map 31b.

31. The recently published Jarvis and Mackay map was the first to show details of the Mandan and Hidatsa villages. Made in 1791, the chart illustrates the trek of Donald Mackay to these villages in February 1780. See Jackson, "Inland from the Bay," 42; and Ruggles, "Mapping the Interior Plains," 152–65, fig. 3. Ruggles was reprinted in Luebke, Kaye, and Moulton, *Mapping the North American Plains*, 145–60, fig. 9.3. Details from the Jarvis and Mackay map were copied onto Arrowsmith's great map of 1795 a few years later. See Wood, *Atlas of Early Maps of the American Midwest, Part II*, plate 11. A copy of that map is in the Library of Congress, Washington, D.C. It is discussed in Wheat, *Mapping the Transmississippi West*, 1:155, 175, 242. A small part of Arrowsmith that shows this region is illustrated in Allen, *Passage through the Garden*, fig. 9.

32. Nasatir, *Before Lewis and Clark*, 2:417 n. 4. *Glorieux* refers to the French king Louis XIV.

33. Ibid., 2:493.

34. O'Shea and Ludwickson, *Archaeology and Ethnohistory of the Omaha*, 7.

35. Perrin du Lac, *Voyage*; Wood, *Atlas of Early Maps of the American Midwest*, plates 9, 5b.

36. Diller, "James MacKay's Journey in Nebraska," 123–24. The King map is illustrated in Tucker, *Atlas*, plate 31.

37. The annual Omaha bison hunt was accompanied by a great deal of ceremony. See Fletcher and La Flesche, "The Omaha Tribe," 275–83.

38. Wood, *Náⁿza*, map 1.

39. This translation and those following are by Aubrey Diller and found in his article "James MacKay's Journey in Nebraska."

40. Wood, *Atlas of Early Maps of the American Midwest*, plate 10; Nasatir, *Before Lewis and Clark*, 1:110 (opposite), 316–17.

41. Clark's 1810 manuscript map is reproduced in readable format in Moulton, *Journals of the Lewis and Clark Expedition*, vol. 1, map 125; the 1807 Frazer map is in ibid., map 124; and the 1843 Nicollet map is the subject of Bray, *Joseph Nicollet and His Map*.

42. Johnsgard, *This Fragile Land*, 65.

43. Fletcher and La Flesche, "The Omaha Tribe," 88.

44. Kahl, "Plants," 135, 140.

45. Dorsey, "Omaha Sociology"; Dorsey, "Migrations of Siouan Tribes"; Fletcher and La Flesche, "The Omaha Tribe," 85–86; O'Shea and Ludwickson, *Archaeology and Ethnohistory of the Omaha*, 20–21; Wedel, *Introduction to Pawnee Archeology*, map 2; James, *Account of an Expedition*, 1:300; Wedel, *Introduction to Pawnee Archeology*, 29, 33–34; Grange, *Pawnee and Lower Loup Pottery*, 25–26.

46. Wood and Thiessen, *Early Fur Trade*, 172–92, map 3.

5. DÉNOUEMENT AND DISILLUSION

1. "Selected Documents, 1795–1822," doc. 9.

2. Nasatir, *Before Lewis and Clark*, 1:331; Thiessen, "Historic Trading Posts," 49.

3. Wood, *Atlas of Early Maps of the American Midwest*, plate 5.

4. James, *Account of an Expedition*, 1:200.

5. Williams, *Search for Beulah Land*, 118.

6. "Selected Documents, 1795–1822," docs. 6, 11; Nasatir, *Before Lewis and Clark*, 2:461–62.

7. Nasatir, *Before Lewis and Clark*, 2:479, 474–75.

8. See "Selected Documents, 1795–1822," doc. 4.

9. "Selected Documents, 1795–1822," doc. 8.

10. Wood and Thiessen, *Early Fur Trade*, 97.

11. Moulton, *Journals of the Lewis and Clark Expedition*, 3:237.

12. Williams, "John Evans' Strange Journey," 524–25.

13. Wood and Thiessen, *Early Fur Trade*, 93–128; James, *Account of an Expedition*, 1:200. James made mention of the post much later and through hearsay.

14. Wood and Thiessen, *Early Fur Trade*, 37.

15. Abel, "New Lewis and Clark Map," 329–31.

16. Zenon Trudeau to Gayoso de Lemos, Jan. 16, 1798, printed in Nasatir, *Before Lewis and Clark*, 2:515.

17. Zenon Trudeau to baron de Carondelet, May 26, 1797, in ibid., 520.

18. Jacques Clamorgan to Andre Lopez, Oct. 14, 1797, in ibid., 520 n. 6.

19. Nasatir, *Before Lewis and Clark*, 2:545.

20. Zenon Trudeau to Gayoso de Lemos, Mar. 5, 1798, in ibid., 545 n. 3.

21. Mackay to Gayoso de Lemos, June 8, 1798, in ibid., 563.

22. Johnson and Malone, "Daniel Clark," 2:125–26.

23. Carter, *Territorial Papers of the United States*, 9:29.

24. William Henry Harrison to Clark, Nov. 13, 1803; and Meriwether Lewis to Thomas Jefferson, Dec. 28, 1803, in Jackson, *Letters of the Lewis and Clark Expedition*, 1:135, 136 n. 3. John Rice Jones was a lawyer practicing in Vincennes, Indiana, and Kaskaskia as well as postmaster at Vincennes. A merchant and trader, John Hay was also the postmaster at Cahokia.

25. Wood, "The John Evans 1796–97 Map," 39 n. 51.

26. Wood, *Atlas of Early Maps of the American Midwest*, plates 8, 10; Hackett, *Pichardo's Treatise*, vol. 1.

27. Hoffhaus, *Chez les Canses*, 127.

28. Thwaites, *Original Journals of the Lewis and Clark Expedition*, vol. 1, pp. li–liii, vol. 8, maps 5–11, 13; Diller, "Maps of the Missouri River," 516.

29. Diller, "Maps of the Missouri River," 516; William Henry Harrison to Clark, Nov. 13, 1803; and William Henry Harrison to Jefferson, Nov. 26, 1803, in Jackson, *Letters of the Lewis and Clark Expedition*, 1:135, 136 n. 3, 140. See also Allen, *Passage through the Garden*, 137–39. The Jefferson letter to Clark is reprinted in Jackson, *Letters of the Lewis and Clark Expedition*, 1:163.

30. Nasatir, *Before Lewis and Clark*, 1:106–8. See the appendix for a concordance of Evans's names and modern equivalents.

31. Diller, "Pawnee House," 304.

32. Moulton, *Journals of the Lewis and Clark Expedition*, vol. 2, pp. 122–23, 129; vol. 1, map 23. I am indebted to Bob Saindon, who has made an exhaustive study of Clark's sketches, for this observation about the horse image.

33. Moulton, *Journals of the Lewis and Clark Expedition*, 2:152.

34. Ibid., 2:185–86. See also Tabeau, *Narrative of Loisel's Expedition*, 124–25.

35. Moulton, *Journals of the Lewis and Clark Expedition*, 2:194.

36. Nasatir, *Before Lewis and Clark*, 2:533.

37. Osgood, *Field Notes of Captain William Clark*, 16 n. 7.

38. Wood, "The John Evans 1796–97 Map," 48–49; Lehmer, Wood, and Dill, "Knife River Phase"; Wood, "David Thompson at the Mandan-Hidatsa Villages," 337–38.

39. Allen, *Passage through the Garden*, 143.

40. Nasatir, *Before Lewis and Clark*, 2:494.

41. Thorne, *Many Hands*, 110–11.

42. Moulton, *Journals of the Lewis and Clark Expedition*, 2:259, 260, 277, 279, 286–87, 294, 300, 3:34, 151, 154, 155, 181–82.

43. Brief but authoritative biographies of both men have been published. See Nasatir, "James Mackay," and "John Thomas Evans."

44. Nasatir, *Before Lewis and Clark*, 2:585–86.

45. Houck, *History of Missouri*, 2:71–72 n. 147. Another man, almost lost to history, said that he had been to the Mandans before Lewis and Clark. In his Camp Dubois journal for January 1, 1804, Clark mentions a visit by a blacksmith named Hannerberry, a

man who had "traveled far to the north, & Visited the Mandols on Missouris." Moulton, *Journals of the Lewis and Clark Expedition*, 2:144. Ernest S. Osgood tells us that a Patrick Henneberry was one of the early settlers above St. Louis on the Illinois side of the Mississippi and may be the man in question. *Field Notes of Captain William Clark*, 11 n. 4. But with whom, and how, had Henneberry gone up the Missouri, as a member of the Mackay and Evans expedition, with Truteau or D'Eglise earlier, or as an independent trader? Known sources do not say.

46. Brackenridge, *Journal*, 41 n. 11.

47. Bray, "Boone's Lick Salt Works," 18. Bray cites "Interview with Jesse Morrison," 30-C:86-95, Draper Manuscripts, Joint Collection, Western Historical Manuscript Collection, University of Missouri–Columbia, and State Historical Society of Missouri Manuscripts. The original manuscript interview (30-C:106 [1851]) is in the State Historical Society of Wisconsin, Madison. For a summary of Mackay's Cuivre River claim, see Warren, "Environment and Natural Resources of the Lower Cuivre," 38–39.

48. Little, "Ulysses S. Grant's White Haven."

49. Gaylor Sava and Peggy Dupree, *St. Charles Borromeo Church, St. Charles, Mo.: Translations of Parish Records, 1792–1809* (St. Charles, Mo.: Parish of St. Charles Borromeo, 1991), 1:105; Bryan and Rose, *Pioneer Families of Missouri*, 173. St. Charles Borromeo was the spiritual patron of the King of Spain, Charles IV, after whom the town was named. Until November 1791 the town had been called Les Petites Cotes ("The Little Hills"). It was purportedly founded around 1769 by a French Canadian trader named Louis Blanchette. Emmons, "Founding of St. Charles."

50. Bryan and Rose, *Pioneer Families of Missouri*, 173–74.

51. Little, "Ulysses S. Grant's White Haven," 24–26.

52. Marshall, *Life and Papers of Frederick Bates*, 1:330.

53. "Selected Documents, 1795–1822," doc. 12.

54. Scharf, *History of Saint Louis*, 1:151.

55. Chittenden, *American Fur Trade*, 1:262–63.

56. Nasatir, "James Mackay," 114. For Evans's texts on this subject, see "Selected Documents, 1795–1822," docs. 9–10.

57. Williams, "John Evans's Mission," 593; Nasatir, "James Mackay," 114; Williams, "John Evans's Mission," 594.

58. Orser, "Explorer as Ethnographer," 19; Nasatir, *Before Lewis and Clark*, 2:586.

59. Williams, "John Evans's Mission," 595; U.S. Congress, *American State Papers: Public Lands*, 6:719.

60. Boyd, *Introduction to Malariology*, 21–22. See also Danisi, "'Ague' Made Him Do It."

61. Williams, "John Evans's Mission," 596; Deacon, *Madoc and the Discovery of America*, 148–50.

62. Catlin, *Letters and Notes*, 2:259–61; Brower, *Mandan*, xi; DeVoto, *Course of Empire*, 71.

63. Nasatir, *Before Lewis and Clark*, 2:585–86.

64. Tucker, *Atlas*, plate 31. See also her discussion on page 10.

65. Burpee, *Journals and Letters of Pierre Gaultier de Varennes de la Vérendrye and His Sons*; Smith, *Explorations of the La Vérendryes*; Bolton, *Spanish Exploration in the Southwest*.

Bibliography

Abel, Annie Heloise. "A New Lewis and Clark Map." *The Geographical Review* 1 (May 1916): 329–45.

Allen, John Logan. *Passage through the Garden: Lewis and Clark and the Image of the American Northwest*. Urbana: University of Illinois Press, 1975.

Anderson, Thomas G. "Personal Narrative of Capt. Thomas G. Anderson." In *Wisconsin Historical Collections*. Vol. 9, 136–206. Madison, 1882.

Arader, W. Graham, III. "The Most Important Eighteenth Century Map of the Missouri Valley." In *Highly Important Manuscript Maps of America*. Catalog 49. Philadelphia: W. Graham Arader III, 1984.

Archivo General de Indias, Seville. Soulard to Gayoso, December 15, 1797 (PC 213). Audencia de Ste. Domingo, legajos pertaining to Upper Louisiana. Papeles Procedentes de Cuba, legajos pertaining to Upper Louisiana.

Arrowsmith, Aaron, and Samuel Lewis. *A New and Elegant General Atlas of North America*. Boston: n.p., 1804.

Baldwin, Leland D. *The Keelboat Age on the Western Waters*. Pittsburgh: University of Pittsburgh Press, 1941.

Blaine, Martha Royce. *The Ioway Indians*. Norman: University of Oklahoma Press, 1979.

Bolton, Herbert E. *Spanish Exploration in the Southwest, 1542–1706*. New York: Charles Scribner's Sons, 1916.

Boyd, Mark F. *An Introduction to Malariology*. Cambridge: Harvard University Press, 1930.

Brackenridge, Henry M. *Brackenridge's Journal up the Missouri, 1811*. Vol. 6 of *Early Western Travels, 1748–1846*, edited by Reuben Gold Thwaites. Cleveland: Arthur P. Clark, 1904.

Bradbury, John. *Travels in the Interior of America: In the Years 1809, 1810, and 1811*. Vol. 5 of Early Western Travels, 1748–1846, edited by Reuben Gold Thwaites. Cleveland: Arthur P. Clark, 1904.

Bray, Martha Coleman. *Joseph Nicollet and His Map*. American Philosophical Society, Memoir 140. Philadelphia, 1980.

Bray, Robert T. "Boone's Lick Salt Works, 1805–1833." *The Missouri Archaeologist* 48 (December 1987): 1–65.

———. "The Utz Site: An Oneota Village in Central Missouri." *The Missouri Archaeologist* 52 (December 1991): 1–146.

Brower, Jacob V. *Mandan.* Vol. 8 of *Memoirs of Explorations in the Basin of the Mississippi.* St. Paul: McGill Warner, 1904.

Bruner, Edward M. "Mandan." In *Perspectives in American Indian Culture Change,* edited by Edward H. Spicer, 187–277. Chicago: University of Chicago Press, 1961.

Bryan, William S., and Robert Rose. *A History of the Pioneer Families of Missouri.* St. Louis: Bryan, Brand, 1876.

Burpee, Lawrence J. *The Search for the Western Sea: The Story of the Explorations of North-Western America.* Toronto: Musson, 1908.

Burpee, Lawrence J., ed. *Journals and Letters of Pierre Gaultier de Varennes de la Vérendrye and His Sons.* Publications of the Champlain Society, vol. 16. Toronto: Ballantyne, 1927.

Carlson, Gayle F. "The Nebraska State Historical Society Fort Charles Survey Project, 1987–90," with an appendix, "Geomorphological Investigations of Fort Charles, Northeast Nebraska," by Rolfe D. Mandel. Unpublished report on file, Nebraska State Historical Society, Lincoln, 1991.

Carter, Clarence Edwin, ed. *The Territorial Papers of the United States, Orleans Territory.* Vol. 9. Washington D.C.: Government Printing Office, 1948.

Carver, Jonathan. *Travels through the Interior Parts of North America, in the Years 1766, 1767, and 1768.* London: n.p., 1771.

Catlin, George. *Letters and Notes on the Manners, Customs, and Condition of the North American Indians.* 2 vols. Minneapolis: Ross and Haines, 1965.

Chapman, F. H. *Architectura Navalis Mercatoria.* New York: Edward W. Sweetman, 1768.

Chardon, Roland. "The Linear League in North America." *Annals of the Association of American Geographers* 70 (June 1980): 129–53.

Chittenden, Hiram Martin. *The American Fur Trade of the Far West.* 2 vols. Stanford, Calif.: Academic Reprints, 1954.

Clark, William P. *The Indian Sign Language.* Philadelphia: L. R. Hammersly, 1885.

Collot, Georges-Victor. *A Journey in North America.* 2 vols., 1 atlas. London, 1924.

Cotter, Charles H. *A History of Nautical Astronomy.* New York: American Elsevier, 1968.

Cox, Isaac Joslin, ed. *The Journeys of Rene Robert Cavalier, Sieur de La Salle.* 2 vols. New York: Allerton, 1922.

Danisi, Thomas C. "Honor without Title: James Mackay." Draft manuscript in possession of the author, January 1992.

———. "James Mackay (1759–1822)." In *Dictionary of Missouri Biography,* edited by Lawrence O. Christensen, William E. Foley, Gary R. Kremer, and Kenneth H. Winn, 511–12. Columbia: University of Missouri Press, 1999.

———. "The 'Ague' Made Him Do It." *We Proceeded On* 28 (February 1, 2002): 10–15.

Deacon, Richard. *Madoc and the Discovery of America.* New York: George Braziller, 1966.

Delanglez, Jean. "The Cartography of the Mississippi, Part I." *Mid-America* 30 (October 1948): 257–84.

DeVoto, Bernard. *The Course of Empire.* Boston: Houghton Mifflin, 1952.

Diller, Aubrey. "Maps of the Missouri River before Lewis and Clark." In *Studies and Essays in the History of Science and Learning*, edited by M. F. Ashley Montagu, 505–19. New York: Henry Schuman, 1946.

———. "Pawnee House: Ponca House." *Mississippi Valley Historical Review* 36 (September 1949): 301–4.

———. "James MacKay's Journey in Nebraska in 1796." *Nebraska History* 36 (June 1955): 123–28.

———. "A New Map of the Missouri River Drawn in 1795." *Imago Mundi: A Review of Early Cartography* 12 (1955): 175–80.

Dorsey, James Owen. "Omaha Sociology." In Bureau of American Ethnology, *Third Annual Report for 1881–1882*, 205–370. Washington, D.C., Government Printing Office, 1884.

———. "Migrations of Siouan Tribes." *American Naturalist* 20 (March 1886): 210–22.

Draper Manuscripts. Interview with Jesse Morrison, 30-C:86–95. Joint Collection, University of Missouri, Columbia, Western Historical Manuscript Collection, and State Historical Society of Missouri Manuscripts, St. Louis. Original manuscripts in the State Historical Society of Wisconsin, Madison, 1851.

Driver, Harold E., and Massey, William C. *Comparative Studies of North American Indians*. Transactions of the American Philosophical Society, vol. 47, no. 2. Philadelphia, 1957.

Duckworth, Harry W. "The Madness of Donald Mackay." *The Beaver* 68 (June/July 1988): 25–42.

Dunbar, William. *Life, Letters, and Papers of William Dunbar, 1749–1810*. Edited by Mrs. Dunbar Rowland [Eron Rowland]. Jackson: Press of the Mississippi Historical Society, 1930.

Ekberg, Carl J. *Colonial Ste. Genevieve: An Adventure on the Mississippi Frontier*. 2d ed. Tucson, Ariz.: Patrice Press, 1996.

———. *French Roots in the Illinois Country: The Mississippi Frontier in Colonial Times*. Urbana: University of Illinois Press, 1998.

Emmons, Ben. "The Founding of St. Charles and Blanchette, Its Founder." *Missouri Historical Review* 18 (July 1924): 507–20.

Ewers, John C. "The Indian Trade of the Upper Missouri before Lewis and Clark: An Interpretation." *Missouri Historical Society Bulletin* 10 (July 1954): 429–46.

Farrell, Robert C. "Standing Rock." *Museum News* (W. H. Over Museum, University of South Dakota, Vermillion) 14 (October 1953): 1.

Finiels, Nicolas de. *An Account of Upper Louisiana*. Edited by Carl J. Ekberg and William E. Foley. Translated by Carl J. Ekberg. Columbia: University of Missouri Press, 1989.

Fletcher, Alice C., and Francis La Flesche. "The Omaha Tribe." In Bureau of American Ethnology, *27th Annual Report for 1905–06*, 17–672. Washington, D.C.: Government Printing Office, 1911.

Flint, Timothy. *Recollections of the Last Ten Years*. Edited and with an introduction by C. Hartley Grattan. New York: A. A. Knopf, 1932.

Foley, William E., and C. David Rice. *The First Chouteaus: River Barons of Early St. Louis*. Urbana: University of Illinois Press, 1983.

Garraghan, Gilbert J. *Chapters in Frontier History: Research Studies in the Making of the West*. Milwaukee: Bruce, 1934.

Gass, Patrick. *A Journal of the Voyages and Travels of a Corps of Discovery, under the Command of Capt. Lewis and Capt. Clark of the Army of the United States, from the Mouth of the River Missouri through the Interior Parts of North America to the Pacific Ocean, during the Years 1804, 1805, and 1806*. Pittsburgh: n.p., 1807.

Gates, Charles M., ed. *Five Fur Traders of the Northwest*. St. Paul: Minnesota Historical Society, 1965.

Gaylor, Sava, and Peggy Dupree. *St. Charles Borromeo Church, St. Charles, Mo.: Translations of Parish Records*. Vol. 1, *1792–1809*. St. Charles, Mo.: Parish of St. Charles Borromeo, 1991.

Gilmore, Melvin R. *Uses of Plants by the Indians of the Missouri River Region*. Lincoln: University of Nebraska Press, 1977.

Grange, Roger T. *Pawnee and Lower Loup Pottery*. The Nebraska State Historical Society, Publications in Anthropology 3. Lincoln, 1968.

Grinnell, George B. "Who Were the Padoucas?" *American Anthropologist* 22 (July–September 1920): 248–60.

———. *The Cheyenne Indians: Their History and Ways of Life*. 2 vols. New Haven: Yale University Press, 1923.

Gunnerson, Dolores A. *The Jicarilla Apaches: A Study in Survival*. DeKalb: Northern Illinois University Press, 1974.

Hackett, Charles Wilson. *Pichardo's Treatise on the Limits of Louisiana and Texas*. Vol. 1. Austin: University of Texas Press, 1931.

Hafen, LeRoy R. *The Mountain Men and the Fur Trade of the Far West*. Vols. 3–4. Glendale, Calif.: Arthur H. Clark, 1966.

Haites, Erik F.; J. Mac; and G. M. Watson. *Western River Transportation: The Era of Early Internal Development, 1810–1860*. Baltimore: John Hopkins University Press, 1975.

Hamilton, Raphael N. "The Early Cartography of the Missouri Valley." *The American Historical Review* 34 (October/July 1934): 645–62.

Henning, Dale R. "The Oneota Tradition." In *Archaeology on the Great Plains*, edited by W. Raymond Wood, 345–414. Lawrence: University Press of Kansas, 1998.

Henning, Elizabeth R. P. "Guillaume Delisle, c.1714." In *An Atlas of Early Maps of the American Midwest*, compiled by W. Raymond Wood, 1. Illinois State Museum, Scientific Papers 18. Springfield, 1983.

Henry, Alexander. *The Journal of Alexander Henry the Younger, 1799–1814*. Edited and with an introduction by Barry M. Gough. 2 vols. Toronto: Champlain Society, 1988.

Hoffhaus, Charles E. *Chez les Canses, Three Centuries at Kawsmouth: The French Foundations of Metropolitan Kansas City*. Kansas City, Mo.: Lowell Press, 1984.

Houck, Louis. *History of Missouri*. 3 vols. Chicago: R. R. Donnelley, 1908.

———. *The Spanish Régime in Missouri*. 2 vols. Chicago: R. R. Donnelley, 1909.

Holmes, Jack D. L. "Some French Engineers in Spanish Louisiana." In *The French in the Mississippi Valley*, edited by John Francis McDermott, 123–42. Urbana: University of Illinois Press, 1965.

Hurt, Wesley R., Jr. *Report of the Investigation of the Swan Creek Site, 39WW7, Walworth County, South Dakota, 1954–1956*. South Dakota Archaeological Commission, Archaeological Studies, Circular 7. Pierre, 1957.

Hyde, George E. *Indians of the High Plains: From the Prehistoric Period to the Coming of Europeans*. Norman: University of Oklahoma Press, 1959.

Innis, Harold A. *Peter Pond, Fur Trader and Adventurer*. Toronto: Irwin and Gordon, 1930.

Jablow, Joseph. *The Cheyenne in Plains Indian Trade Relations, 1795–1840*. American Ethnological Society, Monograph 19. New York, 1951.

———. *Ethnohistory of the Ponca, with Reference to Their Claim to Certain Lands*. New York: Garland Press, 1974.

Jackson, Donald. "Some Books Carried by Lewis and Clark." *Missouri Historical Society Bulletin* 16 (October 1959): 3–13.

———. "Journey to the Mandans, 1809: The Lost Narrative of Dr. Thomas." *Missouri Historical Society Bulletin* 20 (April 1964), 179–92.

———. *Letters of the Lewis and Clark Expedition, with Related Documents, 1783–1854*. 2d ed. 2 vols. Urbana: University of Illinois Press, 1978.

———. *Thomas Jefferson and the Stony Mountains: Exploring the West from Monticello*. Urbana: University of Illinois Press, 1981.

———. *Voyages of the Steamboat Yellow Stone*. New York: Ticknor & Fields, 1985.

Jackson, John C. "Inland from the Bay: Mapping the Fur Trade, 1791." *The Beaver* 72 (February/March 1992): 37–42.

James, Edwin, ed. *Account of an Expedition from Pittsburgh to the Rocky Mountains Performed in the Years 1819 and 1820, by Order of the Hon. J. C. Calhoun, Secretary of War, under the Command of Maj. S. H. Long*. 2 vols. Philadelphia: H. C. Carey and I. Lea, 1823.

Jantz, Richard L., and Douglas W. Owsley. "White Traders in the Upper Missouri: Evidence from the Swan Creek Site." In *Skeletal Biology in the Great Plains: Migration, Warfare, Health, and Subsistence*, edited by Douglas W. Owsley and Richard L. Jantz, 189–201. Washington D.C.: Smithsonian Institution Press, 1994.

Johnsgard, Paul A. *This Fragile Land: A Natural History of the Nebraska Sandhills*. Lincoln: University of Nebraska Press, 1995.

Johnson, Allen, and Dumas Malone, eds. *Dictionary of American Biography*. Vol. 2. New York: Charles Scribners,1929.

Kahl, Robert. "Plants." In *An Atlas of the Sand Hills*, edited by Ann Bleed and Charles Flowerday, 127–42. Resource Atlas No. 5. Lincoln: Conservation and Survey Division, Institute of Agriculture and Natural Resources, University of Nebraska, 1989.

Kinnaird, Lawrence, ed. "Spain in the Mississippi Valley, 1763–1794." *American Historical Association, Annual Report for 1945*, Vols. 2–4. Washington, D.C., 1949.

Lehmer, Donald J. *Middle Missouri Archeology*. National Park Service, Anthropological Papers, No. 1. Washington, D.C.: Government Printing Office, 1971.

Lehmer, Donald J.; W. Raymond Wood; and Chris Dill. "The Knife River Phase." Report submitted to the Interagency Archeological Services–Denver by the University of Missouri–Columbia and Dana College, Blair, Neb. 1978.

Little, Kimberly Scott. "Ulysses S. Grant's White Haven: A Place Where Extraordinary People Came to Live Ordinary Lives, 1796–1885." Historic Resource Study, Ulysses S. Grant National Historic Site, Missouri. St. Louis: National Park Service, 1993.

Lowery, Woodbury. *The Lowery Collection: A Descriptive List of Maps of the Spanish Possessions within the Present Limits of the United States, 1502–1820.* Edited and with notes by Philip Lee Phillips. Washington, D.C., Government Printing Office, 1912.

Ludwickson, John. "Blackbird and Son: A Note Concerning Late-Eighteenth- and Early-Nineteenth-Century Omaha Chieftainship." *Ethnohistory* 42 (winter 1995): 133–49.

Luebke, Frederick C.; Frances W. Kaye; and Gary E. Moulton, eds. *Mapping the North American Plains: Essays in the History of Cartography.* Norman: University of Oklahoma Press, 1987.

McDermott, John Francis. *A Glossary of Mississippi Valley French, 1673–1850.* Washington University Studies, new series, Language and Literature, no. 12. St. Louis, 1941.

———. "William Clark's Struggle with Place Names in Upper Louisiana." *Missouri Historical Society Bulletin* 34 (April 1978): 140–50.

Mackenzie, Alexander. *Voyages from Montreal, on the River St. Lawrence, through the Continent of North America, to the Frozen and Pacific Ocean.* 2 vols. London, 1801.

McLaughlin, James. *My Friend the Indian, and the Three Missing Chapters.* Seattle: Superior Publishing, 1970.

Marshall, Thomas M., ed. *The Life and Papers of Frederick Bates.* 2 vols. St. Louis: Missouri Historical Society, 1926.

Matthews, Washington. *Ethnography and Philology of the Hidatsa Indians.* U.S. Geological and Geographical Survey, Miscellaneous Collections 7. Washington, D.C.: Government Printing Office, 1877.

Maximilian, Alexander Philipp. *Travels in the Interior of North America, 1832–1834.* Vols. 22–25 of *Early Western Travels, 1748–1846,* edited by Reuben Gold Thwaites. Cleveland: Arthur P. Clark, 1906.

Meyer, Roy W. *The Village Indians of the Upper Missouri: The Mandans, Hidatsas, and Arikaras.* Lincoln: University of Nebraska Press, 1977.

Morse, Eric W. *Fur Trade Canoe Routes of Canada: Then and Now.* Ottawa: Queens Printer, 1969.

Moulton, Gary E., ed. *The Journals of the Lewis & Clark Expedition.* Vols. 1–13. Lincoln: University of Nebraska Press, 1983–2001.

Nasatir, Abraham P. "The Anglo-Spanish Frontier in the Illinois Country during the American Revolution, 1779–1783." *Journal of the Illinois State Historical Society* 21, no. 3 (1928): 291–358.

———. "John Evans: Explorer and Surveyor." Parts 1-3. *Missouri Historical Review* 25 (January 1931): 219–39; (April 1931): 432–60; (July 1931): 585–608.

———. "Jacques D'Eglise." In *The Mountain Men and the Fur Trade of the Far West,* edited by LeRoy R. Hafen, 2:123–34. Glendale, Calif.: Arthur H. Clark, 1965.

———. "John Thomas Evans." In *The Mountain Men and the Fur Trade of the Far West,* edited by LeRoy R. Hafen, 3:99–117. Glendale, Calif.: Arthur H. Clark, 1966.

———. "James Mackay." In *The Mountain Men and the Fur Trade of the Far West,* edited by LeRoy R. Hafen, 4:185–206. Glendale, Calif.: Arthur H. Clark, 1966.

Nasatir, Abraham P., ed. *Before Lewis and Clark: Documents Illustrating the History of the Missouri, 1785–1804.* 2 vols. St. Louis: St. Louis Historical Documents Foundation, 1952.

Newman, Marshall T. "The Blond Mandan: A Critical Review of an Old Problem." *Southwestern Journal of Anthropology* 6 (autumn 1950): 255–72.

Norall, Frank. *Bourgmont: Explorer of the Missouri, 1698–1725.* Lincoln: University of Nebraska Press, 1988.

Orser, Charles E. "The Explorer as Ethnographer: The Anthropological Significance of James Mackay's 'Indian Tribes' as Demonstrated by a Study of the Arikara." *Ethnohistory* 30, no. 1 (1983): 15–33.

Osborn, Henry Fairfield. *The Proboscidea.* Vol. 1. New York: American Museum of Natural History Press, 1936.

Osgood, Ernest S. *The Field Notes of Captain William Clark, 1803–1805.* New Haven: Yale University Press, 1964.

O'Shea, John M., and John Ludwickson. *Archaeology and Ethnohistory of the Omaha Indians: The Big Village Site.* Lincoln: University of Nebraska Press, 1992.

Parker, John. *The Journals of Jonathan Carver and Related Documents, 1766–1770.* St. Paul: Minnesota Historical Society, 1976.

Perrin du Lac, François M. *Voyage dans les deux Louisianes, et chez les nations sauvages du Missouri, par les Etats-Unis, l'Ohio et les provinces qui le bordent, en 1801, 1802, et 1803.* Lyons: Chez Bruyset ainé et Buynand, 1805.

———. *Travels through the Two Louisianas, and among the Savage Nations of the Missouri; Also, in the United States, along the Ohio, and the Adjacent Provinces, in 1801, 1802, & 1803.* London, 1807.

Piazza, Theresa J. "The Kaskaskia Manuscripts: French Traders in the Missouri Valley before Lewis and Clark." *The Missouri Archaeologist* 53 (December 1992): 1–42.

Porter, James Warren. "Notes on Four Lithic Types Found in Archaeological Sites near Mobridge, South Dakota." *Plains Anthropologist* 7, no. 18 (1962): 267–69.

Prucha, Francis Paul. *Indian Peace Medals in American History.* Lincoln: University of Nebraska Press, 1971.

Ramenofsky, Ann F. *Vectors of Death: The Archaeology of European Contact.* Albuquerque: University of New Mexico Press, 1987.

Ray, Arthur J. *Indians in the Fur Trade: Their Role as Hunters, Trappers, and Middlemen in the Lands Southwest of Hudson Bay, 1660–1870.* Toronto: University of Toronto Press, 1974.

Ray, Arthur J., and Donald B. Freeman. *"Give Us Good Measure": An Economic Analysis of Relations between the Indians and the Hudson's Bay Company before 1763.* Toronto: University of Toronto Press, 1978.

Rich, Edwin Ernest. *The Fur Trade and the Northwest to 1857.* Toronto: McClelland and Stewart, 1967.

Ronda, James P. *Lewis and Clark among the Indians.* Lincoln: University of Nebraska Press, 1984.

Ruggles, Richard I. "Mapping the Interior Plains of Rupert's Land by the Hudson's Bay Company to 1870." *Great Plains Quarterly* 4 (summer 1984): 152–65.

Sayer, G. M. *Les Sauvages Americains: Representations of Native Americans in French and English Colonial Literature*. Chapel Hill: University of North Carolina Press, 1997.

Scharf, J. Thomas. *History of Saint Louis City and County*. 4 vols. Philadelphia: L. H. Everts, 1883.

Shimkin, Demitri R. "Eastern Shoshone." In *Great Basin*, edited by Warren L. D'Azevedo, 308–35. Vol. 11 of *Handbook of North American Indians*, edited by William C. Sturtevant. Washington, D.C.: Smithsonian Institution, 1986.

Smith, G. Hubert. *Big Bend Historic Sites*. Smithsonian Institution River Basin Surveys, Publications in Salvage Archeology, no. 9. Lincoln, 1968.

———. *The Explorations of the La Vérendryes in the Northern Plains, 1738–43*. Edited by W. Raymond Wood. Lincoln: University of Nebraska Press, 1980.

Stevens, Thomas. *Madoc: An Essay on the Discovery of America by Madoc Ap Owen Gwynedd in the Twelfth Century*. London: Longmans, Green, 1893.

Stevens, Walter B. *Missouri, the Center State, 1821–1915*. Chicago: S. J. Clarke, 1915.

Syrett, Harold C. *The Papers of Alexander Hamilton*. Vol. 11. New York: Columbia University Press, 1966.

Tabeau, Jean-Antoine. *Tabeau's Narrative of Loisel's Expedition to the Upper Missouri*. Edited by Annie Heloise Abel. Translated by Rose Abel Wright. Norman: University of Oklahoma Press, 1939.

Temple, Wayne C. *Atlas: Indian Villages of the Illinois Country*. Illinois State Museum, Scientific Papers 1, Supplement. Springfield, 1975.

Thiessen, Thomas D. "Historic Trading Posts near the Mouth of the Knife River." In *The Phase I Archeological Research Program for the Knife River Indian Villages National Historic Site*. Part 2, Ethnohistorical Studies, edited by Thomas D. Thiessen, 47–74. National Park Service, Midwest Archeological Center, Occasional Studies in Anthropology, no. 27. Lincoln, 1993.

———. "Excerpts from the Brandon House Post Journals Relating to Trade with the Mandan and Hidatsa Indians, 1793–1830." Report on file. Lincoln, Neb., National Park Service, Midwest Archeological Center.

Thompson, David. *David Thompson's Narrative of his Explorations in Western America, 1784–1812*. Edited by Joseph Burr Tyrrell. Publications of the Champlain Society, vol. 12. Toronto: Champlain Society, 1916.

Thompson, Ralph S. "The Final Story of the Deapolis Mandan Indian Village Site." *North Dakota History* 28 (October 1961): 143–53.

Thorne, Tanis C. *The Many Hands of My Relations: French and Indians on the Lower Missouri*. Columbia: University of Missouri Press, 1996.

Thwaites, Reuben Gold, ed. *Original Journals of the Lewis and Clark Expedition, 1804–1806*. 8 vols. New York: Dodd, Mead, 1904–5.

Tucker, Sara Jones. Atlas: *Indian Villages of the Illinois Country*. Illinois State Museum, Scientific Papers 2, part 1. Springfield, 1942.

U.S. Congress. *American State Papers: Public Lands*. Vol. 6.

Van der Zee, Jacob. "Fur Trade Operations in the Eastern Iowa Country under the Spanish Regime." *Iowa Journal of History and Politics* (July 1914): 355–72.

Villiers du Terrage, Baron Marc de. *La Découverte du Missouri et l'histoire du Fort d'Orléans, 1673–1728*. Paris: Librairie Ancienne Hononé Champion, 1925.

Wagner, Henry R. *Peter Pond, Fur Trader and Explorer.* New Haven: Yale University Press, 1955.

Warren, Gouverneur Kemble. Manuscript map of the Missouri River. 1856. Q579, sheet 14, Record Group 77. National Archives and Records Service, Washington, D.C.

Warren, Robert E. "Environment and Natural Resources of the Lower Cuivre River Valley." In *Middle and Late Woodland Subsistence and Ceramic Technology in the Central Mississippi Valley,* by Michael J. O'Brien et al., 21–65. Illinois State Museum, Reports of Investigations, no. 52. Springfield, 1996.

Wedel, Mildred Mott. "Le Sueur and the Dakota Sioux." In *Aspects of Upper Great Lakes Anthropology: Papers in Honor of Lloyd A. Wilford,* edited by Elden Johnson, 157–71. Minnesota Prehistoric Archaeology Series, no. 11. St. Paul, 1974.

Wedel, Waldo R. *An Introduction to Pawnee Archeology.* Bureau of American Ethnology, Bulletin 112. Washington, D.C.: Government Printing Office, 1936.

———. *An Introduction to Kansas Archeology.* Bureau of American Ethnology, Bulletin 174. Washington, D.C.: Government Printing Office, 1959.

Wheat, Carl Irving. *Mapping the Transmississippi West, 1540–1861.* Vol. 1. San Francisco: Institute for Historical Cartography, 1957.

Will, George F. "Archaeology of the Missouri Valley." *Anthropological Papers of the American Museum of Natural History* 22, pt. 6 (1924): 285–344.

Will, George F., and Thad C. Hecker "Upper Missouri River Aboriginal Culture in North Dakota." *North Dakota Historical Quarterly* 11 (January/April 1944): 5–126.

Will, George F., and Herbert J. Spinden. *The Mandans: A Study of their Culture, Archaeology, and Language.* Peabody Museum of American Archaeological and Ethnology, Papers 3, no. 4. Cambridge: Harvard University, 1906.

Williams, David. "John Evans' Strange Journey." *American Historical Review* 54 (January 1949): 277–95; (April 1949): 508–29.

Williams, Gwyn A. "John Evans's Mission to the Madogywys, 1792–1799." *The Bulletin of the Board of Celtic Studies* 27 (May 1978): 569–601.

———. *Madoc: The Making of a Myth.* London: Eyre Meuthen, 1979.

———. *The Search for Beulah Land: The Welsh and the Atlantic Revolution.* London: Croom Helm, 1980.

Williams, John. *An Enquiry into the Truth of the Tradition Concerning the Discovery of America by Prince Madog ab Owen Gwynedd about the Year 1170.* London, 1791.

Wood, W. Raymond. *An Interpretation of Mandan Culture History.* Bureau of American Ethnology, Bulletin 198. Washington, D.C.: Government Printing Office, 1967.

———. *Biesterfeldt: A Post-Contact Coalescent Site on the Northeastern Plains.* Smithsonian Contributions to Anthropology, no. 15. Washington, D.C.: Government Printing Office, 1971.

———. "David Thompson at the Mandan-Hidatsa Villages, 1797–1798: The Original Journals." *Ethnohistory* 24 (fall 1977): 329–42.

———. "Plains Trade in Prehistoric and Protohistoric Intertribal Relations." In *Anthropology on the Great Plains,* edited by W. Raymond Wood and Margot Liberty, 98–109. Lincoln: University of Nebraska Press, 1980.

———. "The John Evans 1796–97 Map of the Missouri River." *Great Plains Quarterly* 1 (winter 1981): 39–53.

———. "Mapping the Missouri River through the Great Plains, 1673–1895." *Great Plains Quarterly* 4 (winter 1984): 29–42. Reprinted in *Mapping the North American Plains: Essays in the History of Cartography*, edited by Frederick C. Luebke, Frances W. Kaye, and Gary E. Moulton, 27–39. Norman: University of Oklahoma Press, 1987.

———. "Cultural Chronology of the Upper Knife-Heart Region." In *Papers in Northern Plains Prehistory and Ethnohistory: Ice Glider, 32OL110*, edited by W. Raymond Wood, 7–24. South Dakota Archaeological Society, Special Publication 10. Sioux Falls, 1986.

———. "Nicolas de Finiels: Mapping the Mississippi & Missouri Rivers, 1797–1798." *Missouri Historical Review* 81 (July 1987): 387–402.

———. "Ethnohistory and Historical Method." In *Archaeological Method and Theory*, edited by Michael B. Schiffer, 2:81–110. Tucson: University of Arizona Press, 1990.

———. *Náⁿza, the Ponca Fort*. 2d ed.. Reprints in Anthropology, no. 44. Lincoln: J&L Reprint, 1993.

———. "Fort Charles or 'Mr. Mackey's Trading House.'" *Nebraska History* 76 (spring 1995): 2–7.

———. "The Missouri River Basin on the 1795 Soulard Map: A Cartographic Landmark." *Great Plains Quarterly* 16 (summer 1996): 183–98.

———, comp. *An Atlas of Early Maps of the American Midwest*. Illinois State Museum, Scientific Papers 18. Springfield, 1983.

———. *An Atlas of Early Maps of the American Midwest, Part II*. Illinois State Museum, Scientific Papers 29. Springfield, 2001.

Wood, W. Raymond, and Thomas D. Thiessen. *Early Fur Trade on the Northern Plains: Canadian Traders among the Mandan and Hidatsa Indians, 1738–1818*. The American Exploration and Travel Series, no. 68. Norman: University of Oklahoma Press, 1985.

Works Project Administration. *North Dakota: A Guide to the Northern Prairie State*. Compiled by workers of the Federal Writers' Project of the Works Progress Administration for the State of North Dakota. 2d ed. New York: Oxford University Press, 1950.

INDEX